This is a formidable work on the source (
provides a fascinating picture of Klein as a
many of the deepest questions raised by
Narrative of an Adult Analysis, this book may come to rival the *Narrative of a Child Analysis* as a means of understanding Klein's work. Christine English has admirably brought together and commented upon Klein's clinical notes, and the book allows Klein's ideas to be explored in the details of her sessions, providing direct clinical evidence for her theories.

John Steiner, *Training and Supervising Analyst, British Psychoanalytical Society*

Christine English has produced a book of tremendous interest and major importance. It is also gripping to read. This book is the first and for now the only account of Melanie Klein's day to day psychoanalytic treatment of an adult patient, and it is enthralling. Working from her access to Klein's extensive notes in the Melanie Klein Trust archives, the author presents a detailed and expressive account of Klein's highly original way of thinking and analysing. The book will be an important and exciting addition to psychoanalytic studies.

Priscilla Roth, *Training and Supervising Analyst, British Psychoanalytical Society*

With this work, Christine English has taken a hugely important step forward in Klein studies. She has tapped into a very rich seam in the Klein archive, drawing together extensive and detailed sessional notes which illustrate beautifully how Klein thought about and worked with an adult patient, Mr B. This rare and moving account of an adult analysis is a wonderful adult complement to, and will likely become as famous as Klein's analysis of her child patient, Richard. It deserves to be very widely read indeed.

Jane Milton, *Training and Supervising Analyst, British Psychoanalytical Society*

Melanie Klein's Narrative
of an Adult Analysis

Melanie Klein's Narrative of an Adult Analysis offers the first detailed account of Melanie Klein's work with an adult patient, Mr B, which spanned the years 1934 to 1949.

This volume includes fully edited sessional notes made by Klein about her work with Mr B. Christine English has expertly collated, curated, and annotated Klein's original notes from the Melanie Klein Archive, giving the reader clear insight into this fascinating case for the first time. Throughout, English offers extensive critical commentary, as well as a thorough introduction to the case. She gives the rare opportunity for the reader to be privy to the working practice of one of the most eminent analysts of her time, offering a clear and detailed record of Klein's interventions and thinking in her work with one patient over a number of years. This unique and vivid record illustrates Klein's technical approach in the greatest detail, showing her sensitivity and intuition as a clinician, as well as introducing many of her influential theories.

This book will be essential reading for all psychoanalysts, psychoanalytic psychotherapists, and other therapists interested in Klein's work. It will also be of interest to post-graduate clinicians, psychoanalytic theoreticians, academics, and researchers concerned with psychoanalytic ideas and the work of Melanie Klein.

Christine English is a child, adolescent, and adult psychoanalyst in private practice in South Oxfordshire, UK. She is a Fellow of the British Psychoanalytical Society, Archivist of the Melanie Klein Trust, and Honorary Associate Professor of the Psychoanalysis Unit, University College London.

Melanie Klein's Narrative of an Adult Analysis

Christine English

Routledge
Taylor & Francis Group

LONDON AND NEW YORK

Designed cover image: Stormy Petrel by Beccy Kean

First published 2023
by Routledge
4 Park Square, Milton Park, Abingdon, Oxon OX14 4RN

and by Routledge
605 Third Avenue, New York, NY 10158

Routledge is an imprint of the Taylor & Francis Group, an informa business

British Library Cataloguing-in-Publication Data
A catalogue record for this book is available from the British Library

ISBN: 978-1-032-44685-1 (hbk)
ISBN: 978-1-032-44687-5 (pbk)
ISBN: 978-1-003-37341-4 (ebk)

DOI: 10.4324/9781003373414

Typeset in Baskerville
by MPS Limited, Dehradun

Contents

Foreword

Elliott Jaques wrote in his foreword to *Narrative of a Child Analysis*: 'it occupies a unique position in the body of Mrs Klein's work'. With this present volume, *Narrative of an Adult Analysis: Melanie Klein's Analysis of Mr B*, Christine English, the latest archivist of the Melanie Klein Trust, brings us not merely a complement to the earlier clinical example of Klein's work, but also the first detailed example of her clinical work with an adult patient.

Elizabeth Spillius was the first honorary archivist for the Trust over many years. Jane Milton took over this task in 2014–2021. Both have published works based on the Klein archives as have many other analysts who have accessed this invaluable collection of data.[1] The archive includes correspondence, diaries, drafts of letters and publications, case material, photographs, files on the controversies within the British Psychoanalytical Society (1939–1944), family correspondence, and literary fragments.

In her will, Melanie Klein left her notes and papers to the Melanie Klein Trust. They were initially in the care of Hanna Segal, and in 1984 they were given to the Contemporary Medical Archives Centre of the Wellcome Library for the History and Understanding of Medicine. This newest publication from the data of the archive adds not only to the body of scholarly work on Melanie Klein and to an understanding of the evolution of her ideas but adds a significant contribution to the further study of the entire field of psychoanalysis.

As with the case of Richard published in 1961, this account of the analysis of Mr B presents us with the details of Mrs Klein's thinking and her struggle with establishing and developing clinical theory and clinical process. Richard's case extended over a 4-month period during World War II. Elliot Jaques contended that she devoted more intense time and thought to that publication, than to 'any of her other works'. She was working on it still, a few days before her death. With the addition of the Mr B case, Mrs Klein's brilliant legacy as an adult and child analyst is further solidified.

Mr B's analysis spans the period from 1934 to 1949. The notes presented in this book are detailed from a number of points within the analysis, during that time. Here we see the early application of Klein's ideas concerning anxiety, transference, projective identification, and unconscious phantasy. We see these come alive over an extensive course of a psychoanalysis. Christine English has, with this text, provided clinicians with the opportunity of examining detailed clinical material of one of the most original, creative and great minds across the development of psychoanalytic technique and theory.

In this case of Mr B, we see Melanie Klein in the mid-1930s, almost 15 years prior to the case of Richard, working as an analyst with an adult patient, in the kind of detail which we rarely have seen in our literature. We are allowed to examine not a single or even a series of hours. We are given a glimpse of her work over an extraordinary period of her development and the developments within psychoanalysis itself.

Here we see another valuable part of her legacy as a psychoanalyst with an adult. One is almost surprised as to how she was able to work in 1936 with Mr. B. in psychoanalysis, given that she had still to fully elaborate many of the theoretical constructs that would later help her to understand such clinical material. She is interpretive, detailed and consistent as an analyst. The internal world is foremost in her mind, but so are the history and the patient's real experiences. Her understanding of working with and in the transference is still evolving. Yet one can already see how it is crucial to her way of working deeply with her patient. She perseveres, recalibrates and continues in the face of the onslaught of his anxieties and panic and actions. She follows the patient's associations with deeply complex and thoughtful constructions of his internal world and how he lives them out within his external world.

We are allowed to see her struggle with the reality of a patient's life, as she did with Richard years later. Her humanity and kindness yet her insistence on working within her construct of analysis is remarkable. She knows Mr B's history for instance, and his envy of his younger sister. When Mr B is then unsettled by bumping into another child patient who is leaving Mrs Klein's consulting room, she tries to 'fix' the problem by moving the hour. At the start, not yet having a concept of total transference, she describes how Mr B reacts to his hour being taken away. It is a brilliant series of interchanges where Mrs Klein grasps the struggle as an external one only to be pushed by the clinical interaction and analytic material, to see how truly it was an internal unconscious struggle. She came to understand that this internal conflict could only be worked through within the internal world: through interpretation and within the transference and the analysis. Christine English provides us a window into this evolution and development along with rich, real and passionate clinical material. A truly three-dimensional and alive Mrs Klein emerges.

It has been stated that Mrs Klein's writing on theory was difficult to understand. Though I'm not sure that is true, here one sees how completely untrue it is of her clinical interactions. In Richard's clinical case, we were privileged to see how a clinician under extraordinary circumstances was able to establish and work within an analysis. There was a war going on, terrifying things were happening in London and in the world. Yet Mrs Klein and Richard worked diligently. We were permitted to see the drawings, the notes, and both the interaction and interpretations made and this young child's responses.

Analysts have studied Mrs Klein's case of Richard for decades. Years after its publication, Donald Meltzer, one of the last patients of Mrs Klein, himself a child and adult analyst, published a series of texts based on lectures he gave at the Tavistock. In his book, *The Kleinian Development Part Two: Richard Week by Week*, (1989) Meltzer demonstrates and examines the evolution of Klein's thinking based on the way she worked with Richard. In this fascinating case of Mr B, we as readers are allowed to further study Mrs Klein's extraordinary gift to psychoanalysis. As Elliot Jaques wrote about Richard's case, it afforded us a look at Mrs Klein's work life as 'no other of her books or papers'. This present volume will allow further in-depth study of how Mrs Klein's legacy, her creativity and her passion for psychoanalytic thinking and practice continue.

Abbot A. Bronstein, PhD
Editor, Analyst at Work Section, *International Journal of Psychoanalysis*

Note

1 I had the good fortune over many years of consultations with Mrs Spillius to be allowed to look at some material from the archives including lectures and case notes. Some of these Mrs Spillius published in her books based on her papers and the Klein archives (2007).

References

Klein, M. (1961) Narrative of a Child Analysis: The Conduct of the Psycho-Analysis of Children as seen in the Treatment of a Ten Year Old Boy. Vintage.

Meltzer, D. (1978) The Kleinian Development Part Two: Richard week by week. The Harris Meltzer Trust.

Spillius, E. (2007) Roth, P. and Rusbridger, R. (eds.) *Encounters with Melanie Klein, Selected Papers of Elizabeth Spillius*. Routledge.

Acknowledgements

Jane Milton originally encouraged me to explore the Melanie Klein Archive where I encountered Mr B for the first time. Jane seemed fully to expect that a book would follow from my explorations, so in a way, I simply acted in accordance with her expectations in producing this work. I was frequently buoyed by her cheerful support as the project unfolded, and I am also thankful to Priscilla Roth for her ongoing encouragement. Abbot Bronstein's interest in my work gave great inspiration, and I thank him for commenting in detail on, and for writing the Foreword to the book. I am grateful to the Melanie Klein Trust for their permission to publish Klein's clinical notes on Mr B, and for their generous support of this project from its inception to completion. It is a privilege to be part of, and to have been given the opportunity to work as an archivist for the Trust.

The cover picture of the book was painted by Beccy Kean and is called Stormy Petrel. It was inspired by an extremely poignant moment in Mr B's analysis: his painfully moving description of this tiny seabird which struggles so much to get to its young and Klein's connecting of this to Mr B's experience of his mother, whom he felt had struggled so much to feed and nurture him.

This book is for my family, and for Chris Mawson, to whom we all owe so much.

'And to be wroth with one we love,
Doth work like madness in the brain'

Coleridge, 1816, quoted by Melanie Klein in *Love, Guilt and Reparation*, 1937

'If we fall out with those we love, it works like poison on the brain.'
Mr B, p.19, this work.

Introduction

This book is the product of my first serious exploration of the Melanie Klein Archive, and brings to light the record which exists of Klein's long analysis of an adult patient, Mr B. Those readers with a good knowledge of Klein's published works will recognise this patient from her 1940 paper, *Mourning and its Relation to Manic Depressive States*. There, he appears as 'D', and Klein uses material from his analysis to illustrate how early anxiety situations that are revived during mourning may be worked through in analysis. I shall return to the particular clinical material which Klein uses in her *Mourning* paper in chapter 3, and in the concluding chapter of this book.

Mr B was first introduced to members of the British Psychoanalytical Society in 2004 by Elizabeth Spillius, in a talk which described the notes she had found in the archive that Klein had made about psychoanalytic technique. This talk was later published in Spillius' (2007) *Encounters with Melanie Klein*, so we meet Mr B within these pages. More recently, John Steiner (2017) has edited and published Klein's *Lectures on Technique* in their entirety, along with a critical commentary. Here, he discusses Mr B[1] much more fully, since Klein refers to him often throughout her lectures, and presents detailed material from some of his sessions to illustrate her theoretical ideas. Though he is not named there, I am also very confident that Mr B is the subject of Klein's fifth and sixth lectures on technique. I shall return to both Spillius' and Steiner's contributions later. However, with this book, I am aiming to give the fullest possible picture of Mr B and his treatment that is so far available, which I have been able to construct from Klein's day-to-day clinical notes in the Melanie Klein Archive.

Klein often wrote copious and incredibly detailed notes about her adult and child patients, and with the help of Elliott Jaques, she constructed the detailed *Narrative* of her relatively brief (4-month) analysis of 10-year-old Richard, which was published posthumously.[2] However, Klein never published a full or even partial account of the analysis of an adult patient. This, then, is the first such account. Mr B's analysis began in 1934 and continued until at least 1946,[3] possibly until 1949 and beyond. During the treatment, Mr B was called up for service in World War Two, and when he would return to London on occasional

DOI: 10.4324/9781003373414-1

leave Klein would make arrangements to see him, for which he was clearly enormously grateful. The analysis was also disrupted when Klein herself moved temporarily to Cambridge in the autumn of 1939, fearing air raids in London, and then to Pitlochry from July 1940 to September 1941. These interruptions notwithstanding, the months of sessional material which exist in the archive, which span some 16 years, allow us to form quite a full picture of the nature of Mr B's difficulties and the trajectory of his analysis.

Mr B is a fascinating patient who was unquestionably helped by his analysis. Klein's record of her work with him gives the most vivid insight into her highly original way of thinking and analysing. It shows Klein to have had the most remarkable understanding of the internal life of her patient, and of the influence of this on his external life. Her notes reveal the way in which she sensitively used her insight to help him understand the difficulties which hampered him.

In chapter 1, I will say more about Mr B's background and history, but first, a brief note on how his analysis began. Though there are no sessional notes of his treatment in the years 1934 and 1935, we know that Klein began to see Mr B in May 1934, just one month after her eldest son Hans was killed in a mountaineering accident in the Tatra mountains. It is surprising to learn that Klein began a new analysis at this time. However, when she first met him, Mr B was roughly the same age as Hans was when he died, and one wonders if this influenced Klein's decision to take him on, despite his being really very ill, and, as it turned out, difficult to manage.

Thus far, I have not discovered any correspondence between Klein and Mr B from the years beyond the end of his analysis, though he did frequently write to Klein whilst he was in treatment. We don't then know what life served up to him after it, or how he responded. Klein's notes do however detail the extensive working through of many of Mr B's difficulties, and at times show him to be living much more peaceably because of his analysis. The notes reproduced in this book can then be seen as providing strong evidence for Klein's analytic method, and for the theories she had already developed, and was continuing to elaborate at the time of Mr B's analysis. For example, her work with Mr B undoubtedly influenced the development of her highly original theories concerning mourning, the need to excavate love that has become buried under hate, and regarding the profound implications of an individual's conception of the nature of parental intercourse and relations. Mr B is evidently helped to recover some sense of a happier, if fragile union between his internal parents, as some of the late clinical material presented in the final chapter of this book shows. Readers will quickly learn just how much Mr B suffered from a belief that his parents' relationship was desperately unhappy, and at times tremendously destructive. This helps one appreciate how enormously important Mr B's analysis was to him, since it seems in the end to have modified this belief. Mr B is also helped by Klein to begin the complicated process of mourning his mother, who dies early in his analysis.

Mr B's case also helps us to understand more fully Klein's approach to dreams and to transference, her understanding of which was still developing whilst she was treating Mr B. Just as Freud's *Little Hans* gave evidence for his theories of infantile sexuality, we can find within Mr B's analysis the most detailed evidence for Klein's ideas concerning the combined parental couple, phantasies concerning the inside of the maternal body, attacks on objects using bodily products as 'weapons', and the guilt that follows these attacks, which may go hand in hand with a terror of retribution by damaged objects.

Klein's work with Mr B reveals so much about the nature of the fundamental conflict between love and hate, which, as Klein saw it, is first experienced in connection with the breast. This record of Mr B's analysis constitutes a serious study of some of the terrible implications where such a conflict is not well worked out in development. It also provides great insight into what may drive a negative therapeutic reaction, and into the dynamics of, and obstacles to mourning. There is very moving material about the impact of the unexpected arrival of a sibling, and about the way in which love can become almost entirely obscured where hatred has instead been nurtured through grievance. Love, however, as Klein's work with Mr B shows, may in turn be liberated through the rigorous analysis of aggressive impulses and hatred.

Methodology

This work builds on the valuable work that Elizabeth Spillius, Claudia Frank, John Steiner, and Jane Milton, amongst others,[4] have done to bring to light Klein's theoretical ideas and clinical records. As Steiner (2017) notes, Elizabeth Spillius, who was the first archivist of the Melanie Klein Trust, has thus far done 'more than anyone else to make the contents of the archive known to the English reader' (pp. 2–3). When she began working in the archive in the 1990s, Spillius accessed both physical records housed at the Wellcome Library and worked from deteriorating original papers and microfilms, as was customary at that time. In 2014, Jane Milton took over as archivist for the Trust, and worked with the Wellcome to begin the process of digitisation of the archive which was made available to the general public in 2018. Whilst I began working with copies of Klein's typed notes handed to me by Jane Milton, I have largely conducted my research via the digitised archive. In 2021, I took up the role of archivist for the Trust, which has generously supported my effort to bring Klein's work with Mr B to light, including with the help of a Spillius Award.

My first encounter with Mr B in the archive was in file D.14, which is entitled 'Possibly for seminar[s]: Patients B, E, F, G, P, R'. Though fascinating material about all these patients appears here, notes on Mr B's sessions take up half the file, so I had the fullest introduction to him, and my interest in discovering more was stirred. On searching further in the archive, I found six files that were entirely made up of sessional notes of his treatment: B.63, B.64, B.65, B.66, B.67 and B.68.[5] These six files are the ones from which I have primarily drawn in my research, and the notes therein span the years 1936 to 1949.

In her 2004/2007 paper,[6] Spillius reproduces a fragment of Klein's notes on a male patient, dated 1947. These notes appear in file B.98, called 'Theoretical Thoughts', and the fragment itself is headed 'An illustration of the schizoid mechanisms'. Though in this file the patient is only referred to as 'he', I believe this is also Mr B.[7] The material, which captures the patient's experience of being in a trench during the war, is incredibly vivid, and much like that used by Klein in her second *Technique Lecture*. Steiner (2017) calls this latter clinical description a 'tour de force'. He writes, 'there are very few descriptions of this kind to be found in contemporary literature where unconscious phantasies are rarely interpreted so directly or presented in such detail' (p. 13). Further, he says, 'It may be that we are more sensitive to the patient's capacity to follow [such interpretations,] but it is also possible that we have lost some depth and vitality in the process' (Ibid., p. 23). I think the reader will find much of the material I am presenting in this book to be similarly revealing of Klein's imaginative, if challenging, approach.

My feeling is that Klein's work with Mr B shows us what psychoanalysis, at least as Klein conceived it, is about; that is, understanding the deepest layers of the patient's unconscious as these become evident in the here and now of the analytic session. It may be that contemporary analysts do not interpret material in quite the way she did, as Steiner (2017) suggests, but it seems undeniable that the way Klein thought about the nature of the internal world, internal objects and unconscious phantasy, continues to influence, to the greatest extent, the way psychoanalysts and psychotherapists think about their adult and child patients. Klein's unique and at times deeply compassionate way of working is captured vividly in her work with Mr B. Her reflections upon his internal state, which so profoundly influences his external life, relationships and creativity, seem remarkably contemporary. For example, when Mr B's early, traumatic experience of the arrival of a baby sister is reactivated by his bumping into a child patient at Clifton Hill,[8] he can barely bring himself to attend his sessions and is also wracked with guilt about the hostility that has been stirred within him. There are extensive notes about Klein's analysis of this situation, and movingly she records that,

> *I showed Mr B, both in my attitude and in my interpretations, that I quite understood that he could not help staying away since there was too much anxiety connected with the remote possibility of meeting the child [again,] and that altogether he could not bear to be with me for the full time. I had generally interpreted that the main thing was not his disappointment, but the anxiety aroused in connection with his aggression both against the child and against me … and it certainly relieved some anxiety that I said that we would just have to be patient and do at the moment as much work as we could.*

Klein shows herself to be as incredibly understanding of Mr B's predicament as she is determined to reveal honestly to him the turbulence of his mental life and the ramifications of this.

If Klein's use of language (bad penises inside, explosive faeces and burning urine used as weapons against objects) is felt by some to be off-putting or outdated, her work with Mr B largely convinces one that phantastical and primitive conceptions of bodily contents and about what goes on between objects inside the mind and body have the greatest bearing on how Mr B feels about himself, others, and about life in general. Whilst not exactly a metaphor, since Klein seems to have thought that in some sense Mr B felt he had swallowed the bad penis, she meant that he felt himself to be full of bad potency; to have taken in the bad aspects of his father and brother, and so to have become himself worthless, poisonous, and destructive. Such terminology is a vehicle to express aspects of experience which are so intense in the early part of life, that are bound up with bodily experiences, and which never fully leave us.

In the next chapter, I shall introduce Mr B more fully, and will summarise some of the important developments of his analysis. Chapter 2 then brings some of Klein's own reflections on Mr B's formative experiences, many of which are powerfully revived during the analysis, as when Mr B crosses over with one of Klein's child patients. It seems appropriate to reproduce these reflections at this stage in the book, since they too serve as something of an introduction to Mr B. In chapters 3–7, I will present and introduce Klein's clinical notes on Mr B. These have been lightly edited to improve the reading experience and the introductions give some orientation to the contents of each chapter. Whilst I do frame the notes, and in the concluding chapter make a final attempt at drawing things together, I have, in the main, aimed to allow the notes to speak for themselves. Thus, I hope the reader will hear Klein's voice come through most strongly in these pages.

Notes

1 In fact, it was John Steiner who first referred to the patient as Mr B (Steiner, 2017, p. 119), and I have continued to do so. Klein herself called her patient 'B'.

2 Klein, M (1961/1998). *Narrative of a Child Analysis*. Virago.

3 Klein's diaries survive only until 1946. Sessions with Mr B are recorded in Klein's diary until the end of that year. There are no corresponding clinical notes for 1944, 1945, or 1946, however. There are also clinical notes that are dated 1947 (in B.98), 1948 (in B.6), and 1949 (in D.14). It is possible, since there is very little clinical material from these later years, that Klein was simply preparing notes for teaching in those years and drawing on analytic material that took place much earlier. It remains for this to be confirmed.

4 Some decades ago, Pearl King and Riccardo Steiner extensively used material from section E of the archive in their 1991 book *The Freud-Klein Controversies 1941–45*. Bob Hinshelwood and Maria Rhode recently contributed papers to Jane Milton's (2020) *Essential Readings from the Melanie Klein Archives*, based on their research there. Also, in a recent 'Archival Studies' section of the *International Journal of Psychoanalysis* (August 2018, Vol.99:4), several prominent Kleinian analysts, including Rachel Blass, Heinz Weiss, and Michael Feldman, made contributions following the publication by Steiner (2017) of archival material in the form of Klein's *Lectures on Technique*.

5 The notation B here refers to section B of the archive, 'Case Material, child and adult', rather than to B the patient.

6 Spillius, E (2004/2007). Melanie Klein revisited: Her unpublished thoughts on technique'. In *Encounters with Melanie Klein: Selected Papers of Elizabeth Spillius*. Eds Roth, P. and Rusbridger, R. Routledge.
7 Further reference is made to this excerpt in chapter 7.
8 Clifton Hill was Klein's home between 1933 and 1953, and her consulting rooms were also here.

References

King, P. and Steiner, R. (1991) *The Freud-Klein Controversies 1941–45*. Routledge.

Klein, M. (1940) Mourning and Its Relation to Manic-Depressive States. International Journal of Psychoanalysis 21:125–153.

Klein, M. (1961/1998) *Narrative of a Child Analysis*. Vintage.

Milton, J. (2020) *Essential Readings from the Melanie Klein Archives: Original Papers and Critical Reflections*. Routledge.

Spillius, E. (2007). Roth, P. and Rusbridger, R. (eds.) *Encounters with Melanie Klein: Selected papers of Elizabeth Spillius*. Routledge/Taylor & Francis Group.

Steiner, J. (2017) *Lectures on Technique by Melanie Klein*. Routledge.

Strachey, J., Freud, A., and Tyson, A. (1955) *The Standard Edition of the Complete Psychological Works of Sigmund Freud*. Volume X (1909): Two Case Histories ('Little Hans' and the 'Rat Man').

Chapter 1

One who has not been held well

Mr B was in his late twenties when he began analysis in 1934. He was by that time married with three children, and may later have had a fourth child. He was the owner of a large estate that incorporated a farm, outside of London, and he sat on the Board of a company with offices overseas as well as in London. He was, in Klein's words, 'a difficult patient to manage.' He was often silent, frequently late, and typically hostile; full of complaints and grievances.

Klein writes of Mr B that,

> *his upbringing was that of a child of typically Victorian parents in wealthy surroundings in which everything that was best was provided for the children. There was a nurse and nursery maid, and relatively little contact with the parents up to the time they went to school.*

Mr B, according to Klein, 'had never quite grown up from the nursery' and seemed 'unusually aware of feeling haunted by this period of his life.' Something that emerges repeatedly in his analysis is that Mr B feels that since his difficulties began very early in his life, there is no hope of putting them right. Mr B had a brother who was three years older than him, and a sister five years younger. His father worked in the City, and it is likely that the family lived on an estate outside of London. The family was musical. Relations between Mr B's parents were not happy, but there wasn't any obvious conflict either.

Mr B boarded at a prep school from around age eight, and reportedly felt he had been 'turned out' of his home when sent. Indeed, Klein notes that one of Mr B's great complaints about his mother was that she did not accompany him to his boarding school when he went for the first time. This was very likely experienced as a repetition of his being turned out of the nursery upon the birth of his sister, which I shall shortly describe. Connected to this, Mr B conveys in his analysis great ambivalence concerning dependence, something which Klein reported was evident in her first consultation with him. Both Spillius (2004/2007) and Steiner (2017) have discussed this.

Later, Mr B studied at Oxford, though there is no record of which subject he read. He had an interest in classical literature, as well as music, which may have

DOI: 10.4324/9781003373414-2

come from his family or public school education. It seems however that he was interested in psychoanalysis even at Oxford, though he wasn't sure his family would support his treatment, and it would be another decade before he would begin his analysis with Klein.[1] Mr B had an enduring love of the natural world and this is endlessly evident in his material. It illuminates his internal life and often makes reading Klein's notes on the treatment fascinating. At times, it is nature's cruelty and disinterest that Mr B cites to illustrate his emotional states and conflicts, but more often than not, the interweaving of Mr B's knowledge of the natural world with other aspects of his experience simply makes the material incredibly rich.

Klein feels that Mr B is extremely intelligent, and 'very fair and kind in many ways.' His wife, however, Mr B complains, has entirely insufficient regard for him. He, on the contrary, is almost incessantly preoccupied with the state of her health. Klein clearly thought this was a projection of Mr B's own concern about his insides, and that this transference was much in line with his attitude towards his mother, about whom he was often incredibly hostile and in turn terribly worried. There is a brief reference in Klein's notes to indicate that Mr B's wife was herself in analysis. Indeed, on one occasion, she records that Mr B has telephoned his wife's analyst to enquire after the progress of her analysis! As far as his own health goes, it emerges that Mr B had always suffered from severe constipation, and that this resolves during the analysis. Quite late on in his treatment he also tells Klein that he had long suffered from psoriasis, and this again appears to improve during the analysis.

A flat fish mother

Though there is mention of happier memories in connection to his mother; of her reading Homer to Mr B, teaching him the names of flowers, and singing to him, these good experiences are rarely recalled, at least in the early years of the analysis. Indeed, one comes to understand that better memories and more loving feelings about Mr B's mother have been deeply buried under grievance. Much of the work of the analysis could in fact be said to consist of the analysis of his hatred, particularly in connection to his mother, which eventually leads to a freeing up of more loving impulses towards her. As the analysis develops, Klein also comes to understand that much hostility that had more rightfully belonged to Mr B's father, had been projected into his mother who had come to stand for all things neglectful, depriving, and critical.

Mr B was fed by his mother during the first month of his life and he believed that this had been a harrowing experience. He thought he had been extremely frustrated at the breast; that there had neither been enough milk nor time with his mother. He also felt he had been very poorly held, literally, by his mother, and he attributed his own physical awkwardness and ungainly way of holding himself to this. Several years into the analysis he speaks to Klein about 'women who are good mothers and others who are like flat fish.' Klein interprets to Mr B that this fish, with its,

> *eyes in the wrong place and this awkward position of the eyes, is that of the breast which means that baby cannot get well from one breast to the other. It seems again to signify the whole awkwardness and clumsiness of the feeding process.*[2]

When a nanny arrived at the end of Mr B's first month, she reportedly 'found that he had been starved' and 'gave him the bottle.' Mr B then shared the nursery with this nanny, who became overall a good figure in his life, until his fifth year. At this time, Mr B's sister was born and his nanny became her nursemaid. This was another deeply traumatic experience and a loss from which Mr B felt he never recovered.

We know little about Mr B's external mother. She was not English,[3] and Mr B said that she came from a family where there had been great misery. In the earliest notes that exist of the treatment, Mr B refers to a maternal aunt in an asylum, and two suicides in his mother's family.[4] At least in the early years of his analysis, he strongly emphasises his mother's unhappiness, her negative attitude towards men, sexuality, and in particular, the male genital. Mr B very much connected his mother's attitude to his own powerful belief that sexuality, and indeed any sort of cooperation or relationship standing for a sexual exchange, was destructive. Mr B knew that he had turned away from his mother very early on, and felt he had alienated himself from her more and more as his life progressed. Their relationship remained, he thought, 'on a razor edge between love and hate.'

Whilst Mr B doesn't describe his mother as strict or harsh, he does tell Klein that she would 'report' him to his teachers and father, and that his father would then punish him physically. Klein writes,

> *In fact, his father behaved brutally when he was called upon to interfere in the education of the child. He would not try to understand, but after the mother had complained about the child the father would smack him in the face. Then the mother would be sorry, but on other occasions she would ask for the father's interference again (Klein, in Steiner, 2017, p. 47).*

Mr B's hatred of his mother and the guilt he felt about this, Klein suggests, is a kind of reaction formation to the intense, sensual love he felt for his mother, for which he feared he would be punished. There is much evidence in the material for this, as can be seen in chapter 4 in the kingfisher material. Klein clearly thinks that Mr B turned away from his mother in hate partly because it seemed impossible to separate his love for her from sexual desire. Unrelenting complaints about his mother then also serve the function of staving off the fury of a castrating father. It is because Mr B abandons his mother, in his mind, to a deadly intercourse with his father, that he has to modify his whole attitude towards her,

Klein comes to understand. To hold on to his love would have meant having to bear too much sorrow and guilt.

Mr B's mother's death during the analysis leads to much important work, and throws light on the way in which mourning itself can be interrupted by the need to keep hatred alive. Mr B longs to have a more peaceful mother inside of him, one who is not desperately harmed by his destructiveness. Yet as may already be evident, it is problematic for Mr B to 'go on peacefully,' including to work well with Klein, where loving feelings such as those which drive cooperation are felt to be so close to, or even equated with, sexual feelings. In the face of this, Klein suggests, one of the most pressing analytic tasks is to help Mr B recover and preserve a good, loving mother inside of him. Indeed, by early 1937, less than three years into his analysis, Mr B movingly tells Klein, 'mothers, despite all their faults, do have a lot of great advantages.'

Mr B's external father is a more shadowy figure, about whom we know little. As will already be clear, he was at times a frightening and violent character in Mr B's mind. Indeed, in her fourth *Technique Lecture*, Klein says that Mr B's 'phantasies of a dangerous father butchering his mother in intercourse were one of his main anxiety-situations' (Steiner, 2017, p. 65). Later in his analysis however, after the death of his mother, Mr B's homosexual longing for his father emerges more fully, along with his fear of this. He tells Klein that he felt his father never admired him or encouraged him; He may, for example, have wanted Mr B to learn carpentry, but never spent time teaching him, or doing it with him.

As the analysis progresses, Klein comes to understand the extent to which hatred of Mr B's father has primarily been projected into, and directed towards, his mother. Only rarely does hatred towards his father become evident. When Mr B has been in analysis for a couple of years, he does recall that when he was 10 years old and his father was recovering from appendicitis, he leaned on his father in such a way as to cause him great pain. The memory causes Mr B to suffer greatly. He is led to think of the precarious state of his father's health at that time and it becomes clearer that in phantasy at least, he has wrought much damage upon his father. Mr B also tells Klein about a screen memory of sorts, in which his father tells him, with tears in his eyes, to take care not to harm his younger sister whilst he plays at shooting soldiers. It seems clear that at that time, Mr B felt his father had ruefully exposed Mr B's aggression.

Mr B's emotional attitude towards his father can also be discerned through the 'Chairman material' he brings. The Chairman[5] is frequently regarded with contempt and disdain, and Mr B often talks of a plan to oust him from the company. On occasion following such expressions of hostility, a more friendly attitude emerges towards the Chairman. Mr B then works to get relations between them on a better footing, and one can certainly read this as an attempt to reconcile with his father in his mind. There is a very painful and poignant episode in the analysis, akin to the 'shooting soldiers' memory, in which the Chairman takes Mr B aside and speaks to him of how bitter he feels Mr B is, and of what a lamentable feature of Mr B's personality this bitterness is. Mr B is mortified. Here, Klein interprets his feeling that the Chairman, standing for his father, has recognised how poisonous Mr B's attitude towards his father and his parents together is.

The combined parental couple

Klein records that externally, 'the parents, as Mr B felt it, were not at all in harmony but not actually quarrelling. The atmosphere was not happy.' Analysis reveals, however, a terrifying sense of a ruinous intercourse between parental objects in Mr B's mind. Though neither party is unscathed, Mr B's mother is felt to come off far worse. Her death in the second year of his analysis revives very primitive anxieties about what is done to her by a butchering father inside Mr B.

Mr B's internal world is then felt to be a scene of utter devastation, where nothing can be kept alive. The need to keep his parents separate in his mind in order that some life can grow up inside of him comes up repeatedly in the analysis. As one would expect, there are important implications for his relationship with Klein. Mr B essentially feels that if he is to have a good relationship and intercourse with her, some extremely dangerous force will be roused that will destroy them both. This contributes to his lack of co-operation in the analysis, expressed through lateness, silence, and outward hostility, something which Klein is incredibly understanding of. She conveys strongly to Mr B that his obstreperous attitude has less to do with destructiveness than with a terror of doing harm, and this goes some way towards preserving her in Mr B's mind as a helpful object who can help him go on doing the necessary analytic work.

Mr B of course does have some external evidence that his parents could unite against him. Yet Klein does not fail to note that his dread of their intercourse is also connected with the bad and dangerous impulses that are stirred up in him by his awareness of their coming together. This too, she notes, had motivated his repression of almost any aspect of parental sexuality. Mr B tells Klein, clearly convinced of it himself, that he never had any interest in his parents' sexual life whatsoever. This is hard to believe given the devastation he felt about the arrival of his sister, which I shall shortly describe. As the analysis proceeds and some of this repression lifts, however, good aspects both of parental sexuality, and of sexuality in general, are also recovered. As will be seen, the implications of Mr B modifying, through analysis, the internal representation of his parents, who are then felt to be involved in a less destructive sort of intercourse, are enormous. Perhaps the single most important thing that follows from this, is that Mr B can finally begin to mourn for his mother, and indeed for his father who is by this time close to the end of his life.

Siblings

When Mr B's sister was born when he was five, it was, in his words, 'a shattering experience.' Mr B tells Klein that he had no idea another baby was coming; that he was not in any way prepared, rather he just 'woke up, and she was there.' Mr B felt that something absolutely 'monstrous' had happened. Certainly, it was an irreparable loss to be deprived of the attention of his nanny, with whom he had shared the nursery up to that point. Following Mr B's expulsion from the nursery, he shared a room with his brother, though probably only for a short time until his brother left for prep school. A frightening memory of his brother sleepwalking towards his bed suggests some worrying sexual activity during that period. Klein seems to accept this as an external reality, rather than a product of Mr B's phantasy life, but one cannot know for sure. I shall return to this shortly.

It seems Mr B watched silently and with growing hatred all of the ministrations and 'fussing' over his baby sister in the nursery, yet he was apparently prevented from assisting in her care. One wonders whether, had he had been allowed to help, this might have gone some way towards mitigating Mr B's hatred of his sister. Instead, he felt he wasn't trusted to put anything right. Later, he found it agonising that his sister was left to cry, presumably because she was being fed according to a routine, whilst he imagined something terrible was happening to her insides. It was inexplicable to him that he should eat when she was suffering so much and was abandoned to her suffering, just as he felt he had been. Mr B's later preoccupation with his wife's health can clearly be connected to this.

Mr B did become very attached to his sister in time and enjoyed teaching her, perhaps as some sort of reparation for his earlier murderous feelings. He remained however wracked with guilt concerning his early treatment of her. Again, Klein suggests that this guilt might be accounted for by a sexual violation, in external reality, of Mr B's sister by him. In her sessional notes, Klein doesn't reflect upon the role of phantasy in his memory, for example of his brother sleepwalking towards his bed. Indeed, she emphasises on several occasions that there is much evidence in Mr B's material to suggest that sexual activity between siblings did occur in external reality. However, it is clear that the *experience* of sexual desire and activity, even if this only occurs at the level of phantasy, has had a devastating effect on Mr B's psychosexual development. It seems to have contributed to an entrenched and debilitating sense of worthlessness in Mr B, and to have confirmed a fundamental belief in the ruinous nature of sexuality. In Klein's words, Mr B felt that he had 'swallowed the bad penis,' and that this was inside him, polluting all that he did. Perhaps the most problematic aspect of this as Klein saw it, was that Mr B felt he could not keep his good objects safe inside. His depression, as will be seen, was thought by Klein to provide some protection from exposure to poisonous badness inside, which Mr B believed destroyed everything good.

Mr B's belief that he was not trusted to attend to his sister in the nursery also seems to have translated into a susceptibility to feeling wronged, and in turn aggrieved. This comes up repeatedly in his analysis, when he feels accused by Klein in the guise of a strict nurse or blaming mother. For a long time, any interpretation that points to his internal processes and impulses, Klein highlights, is readily felt by Mr B as an accusation. An openly negative transference towards

Klein is helpful, however, to the extent that it gives access to many of Mr B's grievances regarding his upbringing and important relationships.

On occasion, Mr B laments his lack of co-operation in the analysis, which he knows thwarts Klein's efforts to help him. Klein however sees this very much in light of his terror of punishment lest they have a good analytic intercourse; such is his fear of reprisals from a jealous, hostile, internal father. Whereas Mr B feels the treatment 'disintegrates him,' Klein sees that his internal objects, and particularly a combined parental couple, are disintegrating, or being destroyed, inside Mr B. He then feels trapped with dead, dying, and retaliatory objects. He tries desperately to protect or restore these, but such is his belief in his own poisonous destructiveness that the task seems doomed. Mr B's hostility is repeatedly directed towards and located within Klein, and he consequently feels trapped with an analyst whom he believes wishes to frustrate, deprive and harm him. At such times, strong suicidal feelings emerge.

It is important to note that from the beginning Mr B's transference to Klein is mixed. At times much warmer feelings are in evidence. For example, though he cannot shake the deep conviction that Klein is in favour of frustrating the infant/child by not giving enough milk, he is also moved by her understanding of the infant's suffering at the breast. Klein also reports that Mr B was terrified of being sexually attracted to her in the early stages of the analysis, though for a long period, this had gone into abeyance. As his confidence in Klein increases, however, Mr B's distrust and accusations can easily be connected to his attitude towards his nurse and mother, and this facilitates a thorough working through. When Mr B rages at Klein she is on occasion very clear that he is not seeing her as she really is, but as if she is in sympathy with a terrorising, combined parental object that will not allow him to enjoy a good analysis-intercourse with her. Klein's sensitivity to this is very moving, and enables Mr B to co-operate further, over time.

There is an important moment in the analysis to which I shall return in chapter 6, where Mr B accuses Klein of not sufficiently appreciating the impact of his parents' unhappy relationship on him. Klein then discusses with Mr B the relative importance in development of experience and the external environment, and the individual's own impulses, both of which play their part in shaping an individual's life and development. She tells Mr B, 'analysis cannot undo what your mother did, but it can have the effect of clearing up early feelings.' Klein notes that whilst not an interpretation as such, this is an effective intervention. As part of this conversation, Klein also remarks to Mr B that others have had far worse histories than he; that he had for example never known the awful effects of poverty. It seems to have been a helpful if somewhat surprising introduction of a piece of reality that further helps Mr B to recognise something more of his own role in his difficulties.

Feelings of love and gratitude which had been strongly denied, especially in relation to Mr B's mother, begin to emerge following much railing against her, and indeed against Klein who stands so often for her. Klein's rigorous analysis of Mr B's destructive impulses does seem to liberate the love that lies underneath these. Mr B's denial of his mother's kindness, Klein interprets, had also served to protect him from persecutory guilt about not having protected her sufficiently from a murderous father. With the working through of hatred and grievance, however, which sees the emergence of love, guilt to some extent diminishes and mourning begins in earnest. I think one can see that Mr B has begun to install a good mother inside, from whom he can separate more fully. Mother seems no longer to be felt as a deteriorating object inside, with whose fate Mr B is endlessly preoccupied and despairing about. Mr B is then able to turn more towards his wife, whose state he becomes rather less concerned with. Further, the emergence of sexual feelings in Mr B contributes to a diminution of depression. Alongside these developments, there is 'a fundamental alteration of his negative therapeutic reaction,' Klein notes. One is left with a picture of a very full, challenging, and effective analysis.

Before moving on to Klein's clinical notes, it is worth reminding readers that whilst there are no surviving notes for the first two years of the analysis, Klein did discuss her first consultation with Mr B in her second *Technique Lecture*. There, she records her impression that he was very anxious about becoming too dependent upon her, if he was to begin an analysis. He tells Klein that she speaks and even looks rather like his mother, and admits he hadn't wanted to be analysed by a woman at all. His mother, he says, kept him far too dependent on her. A fuller discussion of this first meeting can be found in Steiner's (2017) book, but one can see that the stage is set from the very first meeting for a powerful analytic experience.

Preface to clinical material

The clinical notes contained in the following six chapters, with the exception of those in chapter 2 which are undated, are mainly from the years 1936, 1937, and 1938. A handful of notes from 1939, 1940, and 1943 appear in chapters 5 and 6. In chapter 7, there are notes which are dated 1947, 1948, and 1949.[6] It is unclear, however, whether these pertain to sessions that took place in those years. As I have said, there are very few clinical notes from these three years, and this leads one to wonder whether Klein was preparing material for teaching in the years 1947 to 1949, and merely drawing on earlier material. This may in the future be confirmed.

As will be seen, Klein's notes from the years 1936 to 1938 are copious. I initially thought that I would present just a portion of these to show significant developments in Mr B's analysis, and to illustrate Klein's technique. However, this proved very difficult, since all of the details Klein records seem eventually to get incorporated into interpretations; everything gets connected up or made use of. Indeed, it is remarkable that Klein seems to make something of almost all of the material that Mr B brings, no matter how apparently obscure or unconnected it may initially seem to be. As such, little sessional material could be omitted. This has made for a longer text than was originally planned, but one which more fairly represents Klein's way of working.

Some editing of Klein's notes was necessary. Sometimes I have added punctuation, or a word or two to complete a sentence or render its meaning clearer. Very occasionally I have filled out scant notes, but my additions beyond a couple of words, or where these are more open to question, are always noted in square brackets. Any changes have, in my view, only clarified Klein's meaning. Thanks to the digitisation of the archive, the original notes can in any case be viewed at PP/KLE/B.63-B.68.[7]

Beginning in chapter 2, Klein's original, albeit edited notes will appear either in italics, separated from my commentary, or in inverted commas. Since Klein herself mainly wrote in the present tense, I have kept to this, occasionally changing the tense in her notes for reasons of consistency. Finally, as Spillius (2004/2007, p. 75) noted, Klein wrote at times in the first person, and at others called herself 'K.' Since this is somewhat confusing, I have edited the notes so that she always speaks in the first person.

Notes

1 There is reference in Klein's notes (in B.63) to an earlier experience of another kind of psychological treatment, but this is quickly passed over.
2 In chapter 4, readers will find Mr B's description of the Stormy Petrel, a bird which struggles so much to get to its young, and Klein interprets this material along similar lines.
3 My guess is that she was Hungarian, based on dreams in which a Hungarian music band appears, arousing much pride in Mr B. Reference to various objects from Hungary further support this theory. When Klein discusses her patient 'D' in her 1940 paper, Mourning and Its Relation to Manic-Depressive States, she writes that he was born in America. However, I wonder if she wasn't deliberately introducing some inaccuracy in order to preserve the identity of her patient. She might have done something similar in her fourth *Technique Lecture*, since there she states that Mr B had a sister who died. Nowhere in her clinical notes on Mr B can I find evidence, or even a suggestion that this loss actually occurred.
4 Klein also recalls this aspect of Mr B's mother's history in her 1940 *Mourning* paper.
5 Of the company of which Mr B is also a member of the Board, or indeed which Mr B may own.
6 Notes from 1949 come from file D.14 of the archive.
7 Very occasionally I draw on Klein's notes from elsewhere in the archive, but wherever this is the case, the original source in the archive will be given.

References

Klein, M. (1940) Mourning and Its Relation to Manic-Depressive States. International Journal of Psychoanalysis 21:125–153

Spillius, E. (2007) Roth, P. and Rusbridger, R. (eds.) *Encounters with Melanie Klein: Selected Papers of Elizabeth Spillius*. Routledge/Taylor & Francis Group.

Steiner, J. (2017) *Lectures on Technique by Melanie Klein*. Routledge.

Chapter 2

My army is ready and
I am fully on its side

Klein's notes which are reproduced in this chapter are undated. Though they were found in the last of the 'B files,' they also serve as something of an introduction to Mr B in Klein's words, and as an accompaniment to the introduction I have given. It seems likely that Klein prepared these notes for a lecture or some other teaching, for she first addresses in general terms the impact on a child of the arrival of a sibling. She writes,

> We find patients in whom some experience in childhood seems to have had a dominating influence on their whole development. One frequent experience of this kind is the birth of a brother or sister. With our child patients we often hear that the parents have actually observed that the child changed.

Turning then to Mr B, she writes,

> One of my grown-up patients told me right from the beginning of his analysis that the birth of his little sister had entirely changed his attitude to his mother and to life altogether. Mr B was full of complaints about his nursery life and his parents, especially his mother, whom he accused of a lack of understanding and a prudish, moral attitude he could not stand. However, he had nothing to report about actual strictness or harshness. She was at the same time seducing, preferring him to father and brother. [Mr B felt she] had a strong dislike of males, [which made for] unhappy relations between Mr B's parents … He reported in many details how he felt that his mother had a hate against the male in general and a dislike of the male genital. In this connection he had always felt that there was something wrong in having a male genital. His parents', but especially his mother's attitude towards sexuality, was in the patient's mind largely responsible for the ambivalent attitude which he had developed towards sexuality. I may mention that the patient had no functional sexual disturbances, but certain inhibitions and difficulties about it, in so far as he felt it at times as something bad and nasty, while at other times he was quite capable of sexual enjoyment.

Klein makes a note in the margin here: 'Contradictory: Mother seducing him – her looks unbearable (unable to look into her eyes), liked him so much … the handsome boy.' She continues,

DOI: 10.4324/9781003373414-3

All his complaints about his upbringing and accusations against his mother, which came up over and over again in his analysis, centred around the arrival of his little sister. He was then five years old. He remembered quite well the whole emotional situation, the feelings he had at the time, and he described them to me with full strength. They were experienced again in the analysis in their full intensity. He felt that something absolutely monstrous had happened to him. He had had no idea that a child was expected. He woke up one day to hear that a baby had arrived. He was put out of the nursery which he had shared with his beloved nurse. He had to sleep with his brother instead. Though the nurse was still nice to him, as he objectively stated, he felt he had been deprived of so much of her attention and love that this meant for him an irreparable loss. One of the points he stressed was his hatred of the great fuss made about the baby. He felt all the special care of the child as something quite unnecessary. All the small details of the baby's nursing had been observed by him with annoyance and suspicion. Often, mother and nurse would put their heads together as if something was wrong with the baby. Oil or grease had to be employed or something else had to be done. All this had been felt by the patient as unnecessary and worrying fuss. He also had the impression that his mother could not enjoy the baby enough, that she was herself continuously worried, though the baby was not actually ill or unhealthy. One thing Mr B felt very hurt about was the fact that though he developed very soon tender feelings towards the baby, he was not allowed to lift it or bath it or do any of the things with it which the nurse did … He quite definitely connected this with a lack of trust in him. Mr B was unusually aware of the influence on his development of this whole situation with all its conflicting feelings.

Mr B maintained that he never again gained trust in his mother and though he remained what one would call on the whole a good boy, he turned away from her inwardly and alienated himself from her more and more. He defined it to me in this way: that he had kept as it were all his life on the border between love and hate; on the razor edge, as he called it. With the fact that he knew so much about all this, Mr B supported his feeling that nothing and not analysis either could alter anything, since nothing could wipe out the disappointment, the pain, the hatred he experienced, and the distrust and resentment and all the other difficulties which resulted from these feelings. The dominating influence of his nursery life on his development was proved by the fact that whenever the patient felt put in the wrong by anybody, or came into conflict with somebody, and in all the details of his own domestic life, he felt that again the grown-ups wronged him and that a strict mother and a frustrating nurse had appeared.

I may say that Mr B is extremely intelligent and has a rich personality, very fair and kind in many ways. He was quite aware of the fact that, in responding emotionally in the way I have described, he had never outgrown the nursery. Though he was full of psychological insight, the work was very difficult in this way: Any interpretation which pointed to the internal processes which contributed to his difficulties, was so easily felt as my blaming him … I at once became the nurse or the mother. Nevertheless, we have been able, step by step, to find out about his early aggression and the anxieties arising out of it, and some dreams have brought definite evidence for his feeling that his faeces and urine were poisonous, burning and destructive in many ways. [There were often] difficulties when I connected this with his attitude towards his sister.

Klein now refers to a difficult but important period in the analysis, which begins when Mr B bumps into another patient of hers, a child:

> *Confidence in me had increased, though this easily changed one day to give place to full distrust and to accusations which we could easily connect with the attitude towards mother and nurse. I had been able to make an arrangement by which Mr B did not meet either the patient before him, or the patient after him. I made a special point not to alter his hour since the definite possession of this special hour meant very much to him, and seemed to be partly a compensation for the great frustration which, in repetition of the old situation, analysis brought to him. But [at some point] I had to alter this arrangement for a child patient who could not come earlier. To begin with Mr B seemed to take it reasonably, but he could not maintain this attitude. He became silent only to break out in accusations about how I had disappointed him and let him down. I had promised him this hour and he asked me to remember how strongly he had felt about this promise. When I pointed out to him that he could still have his hour, but that I could not then help his meeting the child, he seemed to take it fairly reasonably.*

> *The next day he came a few minutes earlier, obviously in order to avoid meeting the child, and he waited in the waiting room until the child had gone. He heard me talk with the child in the hall, since I escorted this child to the door partly to make quite sure that he would leave the house, as he was very reluctant to do so. The child, who had meanwhile developed similar feelings towards the grown-up patient as Mr B had towards him, said before he left, pointing at Mr B's hat which he saw in the hall, 'oh, that man has arrived', a remark which was heard by Mr B in the waiting room. Mr B again tried to take it reasonably and attempted a joke about the child, obviously disliking him, but he then became silent and a very critical part of his analysis began. Near the end of the hour, he broke the silence only to accuse me, full of hate and indignation, of having let him down and broken my promise to keep this particular hour for him. When I pointed out that I understood the difficulties which had arisen out of the presence of the other patient, but that I had actually not altered his hour, Mr B replied that I had actually kept him waiting. It is true [that this was] only for a very short while, actually one minute, but still this waiting occurred in his own hour. It appeared that the old situation, namely the unexpected arrival of the sister, had been reactivated with full strength, and Mr B recognized it himself . . . . He even said that had I announced the child to him before he met him suddenly, it would not have made so much difference, because he would nevertheless have felt the deprivation quite as strongly. It [would] not [have] relieve[d] the feelings roused in him. Analysis had become absolutely bad. Everything that I had ever interpreted was wrong. Mr B felt hopeless and wanted to break off his analysis. When, after my interpretation of the whole situation something seemed to loosen, he said 'you will not be able to do anything because my army is ready and I am fully on its side'.*

The notes continue,

> *During the next few days Mr B came very late, nearly at the end of his hour, so that I could see him only for a few minutes. He had repudiated my suggestion to move his hour 10 minutes later so that he would not meet the child because, [he said,] that would mean*

that he had no more the same hour, [that the hour would be] no more his own. Still, he came every day, although during the day he always made up his mind not to come at all and to break off. But those few minutes we had and to which I was able to add another 10 minutes or so of extra time, gave me the possibility of analysing the situation. I may mention that Mr B felt very guilty for coming so late, for keeping me waiting and for losing so much of his time and accepting extra time, and he watched very anxiously my reaction to all this. He agreed with me that his coming so late was partly to show that he would not keep to time since I had not done so, at least this is how he felt, but I did not stress this point much. I showed him, both in my attitude and in my interpretations, that I quite understood that he could not help staying away since there was too much anxiety connected with the remote possibility of meeting the child, and that altogether he could not bear to be with me for the full time. It certainly relieved some anxiety that I said that we would just have to be patient and do at the moment as much work as we could. I had generally interpreted that the main thing was not his disappointment, but the anxiety aroused in connection with his aggression, [that arose] both against the child and against me. I substantiated this with a few remarks he had made. He had said that even if I happened to abolish this child it would not help now any more. In one of these short sessions, he had spoken of feeling like falling into a well with burning pitch and of disaster all around him. He had not lied down, or if so, had soon got up again and sat further away from me or was even standing. After an interpretation he had quoted a line of Coleridge, 'if we fall out with those we love it works like poison on the brain'. He had spoken of the kettle in him which would boil over and which he could not control. I could relate all this to former material in which his words and thoughts were equated to attacks with burning and poisoning, and I interpreted his anxiety of meeting the child on the grounds of his destructive wishes against this child and his anxiety of abolishing the child directly – as well as of the child being destroyed because of his secretive sadistic attacks against it.

Klein quotes this line from Coleridge (which is slightly misquoted by Mr B) in her 1937 paper, *Love, Guilt and Reparation*. There, she writes of the concern and guilt one may experience upon feeling hatred, at times, towards a loved one. I think she must have had Mr B in mind when she included this quotation. In the notes above, Mr B rages at Klein whose arrangements have provoked the re-emergence in him of very early, unbearable feelings of displacement and hatred. He now feels 'on a razor's edge' with respect to the analysis, and Klein's understanding clearly helps him to cling on until the emotional storm passes, or is worked through. In the following chapter, notes from an early point in the analysis find him in a similarly disturbed and muddled state. Then, however, it is his mother's impending death that Mr B is facing.

Reference

Klein, M. (1937) 'Love, Guilt and Reparation'. In *Love, Guilt and Reparation and Other Works 1921–1945*. (1975). Virago.

Chapter 3

Death had all his life been hanging over him

Klein's notes in this chapter pertain to the months of June and July 1936. Though they are the earliest surviving clinical notes, Klein had by now been seeing Mr B for just over two years. The notes are titled 'Mourning and Melancholia,' presumably because they refer to the period immediately before, and then the weeks following, the death of Mr B's elderly mother. However, as the title of this chapter suggests, Klein's feeling is that Mr B has all his life had death 'hanging over him.' This she connects to his belief that he cannot keep his objects alive inside, where a terrifying and deadly intercourse is felt to be happening all the time between his internal parents. Mr B's mother's death reactivates all sorts of anxieties in relation to an internal combined couple, as well as about Mr B's own destructiveness, and his failure to protect his mother from his internal father.

Some of the material that follows, notably the 'bull dream,' is also used by Klein in her 1940 paper, *Mourning and Its Relation to Manic Depressive States*. Mr B is in that paper called 'D,' but the clinical notes will leave the reader in no doubt that this is the same patient.

June 1936.

Klein records that Mr B's mother has fallen unconscious. It seems she has been 'failing' and 'muddled' for months. Klein writes that Mr B's reaction to her imminent death has been to increase hate and accusations against her, in order to evade 'sorrow, pain and anxiety.' For example, in the session immediately preceding her death, Mr B is 'again very negative, speaking of the ways in which women make men unhappy,' and he directly 'accuses his mother of having made his father unhappy.' Mr B reminds Klein of 'the whole family history of his mother': great unhappiness in the family, two suicides and an aunt who is in an asylum. He evidently feels muddled himself, and he says to Klein 'I know you are going to drive me mad and then lock me up.' Klein interprets, 'That the madness, or muddle ... in the family and in his mother is now internalised and felt by him,' and that Mr B's mother's death 'meant to him her going mad and going wrong and being muddled.'

DOI: 10.4324/9781003373414-4

Following this interpretation, Mr B reports a dream:

> *He saw a bull lying in a farmyard. The bull did not look like a bull, but did not look like anything else either. It looked very uncanny – as if it was only the hide of a bull – but ... it was not only that. It was not entirely dead. It looked very dangerous. He was standing on one side of it, his mother on the other. He managed to get away to the staircase into the house, and felt he left his mother behind in danger; he felt that he should not leave her, but he hoped that she would also get away.*

Mr B associates first to blackbirds, rather to his astonishment; blackbirds which had woken him up in the morning. This he had found very distressing. He then recalls a tale of a man who was nearly crushed by a bull, who was trapped underneath it for hours, but who eventually managed to shoot the bull. He notes the roan colour of the bull and describes this to Klein. He thinks of the buffaloes which nearly died out in South America, but which were finally preserved, and then of killing buffaloes in order to eat them. He adds that the setting for the dream had been his own farm, and that the bull had been standing deep in mud. He 'had a flooring made to make it better for the bull.'

Klein suggests that Mr B's dream represents his phantasy of what happens between his parents: that theirs is a dangerous intercourse which is finally killing his mother. Following his thought about eating buffalo meat, and connecting to other recent material Mr B had brought about repeatedly feeling sick, Klein interprets that this destructive parental intercourse is felt by Mr B to be going on inside him. She writes that,

> *All ... [Mr B's mother's] delirious and frightening ways are signs that the uncanny, dangerous bull inside her is at work, and that she, Mr B's mother, is inside him, hence his feeling muddled and mad ... . His being at the side of the bull with her shows that the whole thing is internalised inside him – his farmyard standing for his body. Actually, he had declared that his tenant is responsible for the farm, which I interpreted as his denying that all this is going on inside him.*

As Mr B's analysis progresses, Klein often emphasises his terror of a castrating bull-father whose presence both prevents him from allowing more loving impulses towards his mother, and from protecting her. She tells him that his mother's impending, and then actual death, reactivates phantasies and associated anxieties about the nature of parental intercourse. She highlights his obvious concern for his parents, who are the blackbirds who disturb him in the night but whom he also loves. Following the bull dream, Mr B talks about planting lilies near his home, and he wonders where they will take root. Klein takes this too as evidence of his concern for his parents, and cites his wish to resuscitate his dying mother. She also points to the good aspects of the bull-father that Mr B has implied by referencing it's delicate colouring and 'the rarity of buffaloes'; and she notes his wish to make a flooring to 'make things better' for the bull which is standing deep in the mud.

On the following day, a Saturday, Mr B's mother dies. Though Klein often did see Mr B on a Saturday (meaning she often saw him six times a week), they did not meet on this particular weekend. When Mr B then returns on Monday he doesn't immediately tell her his mother has died. Instead, he emphasises his hatred of Klein and his conviction that analysis will kill him. It is only when Klein says that his hatred, now turned against her, is covering sorrow and anxiety concerning the state of his mother, that he tells her his mother is dead. Klein writes,

> [Mr B] tells me that the day when he got the news, he had had a lot of insight. He reminded me that I had told him that there had never been a death in his near family, but that death had all his life been hanging over him. He thinks he might now feel relatively different because of the work we had done about it. His wish to put his wife right and a very protective attitude toward me showed that he takes refuge in constructive and creative tendencies, in order to keep alive or to resuscitate the dying mother. He also realises how much the situation is an internalised one. He tells me he had felt sick last night after receiving the news, and says there had been no physical reason for this. He had felt this to be a proof of the internalisation of the whole situation.

Wednesday 10 June 1936

It seems that Mr B's mother has already been buried, since Klein records a dream that comes, 'the day after the funeral.' In the dream,

> Dr B and another person (obviously me [Klein]) were trying to help but actually Mr B was fighting for his life against us. Death was claiming him.

Klein writes that there are 'great and bitter reproaches against treatment as disintegrating.' Klein tells Mr B's that rather, it is his internal objects that are disintegrating inside of him. He describes the confusion he had felt during his mother's funeral about where members of his mother's and father's respective families should stand. He had asked himself,

> Who is the main person? He did not know whether it was father or mother. He had to ask himself whose funeral it was.

Klein interprets that Mr B's father is also felt to be dead or dying. Mr B 'repeatedly laughs' at Klein's suggestion that 'his hostility covers grief.' Any distress he does feel, Mr B says, is attributable to Klein and the treatment. 'Then again,' Klein writes, 'after a bit of insight, Mr B asks, if it is so about internal things, why don't I help him?'

Thursday 11 June 1936

Mr B describes an unpleasant exchange with his wife, and Klein interprets that,

> *he had recently been full of hate against me, and that obviously he displaced some of his hate and anxiety about his dead mother onto his wife. Then, Mr B gives one instance which had hurt him very much – that his wife has asked him, 'Whom would you like to have as your guests at dinner?' instead of suggesting 'Whom shall we ask?' He feels this very strongly – it is as though there is something peculiar about him – that he has special likings and wishes – and that he is a wild, frustrated animal in a cage which must be satisfied.*

Klein notes Mr B's anxiety concerning his 'eating tendencies' or oral destructiveness, which she has clearly been analysing. She suggests that his hurt following his wife's comment,

> *connects with his great feeling of guilt about early attacks on his mother's breast, for which we had had much material before. I try to show how feelings of guilt about these eating tendencies disturb his establishing inside him a peaceful mother image.*

Mr B then expresses disappointment that a female cousin he is fond of did not turn up at a dinner he had attended. He complains of the unreliability of women. Klein connects this 'not turning up' to death and absence, and to Mr B's longing for his mother. She recalls his childhood loneliness and anxiety in the dark. Mr B,

> *suddenly thinks of his looking out of the window at [his] father's house the day before and disliking seeing a Jay on a bush, and his impression that this nasty and destructive bird is going to disturb a nest with eggs in. He then thinks of wildflowers … bunches of them which have been thrown down on ground, probably by children.*

Klein interprets,

> *That he looks at himself and his destructive tendencies, which injure mother and the children inside her, with sorrow, and that he is also a child who has picked nice flowers and thrown them away, thus injuring his mother. Again, I note the importance of feelings of unworthiness and feelings of guilt in connection with her death.*

Friday 12 June 1936

Mr B recalls a dream:

> *He saw a bus directed towards him, coming in an uncontrolled and unorthodox way – in waves. I ask him who was driving, and he says, nobody – the bus was driving itself. It came towards him from over there (which means from the direction of my garden.) The bus went towards a shed … . He had a half bird's eye view – somehow he was high off the*

ground. He could not see what happened to the shed, but he knew it was 'going to blazes'. I asked why he could not see it. He said that his position did not allow this, but that he knew quite definitely that this was happening. Then two people coming from over there, from behind (behind my chair) – They were opening the roof of the shed ... like the way in which his desk opens on hinges. (He has had this made because he does not like to push drawers, and by opening the top of the desk he can see fully what is inside.) He did not see the point of people opening the roof, but they seemed to think it helps.

Mr B says that it is obviously he and Klein who are opening the roof. He connects his 'not seeing the point' of this, with his 'continuous complaints that treatment is no good.' He recalls a recent car accident, in which his car had run into a bus. He complains that,

I don't seem to understand what power of intellectual concentration is needed to put together, out of bits, an old object – from little bits – to sort them out of a chaotic mess and put them together into one thing – he uses the word to 'unify' it. He has lost power in analysis, which illustrates its disintegrating effect.

Mr B continues 'making different remarks,' Klein thinks to prevent her from interpreting, so that by the time he has finished the hour is almost over. Klein writes that Mr B,

laughs heartily when I tell him nothing is going to prevent me from giving this interpretation.

She tells Mr B,

...the bus is the same thing as the bull [which was previously seen to stand for father]. The shed stands for his mother, and that at the same time the bus, the uncontrolled, wild, mechanical thing, was directed against him, Mr B. That he got away by being at a half bird's-eye view, and that his being in a position where he could not see what happens, is the same thing as recently when, [as in the bull dream] by going up the stairs, he really could not see what the bull had done to mother.

Mr B removes himself from danger rather than protecting his mother, as in the bull dream, but Klein also makes the point that his father's attacks against his mother are also a danger to Mr B, because,

The dangerous uncontrolled intercourse ... is internalized and eternalized.

She notes that Mr B leaves 'very relieved.' However,

He says that it is very muddling that he feels that I am at the same time the person with the half bird's-eye view, and the person behind who is helping open the roof.

Klein acknowledges the frightening chaos and muddle that Mr B feels is inside of him, as well as his difficulty in trusting anybody, including her.

Monday 15 June 1936

After the weekend, when he had been left with such conflicting feelings about Klein, Mr B,

> *Accuses me in every way of doing harm to him, though when I point out that he seems entirely to dismiss the thought of the death of his mother, he agrees that this must have something to do with his state.*

Mr B then reports a dream, noting first that he and a neighbour had actually been out shooting snipe, but that they had shot very few. In the dream,

> *There were hundreds of snipe killed by the farmer, who did not understand that one must not shoot snipe while they are nesting.*

Klein interprets,

> *That this is again the bad father (the bull and the uncontrolled car) who would injure mother and her babies. He and the neighbour represent here the brother and himself, who have not done so much harm, comparatively, to the babies.*

Klein notes that earlier material has pointed to the equation, in Mr B's mind, of shooting with killing children, a fact that accounts for his deeply ambivalent feelings about shooting. Following this session, Mr B writes to Klein, as he often did after sessions. His letter 'seems to admit that he can't really maintain his view that analysis is the cause of his despair.' He pleads with Klein however, 'that if I am true and that what I say is so, he cannot bear that either.'

Wednesday 17 June 1936

Mr B is 'in a desperate state' and 'breaks down,' Klein writes. He asks her,

> *How can it help him to know that he feels this way about his mother?*

Klein tells him,

> *That it all refers not only to the real mother, but to the dangers to the internalized mother and his peace of mind [or indeed lack thereof,] about this internalized mother.*

Mr B goes on to express 'desperate distress' about his wife and about a business transaction. He should do something about the Chairman, he says, but he cannot. Klein interprets,

> *That all these, the company, his wife and me, are standing for his mother, and that the anxiety is that he will not be able to save her against the bad Chairman, bull, car, etc.*

Mr B then tells Klein that he felt 'the bottom falling out of him' when he overheard his wife arranging to go with her brother to hear some music. Mr B had not been invited. He accuses Klein, saying:

> *I seem to think he does not want to speak or that he has nothing to say, but that he could speak for years on end about music without finishing. It is like embroidery where the pattern is lost and the stitches are rotten, if he described what music meant to his mother, to his father and to him. He is overwhelmed with feeling while saying this and cries. Actually, he can only mention that he found himself breaking down once as a child outside the drawing room, and this reminds him of having seen the butler collapsing on a chair because his mother had been angry with him. He feels quite unable to tell me that his breaking down outside the drawing room door was connected with a reprimand of his mother in regard to his music, but he admits it when I say so.*

This is the first mention in Klein's notes of Mr B's love of, and complicated relationship with music, which was clearly a family interest. It later becomes evident that music, and particularly playing the piano, is inextricably bound up with Mr B's longing for his mother and his 'failure,' as he sees it, to play well and thus to please her.

Mr B reproaches Klein during this hour, accusing her of being 'omniscient, laying down the law, knowing everything – like God.' He recalls that he 'always felt sympathy when the Pharaoh hardened his heart more and more, the more plagues were put on him by God.' Klein notes Mr B's clear identification with the Pharaoh and his frequent feeling of being wronged by the God-like adults. She also however cites his guilt,

> *which had recently shown so strongly, and which he had acknowledged by saying that he was a bloody nuisance, and that he feels rotten about himself.*

Klein remarks,

> *how unsatisfied Mr B always felt at the shortness of the hour, and about the fact that one could not go on for hours if one felt like it. He is feeling deserted by me, and he must in this situation feel that I should be with him during all his waking hours and give him all the relief, and so on, and that this is part of his hardening his heart against me.*

Thursday 18 June 1936

Mr B, 'again speaks about music with great and tender emotions.' He says that though his mother was supposedly musical, she never sang. He speaks with resentment about being made to practice scales, and Klein interprets that,

> *When I ask for his associations or expect him, in however free or understanding a way to give them, I become the person who makes him play scales, while he obviously longs for something else in connection with music.*

She also reminds Mr B that once, 'when speaking about the unspeakable importance of feelings about music,' he had referred to his mother's breast. She suggests that Mr B might very early on have heard music and connected it with his mother. Mr B agrees, and says he 'thinks it possible that his mother might have sung to him when he was quite small.'

Friday 19 June 1939

Mr B begins by reporting a nightmare:

> *There were women, and they were coming near to him, - just women in general, he does not know how they looked nor how many - perhaps all the women in the world. Mr B had to hold them off with his arm, and he points out that he was holding them away from the front of his body. He felt them as very dangerous.*

He associates to 'marmalade tins,' and to 'opening the lids and finding them full of something horrible.' He thinks of blow-flies, and,

> *speaks of a satiric poem which his mother used to recite to him – "Who has put blowflies into the butcher's shop?" – and so on – lots of questions of the kind, and the answer to all of them is 'Napoleon'.*

Klein interprets that Napoleon is now standing for father. Returning to his dream, Mr B recalls the women he was trying to hold off. He says,

> *They were 'terror' – personified terror. He mentions three mythological women, with one eye between them, whom Perseus saw. I show that Perseus was also connected with another woman who, as far as I remember, was not at all frightening. Mr B says, yes, it was Andromeda, whom Perseus saved from the dragon, but that he had not thought of her – only of the terrifying women. I suggested he had only looked at the horrible aspects of the women and that he felt they were actually tins full of horrible poison and other things. I remind him that at times it seems as if he had none but unpleasant memories of his mother or of what she had done for him, and he agrees to that.*

Reflecting on this, Mr B says,

> he had not entirely forgotten [the better memories of his mother] ... . He reminds me of her explaining to him about flowers and teaching him, reading and the happiness connected with that, but that he had really at times entirely lost this.

Klein then speaks to why he loses hold of these memories, or had to turn away from his mother:

> I show that in analysis a similar process takes place, and that at times he denies everything he feels I am doing for him. That he had to deny the relation of Perseus to the woman he saved and only remember the terrorising women because he felt he had actually not saved his mother. [I say that in] the dream of the bull, where he actually went away and left mother in danger with the bull, he repeats the early situation where he felt that he left mother to the dangerous father who put blowflies into her and so on ... and felt he had not protected her. I point out that his anxiety of the father in this situation when he would have protected her was too great, and therefore he had to deny her kindness so that he should not feel so guilty.

Klein clearly feels that recent work in this area is reaching Mr B, for she writes that,

> An obvious relief has set in in the last few days. I point out that his ease of mind goes with friendly memories coming up and his building up the belief in the good mother inside him. Lessening of guilt and anxiety and so on is a condition for that.

Saturday 20 June 1936

Mr B is 'entirely exhausted and deeply depressed.' He despairs that his wife, 'cannot be put right.' Klein interprets that,

> despair about his mother is now put on to his wife. That he has always done so, but it becomes very clear recently.

Thinking then of his mother, and of recent recollections about his piano playing, Mr B speaks 'with great emotion and as if it is impossible to put things into words.' He comments that he had a very nice piano teacher, but that 'she became spoilt by teaching him piano.' He then says,

> He would never force a child to learn the piano – as little as he would cut his head off. If a child asked for an explanation of this marvellous instrument and wanted to know about everything inside and how it comes about, and about how the nice noise gets out of it and how the waves get into the air, and perhaps something of the history of music, then of course he would give it, but it should not be forced in any way.

Klein suggests to Mr B,

that his whole description seems to apply to the whole of the inside of the body, and I remind him of his exploration (masturbation phantasies) of going up into the inside of the body ... . That was not forced on him, that he could do by himself. Mr B agrees that the piano would represent a female object and I interpret that he had felt a connection between the music, which he had recently called a luscious fruit, and the breast, and that his playing on the piano seems to have been like handling the genital or the breast in a way which he wanted and at the same time feared. Any failure and reprimand would show that he had done the wrong thing for his mother's breast and body. It would lead to castration.

Mr B agrees with Klein. He says that 'the piano had been the only thing in which he had failed.' He continues, explaining that,

In every other respect his learning and knowledge had been very much appreciated; and that he could not bear any failure on intellectual lines, because he was in continuous fear connected with his guilt feelings, and intellectualised his potency and his sexual phantasies.

Sunday 21 June 1936[1]

Mr B is late. He feels 'frightful, in despair,' including about his wife's health. He says he can't stand Klein's assumption that she can help him, though neither could he stand it if she were to say she could not;

That would be really as if his mother had told him that she would give up his being taught music.

Klein interprets,

that music seems to be referring to yesterday's material – that his being made to play music was like having to prove his potency – though he would have wanted to prove this, he was horrified of doing so and wanted to dissociate his loving feelings towards his mother from his sexual ones, which he was unable to do.

Klein refers to Mr B's having broken down outside the drawing room, 'after an important music lesson.' She reminds him that he had said he felt castrated then. Mr B then,

turns against me with great hate, saying that this is my jargon, when he would never have dreamt of using this word before. Then he mentions an Austrian woman he knows who had given him some bad news about an accident involving some acquaintance they have in common.

Klein interprets,

> *that my interpretation of castration was taken as the bad news, and that he feels as if the act has been done.*

Monday 22 June 1936

Mr B recalls once having asked Klein to change the time of one of his sessions. He says he hadn't wanted to 'give her trouble' or 'ask favours of her.' Then he says that his wife,

> *wishes for a baby, but that is only an escape because she can't take him into this relation with the children ... [T]hat he would really like to ask her to admit him – to take him in – to these relations, but that is not possible. I pointed out how much stronger his feelings of loneliness and wish for a perfect relationship with his wife are. He did not want to ask his wife favours, in the same way as he did not want to ask favours of me. He would also like me to admit him more and to have a more personal relation with me, especially now he feels more lonely.*

Regarding a baby, Mr B says that 'it is too late now.' Klein says that,

> *'too late' applies really to the death of his mother – that he cannot give her a baby, and that he had wanted to do so. That also would have meant that she 'admitted him', that she had 'taken him in.'*

Mr B's response seems to confirm the interpretation:

> *He mentions rather emotionally that his mother had left certain books to him specially and some jewellery .... He speaks about her love, which he had really never accepted. I remind him of his ecstasy in childhood about playing with her jewellery, and that he feels now that he cannot do this again, because that was one of the memories in which he greatly admired his mother and his aunts. He mentions that he remembers how his mother's mother died. He was grown up, and his mother had talked to him about her mother at the time, and that he remained quite cold. He felt she really wanted him to sympathize with her, and that he upset her.*

Klein connects this to Mr B's wish 'not to upset [Klein's] arrangements' with his request to change the time of a session. She speaks of his evident guilt, and he responds by saying that,

> *he also never wanted to upset the times and order which his mother had. That she kept very much to her times. I then mention that he did not want to upset her with his sexuality, and that order and times also stand for her whole standards and her views, which he would have greatly upset by his sexual phantasies and wishes.*

There is then a long silence, and a range of memories follow. Some are good, some bad, Klein notes. A roof has been damaged at Mr B's home, but they also had visitors with whom they swam. Mr B reflects that he shouldn't burden Klein with his depression, 'that he should not make things so difficult, should not be so difficult.' Klein interprets:

> *There might be an insight which he is not able to admit, which is that while painful things are going on in him, he actually does feel better, and that his feeling he was and should not be so depressed has to do with his feeling that there is some lifting of depression while we are working at the depression. As usual when any step forward is to be recognized he does not admit this.*

Mr B's response again seems to provide some confirmation of Klein's interpretation:

> *He then mentions hay, - he has given orders to make it in a better way, and that while the farmer thought they had no use for it, he [Mr B] said they could put it into bags and carry the bags to feed the sheep, and then they could be used. When mentioning the bags, he reminds me that he had mentioned once that people are human bags ... they are bags full of feelings, recollections and memories. I bring this in connection with the whole way of establishing his mother inside him and processes of introjection.*

Then, for the first time, Mr B expresses a thought about Klein dying:

> *The day before he had, when he came to see me, heard a hammering from a window where someone was doing something to it, and he had suddenly thought that I might be dead, and that he was nailing the coffin.*

As will be seen, subsequent analysis of Mr B's anxiety about Klein's death leads to the freeing up of sexual desire, both towards her and more generally, and this in turn leads to a diminution of his depression.

Tuesday 23 June 1936

Klein writes,

> *The next hour is one of absolute despair. Mr B is quite incapable of speaking for more than half an hour. He does not believe in the least that I can help him, though he has no strength to leave me. He then leaves me suddenly before the end of the hour at the first interpretation, in which I was referring to yesterday's hour.*

Wednesday 24 June 1936

Klein notes only that,

> *[Mr B] did not come, but sent me a letter in which he announced himself for the following day.*

Thursday 25 June 1936

Mr B refers to his absence the previous day, saying he had wanted to get away from Klein, and instead get to his father's home. He 'speaks, as in all these days, in very low voice, deeply depressed and in despair.' When he says it is the treatment he cannot stand, Klein remarks that,

> *he seems absolutely temporarily to deny that he has had a very severe loss and that he feels unable to stand the pain connected with this loss. I also remind him that three days after his mother's death he actually laughed when I told him that his depression and emotional situation are connected with her death ... that while he has in the meantime understood this much better, he still wants temporarily to deny it.*

Klein returns to Mr B's idea about using hay to feed sheep, and to his idea that human beings are 'bags full of emotions.' Mr B says that he, 'does not see why [Klein] should put much importance on this remark,' so she explains that,

> *the importance of it lies in the connection with the present situation and his ways of dealing with the process of establishing his mother inside ... . He had acknowledged, in my view, by this remark that he was doing so, and had expressed in this way hopes of being able to keep her as a good figure; but that any raising of hope is followed by despair in him.*

As if to confirm this, Mr B turns to speak of 'damage done by a thunderstorm,' and other 'manifestations of destruction, hatred and death.' Klein connects his despair to his feeling of being full of hatred and poisoning and burning urine. She says,

> *These dangerous manifestations are connected in his mind with his own hatred, and his belief that he had arranged the intercourse of parents to be so dangerous.*

Mr B speaks of his own son and how helpless he is 'to put his relations to his own parents right.' Klein writes,

> *I interpret this as the wish, in identification with his own son, to renew old situations in connection with his parents and to put things of this kind right. Going back to ... the thunderstorm, I summarize material about the dangerous bull and his mother the night before her death, the shed and the uncontrolled car and his feeling that he cannot save her inside because he had, in his hatred, arranged the intercourse to be so dangerous ...*

Klein reminds Mr B that he had so often in his analysis absolutely denied any awareness of parental sexuality. As they discovered however, 'in his mind, the most awful things were going on in the parents' bedroom.' Despair follows guilt, Klein suggests, since Mr B feels, *he had never protected his mother against the father in intercourse, being too frightened of him as a castrator, and that was shown in his dream in which he actually saved himself and left mother behind with this uncanny bull, hoping that she would get away, but really in the depths being convinced that she would not.*

Mr B then tells Klein,

that he will admit now something which he feels that he can only say because he knows he is going to go in a minute, and that is that in his arranging about the hay is expressed a strong feeling that he does not want it to 'go to hell'.

Klein says that hell is 'the dangerous intercourse of the mother and father,' and that what Mr B has said 'seems to speak for the strength of his belief in his constructive powers.' She notes that Mr B, 'listened to all these interpretations quietly and in rather receptive mood.'

Friday 26 June 1936

First, Mr B tells a joke about a beggar who doesn't even have a car to live in. Then he tells a dream:

He was in a foreign town, probably Paris. He went off with a woman whom he had just casually met. She was not young and not very attractive, but he very much wanted to go to bed with her.

He associates to the way the French will judge a person 'on an individual basis,' whereas amongst the people he knows, it is usual upon first meeting a person to say, 'I know your cousin,' or to make such a connection. There are pleasant things about this, he thinks, though Klein reminds him that at the beginning of his analysis Mr B was very pleased that she was not British, so wouldn't know any of his family or circle. Mr B agrees that,

all this applies to the woman in Paris, who certainly would not know anything about his family, so that he was really judged by his own individual things. He adds that that is already what I do in analysis, I don't know his family; all I am interested in is he himself.

Returning to his dream, Mr B explains that,

he goes with this woman to some hotel and takes a room and then he finds that somebody else is lying in his bed, which he is annoyed about, but not so very much, and he asked for the hotel authorities. The person reminds him of his brother. In the dream the matter did not finish, he had not had intercourse with the woman, but the feeling was definitely very pleasant, and he had the feeling that it would still come off – it wasn't off.

Klein records that on this day, unusually, she had to leave the room for a cough sweet. Mr B then recalled having said once that when the analysis was over, he would ask Klein whether or not she wore scent. Now, he says 'that scent and the lozenge are personal things which I do not want to know about.'

Klein writes that Mr B is himself clear that the foreign woman in his dream stands for her. She interprets,

that his idea was to go abroad with me, and that he had some time ago, before another holiday when we had material of the kind, denied this very strongly. I remind him that the day before, after all these interpretations about the [dangerous parental] intercourse and so on, he had suddenly said, 'I shall die in August when you go away". That in this dream he had simply gone away [and found me]. I had not died.

Mr B reports a second dream:

He was ... sitting at a table with three women ... then three more came in, distinguished and dangerous and attractive ... . He moved from his place to the top of the table and had some gin brought in. He himself had a glass of red wine in front of him, French wine, which he does not really care for at all ... . When the gin was brought in, some person was pouring it in, then it appeared that there was hardly anything in the bottle or the wine glass – but Mr B did not worry – he knew how much gin he had in reserve at home.

Klein writes,

I remind him at end of the hour that he has expressed the same tendency as the day before when he shared some belief in his constructive capacities, since gin, which he had characterized as colourless, stands for his semen, potency and for his feeling that he has got much and will have it, even though at the time being he seems to feel he hasn't got it. He seems greatly relieved and entirely changed following interpretations of the last few days. There is a manic element in this whole attitude, beginning with the beggar, which he actually feels that he is, and that it is he alone who is feeding all these women.

Saturday 27 June 1936

Klein's notes begin, 'Mr B is again in despair.' It is impossible to 'put his wife right,' and there is further 'despair about the relations between children and parents.' Mr B 'imagines how much he himself has been the source of worry in his parents, being the worrying child.' He is full of hatred and accusations towards Klein. She writes,

When I refer to the material of the last hour in which the silent woman was pleasant and he trusted her and made preparations for intercourse, he said very definitely that this dream was quite all right and she was also all right, and would it not be best to leave such things alone. One does not say to a bud that it need hurry to be a flower, one need not even reassure it, and that the analysis is not yet over.

Klein writes,

> *He makes it quite clear that he was not just going to have intercourse with [the woman in the Paris dream]. He first went with her to a kind of park or playground, and associates to a playground which is being built in the country which is going to be awful and looks unpleasant. He first wanted to talk with this woman and to be in her company; and when I say that there was an atmosphere of friendly feelings and trust in the dream in connection with her, he says there was also affection.*

Klein adds that,

> *Actually, the relation to this dream seems to have been an extremely affectionate one – Mr B treats it like a dear possession and agrees when I tell him so.*

The playground too has to do with analysis, Klein tells B. Analysis is 'developing like a bud,' if it also has unpleasant aspects. It brings to light the 'pleasant games of childhood and pleasant relations with his mother.' When Klein makes a connection to the friendly woman of the dream however, Mr B is again indignant. He stresses that intercourse did not happen in dream, but that he was not denying he wanted it. He turns then to another topic:

> *He speaks of a publisher having suggested to him that he should write a book about life in general, and different views he had expressed. He says he cannot do it. I point out that writing the book is along the lines of the bud. He feels things developing and that is the penis developing. I remind him that in the dream, when entertaining women, he was obviously not grown-up because he was so grand about attaining so many. The gin was not there. He knew that he had a reserve, however … . He felt confident that he would have it, as a child feels his penis will grow and that he will be able to do all the things he might be able to do when he is grown up.*

Klein also reminds Mr B 'that there was some belief in his constructive powers when he spoke of having the hay made the right way … to feed the sheep,' and he responds affirmatively:

> *He explained to me in detail about this matter of the hay, and said that there was also the idea that the hay should be eaten by an animal which would appreciate it. It was to be prepared in the right way and also taken in in the right way.*

Klein comments,

> *that this seems to have something to do with analysis, and that he wants me to appreciate his associations; I point out to what extent semen is equated with mental products, which are felt to be gifts.*

Concluding her notes, Klein records that,

> *This material was especially impressive in the way in which the dream itself was treated as an internal object and as a possession.*

Monday 29 June 1936

Mr B has had 'a devastating quarrel' with his wife and is again very depressed. He refers first to a dream which had involved meeting a man, now dead, whom he knew at Oxford. He was a very kind man, though he had been against psychoanalysis. In the dream, this man,

> *looked as if he had come out of the grave, and it made Mr B think of Homer and Odysseus, who met the dead, who were cold and miserable and vague.*

He then breaks off from the dream, telling Klein,

> *That he slept alone last night and wasn't the noise of the rain awful. Then gives me the reasons for the quarrel with his wife, who was going away for the weekend and he felt deserted by her. I interpret his despair about the good mother who left him, deserted him, and that he was taking this as a punishment ... [H]e continuously says that it is quite clear that if he dreams of a person coming out of the grave it must be his mother, and that this very kind man stood for her. I suggested his feeling of despair, of being left alone by his wife, and by me over the weekend, and also of the holidays coming near, connects with feeling of loneliness every night, when he was afraid of his mother's death, and felt left alone. I also connected his feelings of anxiety about the awful rain with former material about dangerous urine and his being dangerous because of urine ... . This appearance of vague, miserable, cold people is a picture of his mother inside him whom he cannot protect because of the dangerous contents of his body and his incapacity to save her.*

In this moving and condensed interpretation, Klein manages to speak to Mr B's sense of being poisonous inside, to his horror of having done harm to his internal mother, and to his dreadful loneliness. Klein connects these feelings both to his mother, his wife, and to her, and the following session seems to confirm that Mr B has felt very much understood by her.

Tuesday 30 June 1936

Klein writes that Mr B's mood is 'entirely different'; he is clearly less depressed. He says, 'he thought it would be a good thing now to leave the analysis, since he could do without it.' Klein suggests that, feeling helped by the analysis, Mr B wants now to leave her whilst she is a good object in his mind, thus saving her. Mr B is not pleased with this thought. He demands to know, 'why he should admit that analysis helps him, when [Klein] never admit[s] that it does harm to him too.' Klein again responds in a most touching way:

I put it carefully to him that I am quite aware that he feels at times worse because of analysis – that it stirs anxiety and so on, but I do not really believe that it makes him worse, though he might feel it so at times. Instead, it is his feeling that grown-ups should not always claim that they are right and the child wrong – that analysis stands for things which his objects did badly … and that is what he would like me to admit.

This again seems to bring Mr B some relief, for he then reports some good business news and a plan to go away on business in the near future, even to take his wife with him. He then recalls a dream:

He went through a room where there were air officials. They were dressed rather like a Hungarian band, and the room was also like a music room.

In association, Mr B recalls a garden party his mother hosted, where a Hungarian band had played. He had been very interested in the band, and 'proud, but much too frightened to speak to them.' Klein interprets,

these air officials and the Hungarian band stand for the father, but represent a pleasant intercourse of the parents, which he has also believed in, besides its frightening aspects.

At this point, Klein writes, 'Mr B got frightfully indignant and went out of the room.' Nonetheless, she is able when he returns to highlight,

His greater feelings of independence from his mother and the wish to turn to contemporaries – in this case, to his wife (going away with her from me) … . He seems not so tied to conflicts about mother and his anxieties about his internalized mother.

Mr B remarks that,

the Army was always a very impressive thing to him – ancient and always very impressive, and there were great emotions connected with it. There are also associations in connection with the old house of his father. I link this ancient thing, the army, and great emotions up with the admired parents and their impressive intercourse.

Klein evidently felt it important to acknowledge Mr B's emerging sense of a different kind of intercourse between his internal parents, and his recognition of them having admirable qualities, even if there is a somewhat manic element to some of the material.

Wednesday 1 July 1936

The analysis does seem to take a quite different turn at this point. Though the material is apparently not new, it is the earliest mention in Klein's notes of phantasies about sexual activity between Mr B and his sister. Mr B is late, having forgotten his session was at an early hour. He comments first that though he is quite happy with his wife, 'she is really like a worried little girl.' He then reports a dream:

> *His wife's doctor was asking him how his wife was. They are in a public room and he finds it difficult to answer – so very embarrassing – but at the same time he is pleased that the doctor should consult him.*

Returning to the relationship with his wife, Mr B remarks that,

> *he had the impression in former years, because his wife is so much like a little girl, that after sexual intercourse it was as if he had raped a little girl.*

Klein reminds Mr B of 'the whole material of the rape of his little sister, which he so much resented.' She says that,

> *this remark about his wife seems to confirm that he has turned away in the past from the conflicts and anxieties about parents to his wishes towards his sister, but that he felt frightfully guilty because she was younger.*

This interpretation provokes an angry response from Mr B, who says,

> *that I am always accusing him and that he will never be on a good basis with me, and that analysis always seems to stress sexuality and does not seem to understand anything else.*

Mr B turns to speak of a novel he has been reading:

> *a detective story in which somebody to do with a company had been found in the water, chained and with a bullet through the head. Members of this company had been asked to identify the body. A person who had been asked to do this had been very upset and the detective had begun to wonder if he was the murderer. When I ask if this person was really the murderer, he says he does not know yet, he has not yet finished the story.*

Klein interprets,

> *that he feels that I am the detective – since he has mentioned that I am accusing him all the time – and the story not being finished is that the analysis is not yet over … . He is continuously frightened of analysis finding all that he has done in the past to his sister and to his mother. He had made a remark himself during these associations which showed that*

he thinks of himself as the murderer, and I point out that there is also the question that somebody else could be the murderer and that the other person is really father, who might have been another member of the company, since he was never quite sure whether father (the bull) had injured mother, or if he, Mr B, had done so in his phantasies.

Thursday 2 July 1936

Klein writes that Mr B is, 'in great despair and feels definitely frightened.' He asks,

Could I not give him a little peace? He has again been unhappy with his wife and says that he feels like a boiling pot in which something is stewing, and from time to time an unseen hand takes the pot away from the fire, and then he feels a little peace. Speaking about the hand, he quotes Hamlet, who, on being asked how his father died, answered, 'Sleeping, by a brother's hand'. I remind him of his memory that his brother once walked over from his bed to Mr B's bed, and he had been horrified, and that he had quite consciously been frightened of his brother in sleep.

Klein writes that Mr B continues to complain bitterly, asking,

Why should children be so unhappy and why should not mother give them peace? He says that I am only blaming him ... I will never understand that mother can be wrong.

Klein interprets,

that I seem now not to stand for his mother at all but for the bad brother and bad father, from whom he always displaced anxieties and blame on to his mother, and that it is my castrating hand which he had been frightened of.

Mr B agrees with Klein. He says that he had only 'recently wondered whether I am always just standing for his mother – just yesterday he had thought this.' Klein writes,

I then tell him that we have had much material showing that I was a very mixed figure and that the parents in his mind always were mixed up with each other. Mr B says very strongly that they were always allied and remembers an incident which he had often mentioned before when he was not as high as a door handle, and he and his brother had done something wrong in the park, and nurse asked them to go to their parents and apologise. Before they came to the door his brother, three years older, said 'never mind, I will arrange the whole thing'. They went into the room and his brother never said a word – never apologised, and then they went out again, and his mother and nurse were dissatisfied. Had he really apologised then his mother would have forgiven him, and he would have felt peace, and he felt that his brother had let him down so badly.

Friday 3 July 1936

After the previous day's session, Mr B had written to Klein, telling her of more upsetting things he had not had time to share during his session:

> *Some physical illness which the doctor found in one of his children needs attention. Mr B is inclined to take it psychologically, and thinks that his wife does not want to see that. He blames both her and me for not attending to the child in the right psychological way. When I refer to this letter he says quietly that he is quite aware that all his external troubles – children, wife, business worry, etc are only something for his inner misery to rest on.*

Later, he remarks,

> *how many fewer people they now see – to dinner, going out with people … I interpret that this refers also to feeding people and having people alive, and he agrees to that. He says that one can also say that it would be nice to think of a live child and to create one, but that he feels that this could not be right.*

Saturday 4 July 1936

Unusually, Mr. B 'comes in good time, if not a little early, to the early hour.' Again however, he blames Klein. He didn't have enough money to tip the taxi driver, and it worries him. Klein interprets,

> *that he came early and obviously was trying to do his best in analysis, but that he got upset because he knows that he could not satisfy the father-taxi man, and that this made him turn against me.*

Mr B reports a dream. He is very concerned that Klein must understand the details absolutely correctly. Klein's notes are rather difficult to follow at this point, but the setting for the dream seems to be the grounds of a castle. Mr B is himself standing atop a grassy bank, beneath which there is a moat:

> *From there he was looking down into water, which was like inky soup, full of old trees. He said, 'We were looking down and then I wanted to borrow the glasses from somebody behind, but then found that I did not need them'. He goes on explaining that it is no good looking through the glasses if you do not both see the same thing. What he was seeing was that the water was splashing and up came the salmon. He felt awfully thrilled about seeing salmon, which are only found in running water. What a surprise it would be to his friends if he told them that. When I asked him who it was he meant when he said 'we were looking', he said, 'The same person was there as is now here in the room.'*

Mr B associates to the moat: In another dream, he had seen dead people in a moat, including 'his wife and another person, standing for father, mother, brother, and his whole family, and they were resurrecting.' Klein remarks that,

> *Mr B's belief that we are seeing something and that he need not borrow glasses from me, implies his belief that we are actually cooperating and that also I am internalized as a person who cooperates, because I am with him.*

Further, Klein suggests,

> *that this moat, as we have seen before, represents the inside of his body and the inside of his mother's body, and that the salmon are coming up in connection with recent associations about people whom he wanted to feed and the 'nice child', which is the live child coming up in the body where all this death is lingering. When I said that this regret that so few people were coming to dinner and they were going out so little – that this means life and feeding – he said that of course a nice child would be the greatest help against death; he agreed to what I said.*

Mr B recalls another part of the same dream:

> *he saw an old couple … there were a lot of other people there as well and they were embarrassing with this couple and he wanted to put the couple out of the way, but we don't know what to do with them. It was as if the man was a Colonel. Then he gives associations about the Chairman with whom he must try to [agree] terms, and of his worry about that. Then he mentions Lady S and that he might see her again, and then that she is unhappy in her marriage – but he wanted to tell her that she anyhow had a very nice wedding – as if this would comfort her – and says that it is not quite out of the question that he might see her again sometime.*

Klein interprets,

> *his wish to comfort and put right his mother. He had seen Lady S standing both for his mother and me, but he does not know what to do with the couple if the parents are united, because this would become the bull, the shed and the car, etc, and he could only try to preserve his mother if he could keep her separate. Only then does he feel that life can come up in him.*

Monday 6 July 1936

Mr B begins by complaining bitterly about the treatment. If only he could go and leave Klein, he says. He then reports a nightmare:

> *I was defaecating. Then says, 'No, I was not, rabbits were running up under my shorts and they were falling down in bits from my legs as if I had defaecated them. They looked like bits of food on a dish'*

Mr B is very concerned that Klein appreciates that he has not defecated the rabbits, but that it was *like* defecating. Klein writes,

> *I make it quite clear that … I know this, but that he has likened the bits falling down from his legs to defaecating. The reason why he must deny defaecation is to do with his wish to let me see the thing as it is and his anxiety of acknowledging it. He then reluctantly says that the rabbits remind him very much of the penis. If one has a small rabbit in one's hand it is like having the penis in one's hand.*

Klein interprets,

> *that this association explains why he should not have defaecated the thing, because first of all it came like food into his mouth – the bits of the dish. I remind him of his thought, 'sleeping, by a brother's hand', and that obviously this thing creeping up his shorts and the penis in his hand have to do with the brother's hand and the brother's penis, also in his mouth. I remind him of the ginger beer which a brother figure was offering him [in an earlier dream], and which he himself identified with the penis.*

At the start of the hour, 'after blaming the treatment and [conveying] his wish to leave,' Mr B had also said 'that that, however, was not what he intended to tell me.' Klein asks, what did he want to tell her?

> *He says he doesn't know, 'but if you say 'I throw an apple at you', that does not mean that one wanted to throw something else.' I interpret that he feels his associations to these … rabbits – as bad defaecation – actually represent the bad penis inside him which is again put out as bad defaecation and which he throws at me when he associates.*

Mr B has a further association to the apple:

> *He says it is connected with Paris, who handed the apple to the goddess and that this certainly was not a bad apple. I interpret that in this association, the apple is likened to the good penis and I to the good goddess. The other aspect, however, is that he throws bad dangerous faeces at me. I interpret his alternating so much now between hate and despair about the treatment and again positive feelings. That now I seem also to stand so much for the bad brother and the bad penis who injured his inside and made him all bad and incapable of giving me, his mother and his wife, the good penis … this all seems so much confirmed by his wife's difficulties about intercourse.*

Tuesday 7 July 1936

Mr B is again in despair. He is,

> *quite unable to decide what he should do. He would like to die. He cannot stand hearing my interpretations, which are awful rot. He is fed up and cannot get away. He puts his*

hankie over his eyes as he used to do in former times and also covers his ears, so that if I speak, he can only hear a vague noise. I tell him that now my words and interpretations are expected to be like the apple, the rabbits, which his associations stood for yesterday, that is, as things thrown at him, or as bad defecations, and that he must preserve all openings of his body against bad and dangerous faeces which might enter him.

Mr B responds in the following ways. He reports some things to do with his business, 'some arrangements, some attempt at a solution he has made with the Chairman which seems to allow a peaceful solution of the whole problem.' He also describes in much detail the situation with his wife and 'his despair that he cannot put her right.' Then, he tells Klein that 'his constipation, which had been very strong when he began the treatment, has entirely stopped.' He finally expresses a view that his wife could also be cured. Klein notes that he is expressing some belief and hope in his own cure, even 'at a time when he seems continuously to point out that the treatment is his whole evil.'

Thursday 9 July 1936

Klein writes that as on the previous day, Mr B is extremely depressed. He,

Accuses me of always having good reasons why he should be depressed. First it is his mother's death – then the holidays, and so on. Repeatedly, he expresses the wish to die, 'with a nice little grave.' He finds it quite impossible to stand me any longer and the treatment, but he cannot go.

Klein speaks of the forthcoming summer break, saying that,

the holidays coming nearer must be on his mind, as well as his anxiety of my death, which had suddenly appeared some time ago in the idea that the workman he heard hammering was nailing my coffin … . He admits that the holidays seem to be hard … . Then he mentions his sister for the first time since the death of his mother. When I press him about his sister – whether she is worried and if this worries him – he says, no, she has enough to do to look after her father, but then suddenly says that she seems quite lost. With strong affects he speaks of whether people in the street know that if their mother dies everything is finished, and they are quite useless for anything else. I point out that his feeling of being useless is that he feels incapable of restoring his mother and his anxieties about his children and his wife increase fears of not being able to repair them.

Klein asks Mr B,

if he means that people who underrate the importance of such a death are pretending? He agrees that this is what he must have meant. Then says he must really always have been awfully frightened of his mother's death and found it very difficult to be without her. He then tells me about his own holiday plans, which he had withheld from me. He does not want to know when I come back because he is afraid that it might be before he is back and he does not want to know that I am available when he cannot come. He then speaks of his pleasure about things he is going to do on holiday and that his daughter was pleased. Finishes up in quite a friendly mood.

Friday 10 July 1936

Klein notes a 'change in attitude' in Mr B. She reports that he,

Feels that I am concerned about him with regard to the holidays, and that I was friendly about that; that he had the feeling that I am not after all going away just because I am nasty and so on. He then refers to an article in The Times which discussed Russia. Russia, which was formerly compared to a bear now seems more like a hippopotamus, 'which keeps itself under the water and just shows the top of its head; Makes itself unassailable because in its own element it cannot be attacked'.

Mr B notes that 'he has had dreams which flew away like butterflies.' He saw a production of The Tempest the evening before and now quotes Ariel saying to Prospero, "Here I am master.' Prospero had saved Ariel from the most awful tortures, and though Ariel has for some time to go on serving Prospero, he will soon be free. Mr B feels this has to do with the analysis. Klein notes that,

His willingness to give me dreams which had flown away shows he is Ariel who serves me in the work with his cooperation. But he also implies that I have saved him from the most awful tortures, which I suggest are deep anxieties about his insides, which seem to be lessened. That his serving me until he becomes free is going on with his analysis for some time.

Klein reminds Mr B,

that some few weeks ago he had said that when analysis is over he would ask me a question about myself. This is the first time he has been able to face the fact that analysis will be over. Then I seem to play the role of the good father, the magician, for it was Caliban and not Prospero who had made Ariel suffer the awful tortures. I cited the beginning of the session where I had been quite good, in his mind, and he had recognised that I was not torturing.

Klein then refers to the Russian bear which becomes a hippopotamus, connecting this change to an improvement in Mr B, to his objects inside and his feeling about Klein. Mr B,

does not quite agree to that because he said he always had a special affection for the bear, though he agrees that the writer of this article meant an improvement, comparing the bear with the hippopotamus, and that he had quoted him in this sense. I point out that of course there is lots of doubt in the goodness of the bull, bear, hippopotamus, but that his association about tortures seems to mean that I help him to improve objects.

Finally, Mr B speaks of a solution that has been found in the company, since members cannot agree to oust the Chairman. Two more people will join the Board. Klein suggests that though the Chairman isn't felt to be 'a very good father, [another solution is] to get better objects in him to help the whole inner as well as external situation.' Mr B says 'it had always seemed to him he must get the Chairman out, and he felt guilty about this.'

Saturday 11 July 1936

Mr B reports a dream, again stressing that Klein should understand very clearly the actual situation:

> *There was a field with grass – but the grass was eaten off like turf. He was looking down and saw rabbit runs. He was trying to find their holes by kicking with his foot against the grass. Then he saw a rabbit hole and he knew there was a multitude of rabbits there, but actually he seemed only to see three. He caught one with his hand and killed it, in the way he used to kill rabbits with great gusto as a child, when chasing them with his dog. Mr B catches it behind with his left hand and, as he says, 'The poor little thing put up its head', he gives it a hard blow with right hand … . Speaking of rabbits he calls them 'fascinating little creatures'. The important thing in catching a rabbit is to pull it the right way out of the hole. After having killed this one rabbit, he had not felt able to decide to kill the other two, he says probably because he was not sure that he would pull them out in the right way.*

Mr B feels this material has something to do with analysis. Klein suggests it 'has something to do with childbirth - with how to pull the baby out the right way … its position, and the way it comes out.' Mr B has various associations to Klein's thought:

> *He saw some beautiful thistle, the milky thistle, which he is very fond of. Then, speaking about thistles, he mentioned the stalkless thistle which, he said, is very clever because it grows so low to the ground that no horse or donkey can eat it. Then speaks of umbels, then he suddenly says that seems to have to do with childbirth. The word 'umbels' reminds him of something, and he asks me to help him. He seems very ignorant about all such facts. When I suggest 'umbilical' cord, he says that is what he meant. Speaking of umbels, Mr B says they are also poisoning – remembering that Socrates was killed by an umbel, and says how different his feelings are as soon as the flora changes.*

Associating again to rabbits, Mr B recalls,

> *a man who works for his firm, who works so hard and is like a ferret getting out the rabbits (customers) and putting them into your hand. He is a reliable man … restricted in other ways – but just excellent about his work. This reminds Mr B of another person whom he had recommended to the firm … he proved to be quite incapable of getting on with people, and it appeared he had taken money and had to be sacked. He never wanted really to be*

helped … . If this man had agreed to be helped, and had confessed about the money … it would have been better, but he did not do this – he was just hurt, and had not the insight to see his fault. Mr B then says that he has a feeling as if he would withhold from me other things which went on in the dream. [These things are] 'like mountain tops behind mist' – but he cannot tell me … . About the ferret he had an association to the Lady with Ferret, a picture by Leonardo de Vinci, and says she seems to hold the ferret against her breast.

Klein's interpretation makes reference to the death of her own son, Hans, who died on a mountain. She suggests that Mr B's,

feeling that he is withholding something awful from me 'like mountain tops' seems to have to do with killing the one rabbit. It is quite obvious that these 'innocent creatures' stand for children, and that in the field … his kicking grass is an attack on the inside … . It is a question of pulling babies out, and he had already killed one. Now in his family no child had died, but the rabbit and mountain tops seem to connect with my son who died in the mountains; and Mr B's being reluctant about killing others … . His guilt and anxiety seem to apply to my other two children and this connects with the whole question of where, since I had mentioned to him that I am going for my holiday … . He probably – as he had done on other occasions – thought of my going away with my son. I suggested jealousy had come up and anxiety of attacking me, hence this danger of killing the other two rabbits. He says that in his family also there were three children, himself and two others.

Mr B notes that the thistle is 'characteristic for Scotland,' where Klein has told him she will spend her holiday. Klein continues:

I suggest that the multitude of rabbits which he knew were there are the children inside his mother's body whom he knew were there; but in his feelings he had attacked them … . The rabbits are here conceived as innocent, but very dangerous children, since they had eaten up the whole grass of the field, and this is a secondary reason for him to attack them inside their mother's body and to destroy them, because in his phantasy and because of his own wishes, they would eat up the inside of the mother. But he himself is the ferret, and is here compared with the good man who does the right work, and so on, but the lady who puts him to her breast will be in danger too.

Klein says that Mr B is then like the man in his company who had stolen the money; he steals the rabbit baby from mother, even kills it, and is then wracked with guilt. She notes that Mr B's identification with this man who cannot admit having stolen, is revealed in his recollection of the occasion when his brother would not allow him to confess to their misdemeanour in the park, which mother and nurse wanted and would have appreciated. Returning to the milky thistle, Klein remarks that,

Mr B's first association had been that it seems to be symbolic for the penis … . He actually wanted to get hold, [inside the] mother's body, of the good penis, the milky one which changed into a poisoning umbel … . He had said that his whole feelings changed with the

flora, which seems to apply also to the state of his inside, because good, milky thistle, standing for the beautiful, admired penis, changed into a poisoning thing inside and made him bad.

Klein reminds Mr B of another of his dreams, in which:

A young man approached a sickly-looking old man, who was sitting at some place where just before an attractive woman to whom Mr B had made advances was sitting … . This young man was pulling out something like a pair of socks – and at the same time he knew, and the old man knew, [that the old man] would be poisoned. This nightmare was connected with the penis, and here, the young man who seemed simple and business-like in the dream, was poisoning [the] old man with his penis.

Klein suggests to Mr B that,

he was identified with the young man who was poisoning, and was at the same time turning away in horror from the scene … protecting himself from a dangerous attack through not wanting to see what happened … Socrates is also a father who dies because he has poisoned him. I connect this whole situation with anxiety and feelings about the death of his mother … . He is unable now to confess to her and to put her right, because of having robbed her and done harm to her children … I also say that his wish to get away from me which he was expressing but was unable to do … connects with anxiety of attacks of the kind on me and on my children, and of the wish to save me.

Monday 13 July 1936

Mr B is deeply depressed and 'full of hatred against' Klein, whom he says, 'seems to claim progress about sexual phantasies, but the contrary is true – that things have got worse with his wife.' He says his wife seems not to want to do things with him alone, but wants always to include their daughter. She also seems not to be grown up herself, but to want 'to be the child.' He reports a dream to which the foregoing comments are clear associations:

He was going to bed with his wife and it was quite pleasant, but he never had intercourse with her, because it was as if their eldest child was behind them –they could not well do the intercourse with her there.

Klein interprets that in the past, when Mr B had seduced his sister, he had really wanted his mother. His wife is now standing for his sister, yet what he wants is a relationship with a grown-up woman, standing for mother.

I remind him that for the first time recently he mentioned that when he had intercourse with his wife it was as if he had raped a child. He now feels strongly a wish for a relation to [an] actual mother.

Klein then suggests that,

> *this situation in the dream where the child appears when the parents have intercourse, seems to be a reversal of the situation where he himself would disturb the intercourse of the parents, and also where he, in being with sister, would be found out by somebody else.*

Mr B says,

> *I always have to find something against him.*

Tuesday 14 July 1936

Klein again notes Mr B's 'change in attitude' towards her. He acknowledges that he had been furious the previous day, but now admits that lately he has managed some very successful negotiations in his company. The implication is that Klein has helped him. A doctor also seems able to help his wife. Mr B says, 'that it is already a great step to make her see that this trouble is there and has to be dealt with. Understanding about it is the first step.' Klein comments that,

> *this also applies to Mr B and also, there is guilt about his own not wanting to see things which I tell him. He felt guilty about his rage against me. I then point out that this company business, as all material of the last few days shows, seems to show that this process of him being put right goes with having his objects put right … . He feels that I am improving his objects inside him, which are reflected in his external objects … . The line of progress seems to be that of taking better objects in, establishing better relations to his mother, acknowledging the bad things as well as the good ones, and not keeping these so much apart but bringing them nearer to each other.*

Mr B says he has decided not to accept any payment as a member of the Board, since the company is currently not making good profits. He says, 'the Director should do what is often done, either have fees reduced or not have any.' Klein interprets that Mr B also wants her to lower the demands she makes upon him, though not meaning in terms of fees. She says:

> *If I claim that I am helping him, then it means stirring in him all these emotions which connect with love towards his mother, feelings of guilt, anxiety and so on … . Actually what he wants me to do is to not make such large demands on his gratitude and good feelings. He has mentioned always that he could not stand love and had to be between love and hate.*

Mr B is 'very dissatisfied' with this interpretation, which in some sense he misunderstands. He tells Klein he 'does not want at all … that she should reduce her fees.' He says he feels 'very depressed, speaks of dying and is all dissatisfaction – that everything is wrong, and then says 'my relations to you are fundamentally wrong and cannot be put right.' Klein tells Mr B,

> that my interpretation has stirred in him the anxiety that he cannot any more put his relations to his mother right because he had not wanted to satisfy these demands on love and gratitude – feelings which he always had about mother but had repressed …. . He feels that if relations to me cannot be better, then all his relations cannot be put right … that there is so much distrust in him about me.

Wednesday 15 July 1936

Mr B begins with 'bitter complaints.' He tells Klein, 'an old lady [was] in front of him in Clifton Hill. He could not walk as slowly as she, but he did not want to pass her because he did not want her to see him coming into my house.' He is furious that someone might know he is going for treatment. He then reports a 'horrible dream':

> It was in a house which he knew to be Dr W's house, but it did not look like it. Miss W was showing him two ornaments which were standing on the mantelpiece, and explained to him, especially about one, how valuable it was. There were two medals, one on top of the other. It represented two figures, one pouring something into a jug which the other was holding. Mr B seemed neither to agree nor to disagree with her thinking that this object was valuable. He simply did not know. He was most embarrassed and frightened, and stressed very emphatically the state of muddle and ignorance in which he felt – this whole dream leaving him in such a state of muddle.

Mr B says the object 'reminds him of something sexual,' and also recalls 'a toy which he had been shown in Hungary which when one turned it round showed a couple in intercourse.'

> Suddenly, Mr B complains about the awful noisiness in the street, the motor cars passing by, the match which I had struck, the matchbox which had been put down, and finally says he cannot bear me to speak any word and stops his ears and covers his eyes, which is unusual. He used to cover his eyes for a long time with his hankie but not his ears. After some time when he has given this up again, I interpret that it seems to be the reactivation of an early observation of intercourse, of which we have had lots of material before …. . He could not look and hear any more because of the state of anxiety he was in. I suggest that he was not wanting to see and to hear anything more because to him this intercourse was not something precious which should be shown to him but something horrible. He quotes Plato who said that one might want to look and to see something and to look away, for example if one sees a heap of corpses, … one might want to see and not to see.

Klein interprets,

> that this comparison shows that intercourse is going to finish with death. I remind him of
> the dream of skinning the bird in which a general castration and his own as well was
> connected with this early phantasy or experience. He reminds me of a nightmare which he
> had told me before that he had had when with his wife in Paris, where he saw on a bed
> vague ill-defined figures – silhouettes – and then intercourse. They were above him as if they
> were raised on the bed, and I suggest that this might have been the position of his cot in
> comparison to the parents' bed. He then says it might also have been that he had been under
> the bed and had got into the room in an unorthodox way, and I connect this with great
> anxiety of being seen by the old woman when entering my house.

Thursday 16 July 1936

Klein records that Mr B arrives 'quite exhausted and frightened.' He says that,

> while he was sitting still in the taxi [waiting to come into his session], a woman passed
> him and stared into the taxi at him. He accuses me of the awful people in this
> neighbourhood, and speaks very strongly against this awful-looking woman, with her
> vacant look, inquisitive, and so on. Describes where she was coming from – she was an
> elderly woman – and asks me whether I think I know her. He is pleased with my saying
> that I don't … she might then, he concludes, just have looked without much purpose.

The somewhat paranoid atmosphere persists, however, as Mr B,

> turns to railing once more about the Chairman and something he 'has done in connection
> with the shareholders without consulting Mr B'. Mr B thinks he may now be trying now to
> get Mr B out, in the same way as Mr B wanted to get the Chairman out of the Board.
> Then mentions reluctantly an attack on the King, but emphasises that it obviously was not
> serious – it was probably only a toy revolver … that constables leading the man away were
> quite friendly, and so on.

Klein interprets Mr B's,

> anxiety of the father whom he has attacked in connection with the early experience [of
> observing parental intercourse], and his [subsequent] anxiety of being observed … . The old
> woman, standing for me, is the bad mother who finds out about his attacks … . I point out
> that now the anxiety about the intercourse has come into connection with the death of his
> mother and the loss of her, which revives [his] old anxiety … that it is an internalised
> situation and … that her death has happened in an awful way.

Finally, Klein highlights Mr B's guilt about the early experience of observing
intercourse, which has become connected with the death of his mother. She

refers again to his dreams of the bull and the shed, which saw his mother coming to harm at the hands of his father. Klein's notes end with the comment,

> *In this hour again, but less than yesterday, Mr B expresses indecision, ignorance, muddle and helplessness.*

Here, Klein's record of work with Mr B during the summer term of 1936 ends. Though there is no suggestion in her final entry for 16th July that this was the last session ahead of the long summer break, Klein's diary suggests that it was. Notes resume again in September 1936 and are presented in the following chapter.

Note

1 Klein's diaries show that she often saw Mr B on a Saturday, and just twice she saw him on a Sunday too.

Reference

Klein, M. (1940) Mourning and Its Relation to Manic-Depressive States. *International Journal of Psychoanalysis* 21:125–153.

Chapter 4

Walking over scorched turf

Mr B's endless criticism of Klein and his analysis, which he cannot bear to bring to an end, fills the sessions of this chapter. During the summer break of 1936, when Mr B is ill, he telephones Klein to clarify when they are due to resume. He finds that she responds in a kindly way, and he then regrets being so frequently reproachful and aggressive towards her. He wants to cooperate, but so often lacks trust in the treatment and in Klein, feeling she accuses him endlessly concerning his 'bad sexuality.' Klein's analysis of this in the following months brings some relief. Mr B's sense that his objects are under constant attack inside, mixed up as they are with a violent parental intercourse, comes to be better understood. It is this backdrop, Klein contends, that accounts for Mr B's need to keep external objects, including his analyst, close, despite his very great ambivalence towards them.

Sessional material clearly illustrates Mr B's preoccupation with the terrible state of his own insides, and with the matter of how to keep his internal objects alive. The 'scorched turf' he walks over in a dream from September 1936, Klein feels, captures his experience of an internal world that cannot support life. Yet, this material is juxtaposed with reflections about a proliferation of life in the form of cistus flowers. Thus, despite his railing against a treatment he claims is destroying him, Klein is able to locate Mr B's hope that his analysis can help him recover good experiences of objects and support his efforts to protect these.

In the period of the analysis covered by this chapter, we also see Klein beginning to connect more fully Mr B's sense of internal destruction with phantasies of sexual activity between him and his siblings. Klein analyses thoroughly the link in Mr B's mind between his own sexuality, and badness and destruction. In the transference, Mr B's dread both of damaging Klein and of being violated by her comes more clearly into focus.

Material also shows that alongside Mr B's sense of a destructive parental intercourse, there is also, deeply buried, a profound admiration of the penis and a nascent sense that intercourse can be creative and curative. There are some terribly moving moments of contact between Klein and Mr B, such as when he speaks to her of his love of birds and the natural world, and tries to explain things to her as he would have done to his very much loved younger sister. Such good contact is however quickly alarming to Mr B, who feels it to be too closely linked

DOI: 10.4324/9781003373414-5

which sexual desire, which is so destructive in his mind. As Klein and her patient struggle to understand this, Klein continues to analyse Mr B's destructiveness towards his objects, which he finds excruciating. When he accuses Klein of having no right to expose the 'horrors inside him,' she says simply that, 'there is no possibility of covering up such feelings if they are there, and they get quite out of perspective if they are hidden away and not brought to consciousness.' This seems very much in line with Klein's belief that love can be liberated where hatred is sufficiently analysed, a perhaps under-appreciated idea of Klein's that Steiner (2017) has recently highlighted.

That hatred, once analysed, can give way to love, is movingly evident in the material of this chapter. Klein's notes begin to reveal a much more nuanced relationship which is developing between Mr B and his internal mother. She is in turn present in Mr B's descriptions of the 'Stormy Petrel', a bird that struggles so much to get to its young, like the 'flat fish mother' who holds her baby so awkwardly; and then in the beautiful and admired Kingfisher which flashes past, stirring such intense emotion. Mr B is now grieving and perhaps beginning to station inside himself a deeply loved mother. Klein talks to him about the way he has always needed to 'put the pleasure element out' of his relationship with his mother, since pleasure is so inextricably connected to destructive sexuality; but she also shows him that through analysis he is getting to know both his parents anew, and revising his past and current relationship to them.

September 1936

The summer holiday has apparently been prolonged, though no explanation is given for this in Klein's notes. Mr B is in a state of despair about his analysis, and depressed, 'as though dead.' Klein interprets that the analysis, 'which he feels he must get rid of, stands for all his badness inside.' Further interpretations along these lines seem to bring some relief, for Mr B then tells Klein about,

> discovering a feather of a bird, an owl … He understood which bird it belongs to, and discussed it with somebody in the neighbourhood who is a great expert. Mr B suggested that it belongs to a bird which is very rare in that part. The expert agreed that it belonged to that bird, but said that that bird is not so rare as Mr B had thought. Mr B says, 'how much one can find out if one understands a little feather.'

Klein interprets,

> that he had been the one who had discovered the feather. I was the expert who could get to so many conclusions from a little feather … and he [responded] by saying how many conclusions one gets in analysis from a little feather.

Several days later, with 'depression very much prevailing,' the matter of the quality of Mr B's internal landscape, and the nature of interactions between objects inside, begins to come to the fore:

Mr B speaks of the Indore process of treating plant waste matter to improve soil, and what a great discovery this was. He says that in England one has quite a good way of dealing with the ground, because cattle which are grazing at the same time provide the manure, and the grazing does not hurt the ground because it gets enriched over and over again by the manure of the cattle. It isn't done so well elsewhere ... Mr B's grounds at X are quite good. However, then he speaks of the problem of willows which get hurt – the bark can be hurt by cattle ... One possibility is to allow the cattle in the same field but to fence in the willows so that they should not be hurt. Mr B mentions that he has learnt that the willow is not male, but is always female. He had always thought it male, but now thinks it is female. These associations had been preceded in the last two days by Mr B's interest in the destruction of the cocoa-moth, which has connected to former material about keeping the good things safe against the destructive bad injured things inside.

Klein interprets that Mr B's problem is 'not analysis and what he is to do with it – is he to keep it on or to give it up – but problem of the ground,' which she clearly states stands for mother, and what he can do about her state inside of him. She says that,

If the child does not destroy the ground (mother) but fertilizes it in the right way, giving good faeces, then mother will not be destroyed.

Klein tells Mr B that really, he is concerned 'with mother's body,' and with the question of how to keep his mother alive inside. She writes that 'this was quite agreed to, because [formerly,] he quite feels he did not know what problems he was talking of, and there were problems.' The following day, Mr B brings two dreams. In the first,

He is travelling with his mother and brother. They are travelling backwards and they both have great trouble in getting her out of the carriage. She is very drowsy and nearly dead.

In the second dream,

He was walking with somebody – a woman – on his left, in the dark, through the parks of London. He was in pyjamas, which is quite a suitable costume if in East Africa, but does not seem the right thing for a London park ... . There were people sitting on benches and he had lost contact with the person on his left – he could see and hear her, but ... (Mr B finds it most difficult to speak and I cannot get much – very unpleasant for him). The person points out to him a cistus. There was not one single bud on it and the whole thing was frightfully gloomy. He was walking over scorched turf ...

Associating to this second dream, Mr B speaks for a time about cistus flowers, as well as of the scorched turf. Klein records,

When speaking about scorched turf, Mr B coughed very much and said that actually he had felt his throat quite burning. He agrees when I point out the connection between scorched

turf and his burning throat. When going out of the door he tells me that cistus is extremely prolific. One morning all the flowers have dropped and the next day a lot of others. In his dream it was very gloomy – nothing there.

Klein's next entry is from mid-October, though she refers to the two dreams described here as if they had been brought very recently, perhaps even on the previous day.

Wednesday 14 October 1936

Mr B is very late. Klein writes that he,

Has been to the seaside for the day because of his cold, and says that from this good air he had to come back to … foul London, adding 42 Clifton Hill. He says this in a low voice, very depressed, but one sees that he feels full of anxiety, that he is terrified of me. I go on not speaking. After some time he says that if I don't speak he does not get less terrified, he seems to get still more terrified.

Klein returns to two dreams above, 'showing him their gloomy atmosphere.' She interprets that,

this person he was going with in the dark and had lost contact with, represents me, who is showing him all the gloominess inside him. I draw his attention to his reluctance to explain what this lack of contact consisted in. I had asked him if it was not hearing, seeing or touching, but he was unable to speak. I suggest his being so terrified when I don't speak has to do with losing contact with me and feeling that I am dead like his mother. Not having contact then means not being able to get in touch with his dying mother inside him, which in the first dream he tries to deal with by putting her out of the railway carriage. But if he puts her out, he loses her. Then he remarks and emphasizes that in the dream he was going backwards … obviously it means childhood and going back to the past.

In the moments before Mr B leaves, he tells Klein part of another dream:

There is a little town, W, which was near the place where he was on his holidays in the north. There is then another town of the same name about 30 miles from there. He has not seen it and it is separated by the sea from this other town W. In the dream he spoke with somebody about this town, but then the second town W was inland and only separated by about 10 miles from the actual place he knows. Somebody was saying something about a boat, and he said "Perhaps it is the boat at the other W."

Klein writes, 'I draw attention to the fact that he has given the dream to me just before he goes.' Mr B is however glad not to have left more time, and tells Klein, 'I have given it to you at the end so that you should not be able to interpret, and so that I shall have time to think it over until tomorrow.' He remarks how much he resents Klein giving an interpretation on the spot.

Thursday 15 October 1936

Mr B is very late and tells Klein that he had 'very strongly wanted not to come.' He 'cannot stand it,' and says, 'the stakes are too high.' Klein tells him that,

> *obviously if he were to leave me now and give up his analysis, which has become the representative of everything destructive and terrifying, he would still not get rid of what is actually the reason for his depression. He says of course he does not believe he would feel happy, but he cannot help feeling that he can't stand it any longer.*

Mr B's comment that the,

> *'Stakes are too high' reminds him of betting, which he never does, and this leads him to recall a very moving line from Homer, which he feels reluctant to quote, but describes. It refers to Hector, who was chased around the town of Troy by Achilles, and was watched by the other Trojans and Greeks. Hector was running for his life – that is, the highest stakes possible.*

Klein says it is clear that analysis has become 'the fight between Achilles and Hector,' and that she too is felt to be extremely dangerous. She suggests to Mr B that his depression has been 'accumulating during the holidays'; that 'he had left in very deep depression, and then the holidays had come.' She reminds Mr B of the very great anxiety he was feeling about his own death and hers. He agrees that in Achilles, Klein appears 'as the most threatening and frightening figure.'

Klein notes that earlier in the session, she had referred to the previous day's dream about two towns with the same name, W. Mr B had at the time,

> *declined to speak, saying he was incapable of saying a word. But after this Homer quotation he speaks with a louder voice and says now he can tell me more about this town W. He expresses now what he had not done before, that this town W is the most charming place one can imagine, beautiful coast, and so on; and that here three places appear, one is real and he knows it, one is real and he does not know it, and the third is not real at all. I suggest to him that this relates to the interpretation I gave about his mother being there and not there inside him. This lovely place which he knows, the unknown place, which is still real, and the phantasy mother, which is both understood and not understood, and this feeling of loss of contact with me … . I say Homer connects with his mother who read it out to him. He agrees.*

Klein records that Mr B is 'a little less depressed when he leaves.'

Friday 16 October 1936

Mr B begins by recalling that Klein has recently mentioned 'the importance of investigating the deeper reasons for his depression.' He says he is 'also very keen to get to understand the deeper reasons.' Whilst Klein can see that this is an expression of a wish to cooperate with her, she thinks better of saying this. She writes that,

> *any time I mention this I am confronted with great difficulties – in the same way as when I show him any change for the better which is connected with his wish to cooperate with me. It is quite true that at times he needs to have it confirmed that he cooperates, but now since the depression has been so strong and the situation so difficult, I refrain from saying that this remark shows a new cooperation.*

Mr B returns to the town of his dream, W. Klein writes that he seems to feel he could 'go on talking and talking about it.' He describes it's 'beautiful position and coast etc.'

> *This leads him to speak about birds, especially mentioning a bird which is found there – the stormy petrel - which actually nests always so that it is towards the Atlantic, which is a speciality of this bird. When it has to feed its young, it has the greatest difficulty, because it is very bad on land – with its feet – which makes it very difficult for it to get to its nest. Mr B seems very sympathetic to the great difficulties of this bird having young, speaking about the awful burden for this bird to have young. Like a poor mother who did not know what to do with her babies.*

Mr B goes on speaking of other birds with 'great pleasure and interest.' In fact, Klein notes, 'he speaks with such pleasure that he leaves me a few minutes later because I find it difficult to stop him.'

Saturday 17 October 1936

Mr B had dined with friends the previous evening and tells Klein that he had continued speaking with them about birds. He seems to feel very guilty about this. Klein interprets that,

> *his feeling of guilt refers to the pleasure he had in talking to me about it. Obviously, he had enjoyed it very much and even wanted to stay on. Mr B agrees that if he enjoys talking with me and if I am interested in what he says and it is pleasant for me, he feels that it is very dangerous. I remind him how much in his relation with his mother he had to put this pleasure element out, and how deeply he enjoyed certain things he had in common with his mother. Also, he agrees that his wish to impress me favourably by his language and the way he is expressing himself increases his feelings of guilt.*

Klein attempts to further understand Mr B's difficulty in enjoying an exchange with her, as with his mother:

> *I raise the question why pleasure makes him feel so guilty, and say that I know he has had sexual enjoyment in sexual intercourse before he came to analysis even. He feels he had more*

before he came, but at the same time we have seen that there is a deep connection in his mind between sexuality and something bad, which he should not enjoy.

Klein notes that in the past Mr B had accused her of underrating his capacity for sexual pleasure, and that this had 'brought about storms in his analysis.' Nonetheless, at this moment, Mr B,

Agrees that sexuality always meant for him something bad – not always, but at times …

Klein reminds him,

that he had given up masturbation entirely at a certain time in his childhood and had not taken it up again. On the other hand he still remembers the time when he masturbated with enjoyment. I also raise the question of what could have happened at this time. He tells me – which he had not done before – that it connects very much in his mind with his first and with his second school – where he had been one term together with his brother, and then the brother left. He tells me a lot about this special summer, which was in between these two terms. There was a very nice boy with them – a friend of his – rather gentle and passive, but very nice. He has no memory, though he was 10 years old, about the house, the arrangement of the rooms, nor about his brother at all in this summer. I had heard before some details about this summer but not about the gentle boy and not the following.

This was that his father had been ill at that time with appendicitis. He had been in bed, and Mr B had been sitting on the bed, and put his hand just on the place which hurt the father, and made him wince. Of course, Mr B says, he did not know that this was just the place which hurt. He passed very lightly over this illness of the father, and I ask him if he had ever seen his father ill before. He answers that this is the first time his father had been really ill. I suggest to him, and had already suggested before in analysis – that something seemed to have happened to him on the line of a sexual attack – reminding him that he had been consciously very frightened of his brother, who had been sleep-walking towards his bed, and Mr B had actually been frightened of an attack on his penis. Also, we have had much material about anxiety of an attack behind.

Klein clearly notes the move from memories of a 'special summer,' and relations with a gentle, passive boy, to the memory of an ill or damaged father whom Mr B harms. She writes,

I mention his having been so terrified of me these last few days and his talking about racing for high stakes, when I appeared to be Achilles and he Hector. He had thought it phantastic when I said I stood for a man. I wonder, however, how much I am here standing for this attacking brother who might in some way have violated him. My interpreting the anxiety of Achilles, etc, had obviously diminished Mr B's anxiety because he could then speak to me so much more freely.

Regarding Mr B's memory of the gentle boy, Klein suggests that it,

> *seems to point to a situation where Mr B played the active role and this boy played Mr B's part, in relation to the raping brother.*

Then, considering Mr B's father's illness, she says,

> *It seemed to have confirmed all Mr B's anxieties of something bad having happened to his own insides, through a relation with the brother. When mentioning this sexual relation with brother, I remind him of material which had been very striking to him – a dream in which somebody he recognized as standing for his brother stood over him with a ginger-beer bottle, and he himself associated to fellatio, the ginger beer bottle standing for the penis. When I say this, he remembers that he had a dream in which there was a lot of beer froth spilt over the floor. He felt rather awkward and did not want to talk about this dream. I interpret that this material having come up at a time when he was terrified of me as the attacking brother who forces him to fellatio and may have robbed him, seems rather to speak in favour of my interpretations.*

Monday 19 October 1936

Mr B begins by wondering whether he really is so depressed. Klein notes that 'he feels very guilty if he pretends to be more depressed than he is.' She records that she had recently told Mr B that 'there were very deep reasons in him against improving or admitting improvement.'

> *I say too that he feels I reproach him that he does not want to become better, but that what I feel about it is that there must be very strong reasons for him to feel that he cannot get out of this depression. I had often before interpreted to him that he is afraid of my underrating the dangers; that he felt always that mother and nurse did this, when they had said 'it is all right – there is nothing in it.'*

Mr B moves to tell Klein that from the place where his maternal grandfather lived, one could see in the distance a landmark, which is a place of special interest for the National Trust. He had surprised himself by making a donation to the Trust in his grandfather's memory. He says that he will however be quite unable to tell his brother and sister about this, though in a way he would like to. He then tells of a visit to a cousin in the country where he met many family members. Whilst his mother's family is 'nearly extinct,' there are a great number of cousins on the father's side. Mr B talks about one particular cousin,

> *who had caught some disease through trying to cure a ferret's wound, which was caused by a rat-bite … When he heard (and here his voice and manner changes) he laughed and said to the person who told him about his cousin: "Oh, have the rats caught him after all?" Mr B tells me that this cousin had been ratting so much that he had killed thousands of rats and that now*

he was himself caught – the rats had got their own back. Mr B does not show the slightest sign of being sorry for this cousin – whom he did not dislike. He then associates to an occasion where his brother and he were in the country near a rubbish heap and were expecting a rabbit to come out of it. They had wanted to catch it, but what came out was a rat which bit Mr B's brother on the finger. Mr B had been fortunate because he had not got bitten.

Klein interprets,

that this multitude of rats is really standing for the multitudes of cousins. That the mother's family which becomes extinct is the mother inside him, which he tries to revive and cannot because the place is over-run with rats. I refer to former material about destroying the moth which injures the cocoa, and also to the problems of last week – how to keep the ground fertile because of the cattle. The manure of the cattle is good for the ground, but at the same time the cattle injure willows.

Klein continues,

I remind Mr B of his own strong feelings about biting and destroying the breast, for which we have had lots of material, as the beginning of everything bad. I say that the rats – the biting rat – are both standing for the dangerous penis, and are now the mother who is going to die because there is no hope against the mass of rats. I told him that he not only has a wish to eternalize, as it were, his grandfather's name, but that the connection of the place – the thing one could see at a distance – is ... the good mother, who seems to be put into the distance so that one can just see her. She is to be eternalized inside. Mr B's anxiety that he will not be able to keep her eternalized, is shown by his trying to eternalize the grandfather's name ... It is the mother herself whom he wants to eternalize and keep going, but cannot because of ... the bad children who are represented through the male side of the family – as if they are the bad penis and bad children who destroy his mother.

Klein finally returns to Mr B's doubt about whether he is really so depressed. She interprets that he cannot 'give in to the hope of getting out of depression,' because of his anxiety that rats or badness or bad children inside will overrun the internal ground and destroy his mother there.

Tuesday 20 October 1936

Mr B begins with a dream:

He dreamt he was at a party. It was not a smart party – although they were in evening dress it seemed something like a picnic indoors, where one drank beer ... Mr B's father also appeared – very weak – the death of his father is very much on his mind. Father is leaning on somebody else whom he had his arm around for support. He says that his father seemed very friendly and was disposed to be nice about everybody. Mr B felt that he wanted to make water and went out to find a lavatory but could not. He went into a place where there were all sorts of obstacles in the way of his urinating, and suddenly discovered that on an old-fashioned counterpane there was a child asleep which disturbed him very much. Suddenly a woman appeared, looking into the room through a window. It was very awkward and frightening. He managed in the end to urinate and went back to the party, and then his father asked him in front of all the people, where he had been or what he had done. Mr B was absolutely enraged by this lack of tact. Just before, he had highly appreciated his father's kindness.

Mr B said the child was found asleep and was an innocent child. There seemed a sort of hurrying in the way he put it, and he spoke in an entirely different voice and seemed rather frightened – then said it was not an innocent child – it was not a child at all. When I tried to find out what it was, he mentions something ... like a doll and then something about a picture which is not Shakespeare but which stands for him. He says this picture does not look at all like a great man. It is not like a man at all – it is as if he had two right arms and it seems all untrue.

Klein connects Mr B's dream material to his probable observation of the primal scene. She recalls,

Mr B's sister being born, the surprise – his not understanding if she was a child or not – and whether there was any connection with the primal scene. I suggest to him that these two right arms ... and a great man represented through a thing which was untrue, suggests Mr B's observations of the primal scene where the limbs of the parents were mixed up. Then, the great man, the father, had become an entirely different figure and ... the child being born, seemed to him such an impossible creature.

Klein suggests that the child of the dream is Mr B himself:

The innocent child who was supposed to be asleep and was not innocent at all, because he was watching the scene with hate and all sorts of feelings which made him seem a rat and not an innocent child. Also, there is a connection between Mr B's urinating and his injuring his little sister, and the mistrust of the women watching him, which he had always felt as mistrust, and which we had in analysis found to be confirming his anxieties of injuring his sister with dangerous urine. Here also a friendly father appears as an interfering figure, who publicly exposes what Mr B has done with his urine. All his anxieties about having been a rat and destroying seem to link now with these early situations of the primal scene and the birth of the sister.

Wednesday 21 October 1936

Mr B is late and then very silent. Klein thinks he has been very disturbed by her interpretation of emerging material. He says he has had 'an awful night.' Though he cannot recall any dream, he feels full of anxiety. Again, he speaks against the treatment, and against Klein, who writes,

I remind him of yesterday's material, especially the dangerous urine, watching woman and innocent child, and his early anxieties being stirred.

She again speaks of Mr B's,

> *original frustration about the baby and all the anxieties connecting with the birth of his sister and his dangerousness to her.*

Thursday 22 October 1936

Mr B is on time, despite Klein having changed the time of his session today, something he has previously hated. He complains about the analysis, and Klein's treatment of him, saying,

> *in a rather low, sad voice, that he feels like being a lot of bad people, and there is no unity in him. He had had a dream two days before in which he was shooting two ferrets, and says that is not a thing one would do in reality, although he would like to shoot his wife's dog because it frightens her so much, and he hates to see that.*

Mr B then accuses Klein of not being willing to help his children who need help, whereas his wife is actually opposed to them having psychological help. He says that his wife wants to take their daughter with them when they visit their son at half term. This, he feels, would be a catastrophe. Klein suggests,

> *that the little girl going to see the brother is a repetition of Mr B's little sister being born, and he does not want that. Mr B then says he wishes he was dead.*

In association, he,

> *Suddenly thinks of lobsters and that one might feel sorry for them. They are alive and put into boxes, very tight together, are taken out … and boiled alive … Then, he suddenly speaks of how he is going to get rid, with the help of other people on the Board, of the Chairman. I interpret that the innocent child [of his last dream], which was not a child but a doll – this was his impression of his unborn sister. I remind him that he had heard from his brother that a child had arrived which looked dreadfully red. That is the lobster, and he had heard or seen something about things getting boiled for the confinement. He felt as if the child was red and from mother's body, and that its being red in this way was an awful thing. His feeling that he would like to be dead connected with the burning urine which he had put into his mother's body. This association had led to the wish to get rid of the Chairman as well as himself, because these parents were too much in their dangerous intercourse. And his death-wish is the result of overwhelming feelings of guilt about what he has done to the babies.*

Mr B had said at the beginning of the hour that he wanted to leave the analysis, but Klein remarks now that what he really wants is to save her from the badness inside of him; from the 'bad eating child' he feels himself to be. She says,

He would then leave me behind in the distance as a loved object. I remind him how often his associations and what he says are felt to be bad and dangerous. He first laughs at the idea that he should want to save me. He seems to feel mostly hate, but then says, 'Well, it is true that my poisonous conduct towards women has done harm to women – to my mother and sister, wife and Mrs X'. He denies that he could be concerned about me.

Returning to his sister at the end of the session, Mr B says,

My parents have not done her much good, have not helped her, through all the fuss they made, just made it all worse.

The implication is that Mr B's sister is psychologically troubled or unwell in some way, though it never becomes clear how. Certainly at times Mr B is overwhelmed by guilt about what he has done, either in phantasy or in external reality, to his sister, and he is dreadfully anxious that his parents knew what he had done. That he was prevented from picking her up or feeding her, he took as confirmation of the adults' mistrust of him. Klein notes here that,

Outstanding in his memory is the place in the country where he had once fed his sister himself from the bottle, because the others were all engaged otherwise.

Following this session, Mr B writes to Klein.

He accuses me that I have not kept to the important terms, because I had suddenly altered his hour, which was his possession and gave him security. This is such a shock that I have to do a great deal of work to undo this shock.

Saturday 24 October 1936

Mr B is again 'very depressed, silent, [and] late.' He says he 'feels so involved,' presumably meaning in his analysis. Klein writes that,

After a break he mentions the dog he had in the summer which he was quite fond of; it once pulled the guts out of a dead sheep – yards of them – and wolfed them. I interpret that he had mentioned his being so involved, and that he also had mentioned before the lot of bad people he consisted of. I suggest the little dog of his wife's which he wanted to shoot and this dog which was eating the dead sheep's guts stand for his own eating tendencies. He strongly disagrees and finds it quite impossible to listen to me.

Monday 26 October 1936

Mr B is full of hate, suspicion, and distrust. Again he says that he wants to leave analysis and,

says that I have no right to expose all these horrors – referring to the sheep, - not even if they were true. I have no right because he had been very ill to 'cut him up'. I give a general interpretation that exposing horrors and so on seems the only way of dealing with them as I do now repeatedly with him – there is no possibility of covering up such feelings if they are there, and they get quite out of perspective if they are hidden away and not brought to consciousness.

Klein then gives a more direct interpretation of Mr B's material, saying,

His expression that I have no right to cut him up refers to the guts the dog has been wolfing, and he expects retaliation for that. Also, that his wish to leave analysis, which is very strong now and repeated every hour, is to save me from his eating me. Then he speaks of his frustrated sexuality, saying or pretending that it is no frustration, because his sexual desires have been so lessened through me and through analysis; that it was I who showed him that they are evil. Here his relation to his wife comes in. I interpret that his wolfing and all this material about urination and the innocent child show that his sexuality has been identified with destruction very early, and putting it cautiously, that he projects on to me his own frustration because of anxiety.

Klein evidently recognises the difficulty in analysing Mr B's oral destructiveness, which for him is so disturbingly bound up with his sexuality. She is clearly treading very carefully, lest he again feels accused by her.

Tuesday 27 October 1936

The session opens with complaints:

Mr B expresses again his strong feeling that I let his children down, and says he knows that it is mad that he should identify me so much with his wife here and accuse me, but that is what he feels. His children need help and do not get it. I point out that he feels that I could help his children, but he continually says that I cannot help him.

Then,

I remind him that he has spoken of mothers who are so attached to their children that they feel as if their children were still inside them – criticizing his wife on that account – and that I am using his own comparison when I say that his children and his wife are his inner objects – brother, sister and mother, father, wife, who are all inside him – connecting with all this material about eating. From this point of view, it is quite logical that he cannot be cured if he has not cured his children.

Wednesday 28 October 1936

Klein's notes of this session are brief, but she reports an interesting observation, made by Mr B, that connects with recent interpretations concerning his 'eating tendencies':

Towards end of hour he tells me that he has connected two things [and that it is] quite amazing that he should only have connected them now ... His daughter, whose teeth are

irregular, was grinding her teeth in her sleep, because of worry … . This irregular position of the teeth is due to the worry & the grinding. I then point out that this anxiety is connected with the eating material – that his daughter's teeth stand here for his own, and that he discovers how deep the worry is about his eating tendencies. In leaving me he is very friendly and says that he would not have thought that I am like these Victorian mothers who suggest that children should be tortured by regulation of the teeth.

Monday 2 November 1936

On this day, Mr B is 'much less silent and depressed,' though he finds it 'difficult to talk.' He wonders, 'Could one give a little poison gas to the people next door?' He has previously felt very disturbed by piano playing coming from the flat next door during his sessions. Earlier material has shown that piano playing stands in his mind for explorations of the maternal body and for sexual exploration. Klein writes,

Then he thinks that poison gas could also be used against rats. He remembers that I had an intention to make the wall soundproof and I tell him that I did so in the summer. He is surprised about this, and then wonders whether the work-people, when they made it sound proof, made a big noise which disturbed the people next door. He did not in the least realise that this association was a wish for revenge against the neighbours for making a noise and disturbing him and me. I then suggest that these are the feelings he had towards the intercourse of his parents. I remind him of his memory of when he was sleeping in the dressing room next door to his parents' room, and woke up once with the nightmare that a dog was attacking his genital. He ran to his mother and found very little sympathy when he disturbed her. I suggest that it was then that he wanted to poison with flatus, and the noise he made was screaming.

In connection with this phantasied attack on the parental couple, Klein interprets that,

Earlier rat material had shown that rats were meant to be both the destructive child and the bad faeces, and now seem to have been the rats next door – the bad parents who also had an eating and dangerous intercourse, and whom he wanted to destroy with poison gas. I remind him of the material where one thing was to destroy the other – the moth destroying the cocoa and then the things used against the moth, which might be dangerous to the good thing inside. I suggest that his difficulty in talking to me is connected with the wish to save me from the poison gas – his words, thoughts, being equated to the dangerous flatus and faeces.

After a silence, Mr B speaks directly of knowing that his father will soon die, though he had found him quite well at the weekend. Klein asks what else Mr B had been thinking during the silence. He says,

He thought of his mother's grave and that his father took him to see it, and told Mr B that he had made arrangements to be buried at her side. How can anybody think of being buried

or being dead? He agrees with me that he feels an awful anxiety about this, and I interpret that his strong suicidal phantasies go with anxiety of death. That death is felt as the rats inside which destroy everything and that less anxiety on this line might obviously give one more serenity about actual death. I also say that the association he had left out was linking up his mother's death – her grave – with my interpretation that he was trying to save me from his destroying me. He then speaks about the distress [he would feel] if his father dies; the house would be sold and so on, and things would be awful. I interpret that the house seems to be standing for the mother and that distress is not only about father's death but realisation that the whole family will break up – that his mother is actually dead.

Mr B recalls a dream:

There was an orphan boy, a very nice child, who was clinging to him. He could not get rid of him. He tried to in many ways. In the end he sent him away with his favourite daughter, who was six feet high and had grown into a most unprepossessing creature. But even that did not help and he could not get rid of this boy's demands.

In association, Mr B,

mentions a girl friend of his wife's who is going far away, and of her throwing herself unsuccessfully at men and still remaining unmarried. He calls her childish, though she is quite grown up, the age of his wife. Then mentions a conversation between his father and himself and his wife, in which his wife said something which was rather childish, and seemed to show she had no idea of legal matters. I then interpret that this favourite daughter seemed to be mixed up with the orphan, and also with this grown up girl throwing herself at men, and with his wife's being childish. They all seem to stand for his sister, who would be an orphan if the father died, and who is actually partly deprived of the family life already by the mother's death. It might have been in his mind what is going to happen to her if she remains alone, since she is unmarried. He says that she will be an awful nuisance and says that he had thought about that. Does not show any sorrow for her, and I interpret that this orphan in his earliest situation was the sister whom he felt would be his responsibility if the parents were killed by poison gas, and how conflicting the situation is when he felt disaster was all around, as he had mentioned before, with some material that his faeces made the whole world artificially green. It shows he felt responsible for everybody in the family, because of his destructive phantasies.

Thursday 5 November 1936

Mr B 'is again deep in depression and despair.' Recent interpretations and a disturbing exchange with the Chairman have stirred up Oedipal anxieties. Klein writes that,

The day before he had mentioned the company board meeting at which the Chairman would have to go, and he had mentioned this very soon after having spoken about his worry about

his father – that he might die. I connected these things, and showed him that the guilt and anxiety comes from the fact that in the deep unconscious the splitting of these figures and displacing to other people in life, etc does not succeed. He agreed, that even with the Chairman he could not say that he dislikes him really; he is a nice old man, inefficient, and actually reminds him of his father. He also knows that when he succeeds in what he has undertaken he will feel very guilty. At the same time his triumph concerning the probable success is very strong. Now he makes himself with the greatest effort tell me that the Chairman had wanted to see him, suggesting having lunch together. He had spoken to him quite frankly and in a friendly way and had asked, is he [Mr B] aware how bitter his words are? The Chairman wondered whether [Mr B's way of being] does not extend also to other areas of life and that his bitterness is part of his character?

This clearly distresses Mr B hugely. He feels in 'absolute despair,' and says that, 'everything is hopeless.' Klein interprets that,

the Chairman's remark has only confirmed in his mind the fact that a friendly father shows him how poisonous his excrements have been and how he has used them to destroy the father and mother. During this talk with the Chairman, Mr B said that he realised that his manners are not always very good, but the Chairman had disagreed with that. He had said 'Your manners are charming, but you are very bitter.' I interpret that bad manners are a harmless thing – a naughty child – while bitterness, connected with poisonous words and actions, is at the root of his feelings of guilt. I showed him that that is why he feels it is quite hopeless, and he will not be able to save father and mother inside him. I also link this up with the rats, poison gas and other material of last hour.

Friday 6 November 1936

Klein notes that,

Mr B was quite changed. He had been kept waiting on the doorstep and mentioned, without anger, that he had heard two women pass by, which he found unpleasant. But he suggested this could not have been important if these women had not meant something frightening to him in connection with the past.

Klein suggests that the women 'were finding out about the poison gas.' Mr B recalls a dream:

He saw a kingfisher. It was flying by but sat down on a post on his left. When showing the position, he was touching the wall to show where the kingfisher was. This was exactly the place on the wall where two days ago he had tapped, asking whether he could not send some poison gas through it. He was speaking to me in the dream and was asking me what kingfisher was called in German, and we talked about that.

He asks me the German name. I tell him that I don't know but I will look it up. He gets excited, and says it is quite impossible to get a conception of a kingfisher from a book. Tells me that when his wife once saw a kingfisher fly by, she nearly fainted, so strong was her emotion. To see a kingfisher is such an experience that one cannot describe it. He speaks with the greatest enthusiasm and admiration of this bird and goes on telling me about it, also where it keeps its young, and seems to insist that I should see it. I suggest that the kingfisher is this marvellous bird which represents mother, & I suggest also father, mother having fished the king. [I note] that he had tapped the wall behind which the parents/neighbours were, who were to be poisoned, but now they are the good parents, the admired ones. I point out how internalization is here represented by the quick passing by of the bird – one nearly doesn't see it, but it comes back. All these are the characteristics of this mother who in his mind is inside him.

Klein continues, noting Mr B's way of speaking to her about the kingfisher:

He is obviously keen to talk to me, to exchange views with me, and to communicate beauty to me. I then stand for the little sister. I remind him of the orphan boy who was such a nuisance. But that now he, in the transference, was comforting his sister and telling her that the good mother is not lost. That though she is dead, she is passing by, she is there, she comes back, and her memory can be kept in the way in which she is felt to be an object inside and that this applies to both parents. He agrees, and says, taking off his glasses, 'some time later', then correcting himself, 'perhaps in another world, you must tell me to whom I should go to do something about glasses. I think that it is all psychological and I could put away my glasses and see without them'. I interpret that this means looking at things with my eyes, in the same way as I do.

Saturday 7 November 1936

Material points to Mr B's concerns about his mother, parental sexuality, and the presence of other children inside mother:

Mr B's daughter had asked him to go into her school to look round, parents being allowed to do this on certain days. Mr B did not want to – hates it, and felt frightfully embarrassed about it, but he went. He was astonished how little space children take up – seeing about 80 children in such a small space. He met there Mrs B, one of the mothers, about whom he is very self-conscious because of her husband, about whom we had certain difficulties in the past. Speaking of this husband he does not call him Dr B but Mr B, which strikes him at once as quite unusual, saying that actually when he had said 'Mr B' he had thought of Mrs B, not of Dr B. I suggest that this great embarrassment while looking at all these children and meeting Mrs B is connected with his phantasies about his mother's pregnancy – how many children fitted into her inside, and what they were doing there. That it might have been a consolation to think that they took up so little space. Also mixing up Dr B (about whom we had so much material, that he represented a father figure to Mr B) with Mrs B shows that the pregnancy was in his mind connected with the mixing up of father and mother, and that his embarrassment in the morning was identical with his embarrassment when he saw the parents in bed and thought of them mixing up sexually and mother being pregnant. Mr B acknowledges the fact that he always felt awkward, and that even now when he sees his wife in bed in the morning, he has quite a special awkward feeling, which he agrees cannot be explained, because he has this feeling without her being ill or for any special reason.

Klein connects this material with Mr B's recent despair following the humiliating exchange with the Chairman:

I remind him of his depression when the Chairman reproached him for bitterness and hostility, because it also meant that he was injuring the babies inside mother especially because none ever came after the little sister, whom he hated so much to begin with.

Monday 9 November 1936

Thinking in the analysis about the sexual mixing up of the parents has stirred great anxiety in Mr B. In this session Klein observes that he is preoccupied with the matter of knowing, specifically about sexual matters. He treats gossip with some contempt:

Mr B mentions a talk with somebody, Mr X, who referred to the husband of the King's mistress. When mentioning this, Mr B says 'Mrs —', nearly saying her name and then stopping. Mr X seemed surprised that Mr B appeared not to know about the matter and said 'You don't mean to say you haven't heard about that? You must have heard her name,' and so on, in the way I sometimes do when trying to prove to him that he knows something which he denies. Mr B himself laughs about this matter because he knew of course all about it … He suggests that not wanting to know Mrs S's name is like avoiding talking about my name and about me. Some time ago he had been extremely disgusted by his wife's mentioning something about me which she had heard at a party – nothing detrimental. He mentions that somebody knew the husband of Mrs S and he is quite a decent fellow. Told me that on the train from Southend they were all talking about it – everyone talks about it, and Mr B, with certain contempt, says he can imagine the journey on the train – how everyone is talking of it.

Tuesday 10 November 1936

Though Mr B says he is 'so depressed,' Klein notes his lack of conviction about this. He says it 'weighs him down to see his wife in bed.' He returns to the matter of gossip. This time Klein explicitly links his distaste of gossip to anxiety about parental sexuality, which in the past and again now, feels so frightening. He tells Klein,

The same Mr X who had mentioned the gossip about the King's mistress had wanted to show him a cutting about something dealing with the divorce. Mr B again appeared not interested, and did not want to gossip with him about it. I point out that this attitude is connected with the children gossiping about the parents' sexuality. Here it appears that he did not want to talk about it; but that the other side, the one where he badly wanted to talk about it with his brother or sister, is repressed. It was so strongly repressed because the intercourse meant something so awful to him that he felt in the mornings the way which we have discussed in the last few hours. He says he does not know what I mean. He had always said that he thought that to his mother, father's sexuality was something horrid, and what difference does it make? I tell him that he of course knew something about that, but what he does deny and has repressed was the whole dangerousness and badness which was produced in his mind by the intercourse. That when he said he would talk to his siblings and make them sit up and listen he had himself connected this with the parents lying in bed and his making them sit up and listen. That he felt that they were in an awful danger, injuring each other and that they did not themselves understand what they were doing.

Klein also challenges Mr B, saying,

did he really not know what I was talking about? He admits that he knew quite well what I was talking about. I then bring in that this whole attitude of denial which he had shown with Mrs S and now shows today with me twice – first, not being convinced that he is really depressed and second, not knowing what I mean – that the child would pretend that it did not know anything about the parents' sexuality if he felt so frightfully guilty about it.

In response, Mr B tells Klein that,

He saw his little son over the weekend, and the boy asked him about the snow bunting, and Mr B found it so difficult to describe this bird. He is going to write to his son and explain to him. He describes the bird as something beautiful, and so difficult to describe. Then mentions that he had dined with friends, and the woman, an old friend of his, had mentioned a letter he had written her about ten years ago in which he sent her some down of an eagle and gave her a vivid description of the country where it came from.

Mr B then recalls part of a dream that reveals more of his attitude towards parental sexuality, including the hostility it arouses in him:

He saw two rabbits in a field. It was quite vague. He thinks that they were separate, not together. He saw a man with a gun who was shooting at them. Then he saw quite vividly a hare run past, squeeze himself over a wall and injure himself. He adds that he feels sure that the hare was dead. Mr B felt strong sympathy with the hare in the dream. The rabbits had come out from holes.

Mr B says his association to the rabbits when he woke up was that Mrs H, the friend to whom he had given the down, told a story about how they were travelling to New Zealand and had met on the boat a Mr and Mrs Rabbit. Another person said that they had never thought that people could be so uncultured, and had mentioned this couple as an instance. Nothing had remained in their memory of what they had seen in London but an artificial apple which they had seen in Selfridges. Mrs Rabbit made it clear that her husband liked to be called Rab<u>bit</u>. Mr B laughs, finding that this pronunciation makes the name still more funny. I suggest that here he treats with scorn, and has made use of it in the dream, the *uncultured parents. The child felt that these parents going to bed together and doing sexual things, are funny, immoral, uncultured, bad. I suggest that the man with the gun is himself, and that the vagueness of these rabbits, the indefiniteness, (he had mentioned that he had seen them only for one moment, passing by), had repeatedly appeared, and suggested the observation of intercourse, which we have had much material for. The hare he was so sorry for shows another aspect of the same theme, the hare standing both for the father's penis, and the father who would be injured in intercourse, as well as for the mother and for himself, if he threw himself into the situation of the parents' intercourse, as he felt he should do, in order to disturb and to save them.*

Klein writes however that there is another side to things; that as well as horror connected to thoughts of the father/penis, Mr B has a deep admiration for both. This admiration has, however, always had to be repressed:

I point out that the eagle, which is an admired bird, and the down which he had described as something so light that one could hardly see it, stands for the admired penis of the father, and so does the snow bunting, which he could not describe to his son. Again, there is this element of just having seen and of not being able to describe it. I suggest that the down is the pubic hair. The eagle is the grown-up penis of the father, while the snow bunting was that of his brother, whom he also admired very much. He agrees to this admiration of his father. He remembers that when his father first told him about something that he did not know, he was most amazed. He had felt that his father was omniscient, and he can still recollect admiration, etc, quite consciously in relation to his father. I point out that this deep admiration of the penis and of the intercourse had to be repressed together with the horrible aspect of the intercourse. I agree that he knew something about his feeling that intercourse could be curative and good, but that again was different from this extreme, deep admiration for the penis, and from the deep horror of it. I suggest that it was the depth and strength of his repression of his parents' sexuality which was the reason why these two extremes could not get nearer each other.

Klein also connects the Kingfisher material to Mr B's sister, and to his phantasies about her conception and birth:

I remind him that the beautiful bird, like the kingfisher, is also the baby sister. We know he thought this baby was horrid when he saw the little sister. He wondered, was it a child at all? And yet he admired her in many ways a little later. This child was born straight after intercourse, in his mind. His brother told him that she was so frightfully red, and also in the dream recently this came in, where the innocent child was lying in bed. He had said, 'Was it really a child?' Here is the conception that intercourse injures the child during the birth; and the hare climbing over the wall is really the child coming out of mother's inside. The indefiniteness has also to do with dying, and with the internal. If things were internal they were fading out. His thinking that the parent-rabbits were separate had also to do with his wish to separate the parents so that they should not be together, [and his wish that] they should both be only with him.

Wednesday 11th November 1936

Mr B is very late for the session and is 'in absolute despair.' He pleads with Klein to 'let him go, he wants to die peacefully.' He speaks of his wife:

> *Her cold had been better, but then she had gone back to bed. He rang up the house and she seemed to hate him. Probably with good reason. He feels that she is justified in hating him and that he has done harm to her. She has got influenza and he cannot stand it. If she would let him help her or do something for her when she is ill it would be a great relief – but she never does, as his mother never did. He takes it partly back, saying that last night she let him bathe her eyes, which relieved her very much.*

Klein says,

> *Mr B's wish to escape from me was really due to his relation with his wife and his anxiety for her. I suggest that he must be frightened that she may die. I remind him that when he complained about his wife's fussing about the children with measles, we found out that he was himself afraid that the children would die. He admits his anxiety of death and tells me a phantasy he had had after the telephone talk, that if his wife were to die, he would commit suicide. People would think that he loves her very much and still it is not true.*

Thursday 12 November 1936

Mr B hadn't wanted to come, but tells Klein he 'feels much relieved' having just spoken to his wife. He reports that,

> *She was better and quite friendly. The doctor had comforted her and prescribed her a good meal, and she seemed quite pleased. Mr B praises the doctor, who is a nice man.*

He then tells a dream, though he tells Klein she will not understand it; that it is 'frightfully complicated and awfully muddled, impossible to describe.'

> *He was looking with somebody at the stage which was in front – pointing towards my garden window. The two of us (and he then suddenly says 'I am sure it was you') were looking at the stage and that was where we should look, but there was nothing whatever to be seen. Nothing went on. From time to time I was glancing over my shoulder and so was he, to the left, (and when saying so he repeatedly taps the wall on the left side of the couch,) and there he saw something. There, Mr A, his business partner, was behaving like a buffoon, gesticulating as if he was conducting a band and the band was playing, but that was not what we actually should have seen. He cannot explain why we should have looked the other way.*

Mr B asks Klein, 'did you get the dream?' and is surprised when she says,

> *It is something quite simple. I remind him that this same wall which he tapped was the one through which he had recently wanted to poison the people next door with poison gas*

because of the music. That this performance of his partner (he mentioned that he is a nice man – that he does not like him at all in the business but he is charming when meets him outside) – his gesticulation, buffoonery and so on, is the parental intercourse; and his wish to poison the noisy people is that of killing the parents in intercourse. That we, he and I, or he and his brother, the children, should not have looked at this performance, but always where there was nothing to be seen. I interpret the connection between his denying attitude towards the sexuality of the parents, and the great wish to see the actual intercourse, but his being afraid of that because of his hate and destruction.

Mr B is very disturbed by Klein's interpretation.

He had been sitting up in a state of anxiety and said that he would not stand it one second longer. He does not know what I am talking about, cannot stand it. Then says he cannot stand the dictatorial ways in which I interpret. The poor patient has nothing to say and must stand everything. Carry on your bloody business, he says, and then again says in the next sentence twice the word 'bloody', and says he wants to run away, and says he will go. I interpret this reaction as the repetition of the old reaction in bed when he could really not stand it any longer –when he felt the parents were carrying on this bloody business, and he felt exposed to anxiety and conflicts by them, without the possibility of stopping them or interfering; I also made clear how much easier the situation is in repetition, because he actually is free to leave me if he likes.

Mr B responds,

He says that in his earlier dream he had thought he might shoot the rabbits, but he doesn't think he did. He thinks the man did. I interpret this as confirmation of his shooting tendencies at the same time as anxiety that the man, the father, also shoots and kills mother and the babies. Mr B covers his ears and eyes with his hankie. (He had left off covering his eyes for a long time, but at one time had done so for a very long time in his analysis). He says that he cannot avoid hearing me. It is very difficult to speak. He isn't going to speak. Why should he? He is only going to give me material for awful accusations. After some time says that it is still worse if I am silent than if I speak.

Klein interprets Mr B's anxiety about her death, if she is silent. When she highlights his doubt in her in recent hours, however, he responds by saying that 'so many people do not believe at all in analysis, but that he is loyal in such cases and does not let me down.'

Saturday 14 November 1936

Mr B is not so late as recently. He reports a dream:

He was sitting in a hotel room on the ground floor in an armchair. His association to hotels is that they are places where there are always unwanted people. He was discussing with an older boy that there were only twenty minutes to go to the top of the mountain. It was perhaps the Snowdon range, all in reach. The other boy said that it is quite impossible to get to the top in this time, and Mr B seemed convinced, though he had never seen the top before. Mr B's association to the older boy is to a man he met in the East, whom he asked about a mountain he wanted to climb. This person did not seem to understand why Mr B wanted to climb the mountain, which Mr B thought would be a great experience for him.

Returning to the dream, Mr B recalls,

He then met the proprietress of the hotel in the corridor, and she tells him where he will find a notice showing how he can get to the top. But when Mr B looks where she told him, he sees lots of signs pointing in different directions and none actually to the top. Mr B connects this with me and the whole dream with analysis – my giving him so many interpretations pointing in so many directions, and none actually leading to the very point which means cure.

Returning to the dream,

Then, Mr B was cross-country running, a race with others. Mr B notes that his father had much approved of his cross-country running, when he wrote to him as a boy. It became very misty, and Mr B thinks this an advantage to him, because he knew the way, but the others did not, so that he would win the race. But the race went partly uphill. Mr B got so tired that he was dragging his legs and became quite exhausted. It was on the way back home he said (meaning the hotel). Then he arrived there and changed his clothes.

Klein interprets,

that the unwanted people are the other patients and my family. That these were the people he was beating in the race. That he has seemed to show a strong belief that he knows his way in analysis and will win, but that the end seems to contradict it because he gets so exhausted and does not know whether he won or not. Also, that all being within reach, the twenty minutes, seems at the same time to cover his anxiety of never reaching the goal, which means not cured, and dead. Also racing to come home, conveys the wish to get back to mother and not being able to find her.

Monday 16 November 1936

Mr B reports another dream:

They were expecting a royal party to come on a visit. Preparations were made for them. Mr B was dressing for it, but found himself in a red hunting coat, explaining to himself that he must have picked it up somewhere, but even in the dream thought that this was not possible, that he had no right to wear it. He was trying to find out from the buttons to which hunt it could belong. Then the party came and the little Princess sat on his left, bringing her face quite near to his. The Queen seemed intrigued by the incident but he did not see her, only knew she was. The princess had a horrible face, screwed up and powdered, and he speaks with strong disgust. Mr B recalls that his wife was hurt when he once pointed out to her that he did not like her to powder herself. He does not know whether this was the face she powdered or some part of the body. He thinks of friends, a little dog belonging to a woman he had lunched with, and that she was warning him when he was playing with the dog and bringing its face close to his own, not to have it too close to his face, in case it bit him.

Klein interprets that,

the screwed-up powdered little face is the woman's genital, his little sister sitting on his left, and something he did to her genital. Also, that the little dog – which was hairy – and the part of his wife's body which he did not remember, all seems to show that it means the woman's genital. Surprisingly Mr B takes it very quietly and says he would not disagree with this interpretation about the genital.

Tuesday 17 November 1936

Mr B is very late, 'so that there is not much of the hour left.' He is,

Quite silent, incapable of speaking, wants to break off analysis. I mention former material in which he said one day he wanted to know whether I was using scent, or whether this was his imagination – he would ask me after the analysis was over. I point out his anxiety of my genital in this relation, and that his being silent and negative was in order not to bring his face nearer, rather to keep himself away from me.

He then reports a dream,

He was standing on rocks. They were red. Only the ones on which he was standing were red, others weren't. He cannot help thinking of blood. Here he had a memory of seeing blood spots in his grandmother's carriage and being told a story that grandmother had picked up somebody who was bleeding – a man whose nose was bleeding, or something of the sort. At the time it seemed to him most thrilling and unbelievable. He had been told some years afterwards that it was quite true. Then he thinks of the war and his taking part in it. He says that it was a mass of rocks, quite smooth, worn down by the water.

There is then a misunderstanding to do with language which sees Mr B almost leave the session. Klein writes,

I, misled by the plural 'rocks' asked how many, or something. He makes a great point that they were not distinct, single objects, referring to my lack of English, and that they had nothing whatever to do with a mess, but were a mass. Here, he is very emphatic about their not being distinct objects, but it was distinct in a way as a mass of rocks. Then he wonders about the plural – why does one say rocks? It sounds as if it was several things, but it was not. He got so annoyed over it that he got up and said he could not stand it any longer, and wanted to go. I explain that I am quite willing to agree that I was misled by my lack of

English, and that I perfectly understand what a mass of rocks is. I have seen them myself. Mr B comes back from the door, but stands near the end of the couch, nearly immobile, a position in which I have never seen him before … He had repeatedly stood up or wanted to walk out, but did not stand before. Mr B does not leave, but is very much on the point of it. Before going out of the room he begins to laugh and says something is extremely funny, and he says that I did not interpret the simplest and nearest thing about the rocks. Didn't I know what it means to be 'on the rocks'?

Wednesday 18 November 1936

Mr B is much less anxious, Klein writes. He tells some other dreams, but also goes back to the 'rocks dream' of the previous day. He says,

He had not mentioned yesterday that he had thought of Odysseus – of the rocks on which Odysseus was stranded – covering himself, being naked, when he saw people coming. He had told this story to his daughter recently, of Penelope who was weaving, and that her weaving would just be finished when Odysseus came home. It is a great memory for him when he first learnt this at school. Also says that his interpretation of 'on the rocks' does not alter the fact that it might mean a lot more. It is striking why one puts them in the plural.

Klein interprets,

His unusual position of standing all the time, as if he was careful about the rocks on which he was standing in the dream. If it is a plural and there is bleeding, it connects with grandmother's carriage and the blood a man has spilt in it, an unbelievable story, which all seems to point to the bleeding parents, and the patient being on top of them, mixed up with them and horrified. If he is stranded on the rocks, he needs my help. I seem to be Penelope who is weaving (former material about some mosaic or handiwork, which analysis was compared to). He laughingly warns me not to compare myself with Penelope, - she had to unpick her work every night. I interpret that I think the simile is right, because I so often seem to undo things – not being able to give the full connections, and so on. But he does not deny that the weaving and Penelope were standing for me and analysis. Also, that he had told his daughter the order in which Odysseus was recognised – dog, swineherd, nurse, son and last of all, his wife. He often feels misunderstood by me and not recognised; but that this was not Penelope's fault, because Odysseus had become so unrecognisable. I bring in also these unwanted suitors of Penelope's – the nuisance, as he called them. She only recognised him after he had killed the suitors. I remind him of the unwanted people in the hotel and the unwanted patients and my family. But that again in the dream, analysis and I seem to be helpful, and Odysseus after all had come home – which also means getting back his mother.

Friday 20 November 1936

Mr B is despairing. He complains,

about his wife not taking enough care of herself – her cold and her not going to bed etc. In her attitude towards his relationship with the children, she is not influenced by him. He should only admire them. His having objected to the smallest child being still in a slobbery state, should not be admitted to meals, but the child is still admitted. Later on in the hour mentions his favourite daughter who so much admires him, treats him as her possession, and mentions that he had gone to say goodnight to the youngest and he wanted to hear a story. Mr B said 'I don't know one', then the favourite daughter came in and said, 'I am supposed by mother and nurse to be in bed, but I heard you were going to tell a story so I came in'. She was sitting down with crossed legs, looking very attractive and self-confident. He then told a very nice story.

Saturday 21 November 1936

Mr B is late, and explains,

He has been to the archaeological exhibition. On the whole he has a friendly attitude. He has often been to the archaeological exhibition and has been unable to leave the person he meets there – his mother-in-law, another time, a French woman. I interpret that in former material archaeological things signify resurrection and the people he is with whom he still keeps as alive, unable to part from them, while I, in the meantime, represent the dying or dead person he is afraid to meet. He mentions that his wife had confessed to him that she had over-spent and had asked for his help to put her accounts right. He is concerned about it as a symptom, but is very friendly, inclined to help and not to mind. Then he mentions he has been with her to a Bloomsbury party, and that the people his wife is interested in or admires were there, but that she did not enjoy herself.

Mr B then brings a dream, the setting for which is some Company premises overseas.

In the dream, the building with the offices, which is now vacated, was still occupied. The manager had a lavatory installed, but in the dream this lavatory wasn't there, but there were lots of pipes and water works to be seen, which stood for this lavatory. He was passing these water works, on a toffee path. He knew it was toffee because when he came to the end of it, he got down and bit a piece of it. It was toffee mixed with nuts like a gravel path. Then he went round, went down the steps to the station on to the platform. Behind his left shoulder (which so often represents my voice and my talk and me) there was an engine driver, who touched him on the shoulder and called attention to himself. He had committed a social crime, and gave Mr B to understand this. But Mr B was quite willing to speak to him, and then went with him down the platform on a walk in the flat country along the open road until he arrived at a semi-circular bench, where he was talking to an elderly fat native woman. He is not sure afterwards if it was one woman or several. Here he took out three things from a bag – scissors and a knife and he doesn't know the third, and doesn't know if it was his bag or her bag. The engine driver seemed to take him away from the toffee path. [The engine driver then] told Mr B that he had taken some scientists to an establishment and they were surprised and pleased. Mr B did not see this route – it was in the distance from the circular bench and hidden by distance and trees. Mr B did not seem interested in this scientific establishment, and it was a rectangular line to the bench.

Associating to the engine driver, Mr B mentions the restaurant he had been to with his wife the night before, which was expensive. He says,

The proprietor is a fat foreigner, very good food, the waiters have dirty nails, and the proprietor said to him that he recognised him. When Mr B mentions the fat foreigner, he says he had a very funny way of calling through the whole place – it was rather empty, and Mr B doesn't know how he conducts his business. He feels very strongly that engine driver is himself. This reminds him of the old dream he brought early in the analysis where an old witch was asking him would he like to see a man who had been dead for 30 years, and he said yes, and he saw the man resurrect, and the man was himself. I agree, and even stress that such a feeling [that the engine driver is himself,] is absolutely convincing, but add that the next association to the engine driver had been the fat foreigner who gives good food, but has a dirty way of dishing it up, speaks bad English, etc. Also the direction from where he was speaking to him indicates that this is me. Mr B had mentioned in connection with the social crime of the engine driver that he does not mind social crimes – that he knows people in the City who have been run in for fraud, and he doesn't mind it so much, but there is in the dream a question of women not having been treated properly.

Klein continues,

that if it has been Mr B in the past, and if his past is resurrecting in analysis and past memories are coming up, the women who had not been properly treated were his sister and mother, and also that the toffee path points to some touching of the genital with his mouth, and that that was felt as a crime towards women. But that he seems to forgive himself, thinking it was not so bad after all. In my interpretation about myself as the engine driver I suggest that he had often felt analysis as something wrong, which people would despise him for, also my social inferiority as a foreigner. I add that taking the scientists to this place might have to do with his having heard something about my work. Mr B dislikes very much my interpretation in which I am the engine driver. When he had explained to me about the toffee path he had been standing up, going more towards the corner of the small room, and having his eyes closed, so that the toffee path was leading directly towards me.

Monday 23 November 1936

Mr B is very late and silent. Klein only notes that he says,

all my interpretations are just following a preconceived idea. That I am always accusing him of sexual acts and that it only makes him worse, and so on.

Tuesday 24 November 1936

Mr B is on time today, but can barely speak a word. He is silent for a long time. Eventually,

> *He agrees with me that this is a false obedience. He has come on time but cannot cooperate. He stresses that it makes him desperate that he cannot cooperate. He feels he is getting worse and worse, and has no trust in the treatment or in me. I interpret that this is connected with being found out about the sexual things which I had suggested that the dreams meant. A few minutes before he leaves he tells me that he could tell me a great lot more about the dreams; that they are his dreams after all, and that he would do so, but that he cannot be hurried by me and cannot be driven about as quickly as I think. I remind him of the engine driver. He also thanks me for a few minutes I give to him because he had just begun to speak about the dreams, and also says in quite a friendly way that he does not mind repeating them all over again and giving all the details, if only I keep to his pace. He sends me by post the same evening a very long and complicated plan of the whole situation and details, obviously making up for his not having said anything, but already preparing me that he might not turn up on the following day.*

Wednesday 25 November 1936

Mr B does in fact attend, though he is again late and reluctant to speak. He is 'depressed and suspicious.' Klein writes,

> *I go back to the engine driver dream and to his letter and plan. That in his letter, which was more friendly than anything that he had ever before written or said to me, I was compared to Joseph and he with Pharaoh. He had said that he doesn't want to behave like the Pharaoh, who threatened Joseph with all sorts of things if his interpretations were not satisfactory. Mr B had forgotten what happened then to Joseph, and I remind him that Joseph had predicted the seven fat and the seven lean years – that he saved the country, and that the Pharaoh was very impressed by this and made Joseph Prime Minister. Mr B is surprised, but remembers. He says that he partly wrote the plan, which as he puts in the letter gave him great pleasure to draw, as a demonstration against my not understanding it enough – wanting to make it as clear as possible, not being disturbed by my interpretations – that he could easily be friendly if I were not there. He explains his remark about his being the engine driver. Then with a low voice, which always implies that he is half guilty about what he says, suggests that what he objects to most to in my work is that I seem to feel so convinced of it. If I had the cynical attitude which most people have towards analysis he would feel entirely different about it. Another thing is that I behave like a mother behaves towards her son – that she cannot appreciate him and let him have his whole importance. I interpret my not appreciating the penis and his manhood, and that he feels that about my interpretations.*

Friday 27 November 1936

Mr B feels 'so desperate' about his wife, 'who will never be well.' He begins to recall a dream, but breaks off, returning to his despair about his wife. When he does return to the dream, he says it was 'horrible':

> *I was giving him a thermometer. He had read that in hot countries if one wants to take a temperature, one first puts the thermometer in a wet cloth, but there was something else as well – a nib – and I told him to put it into his bowel or I put it in. I suggested it and Mr B doesn't know how it happened, but he then saw the thermometer all in bits. He is horrified about the idea of putting a thermometer in the anus instead of the mouth, and tells me the dream with the greatest difficulty. I connect it with the toffee path and suggest that my interpretations are felt like an attack on his anus.*

Saturday 28 November 1936

Klein notes only Mr B's 'great resistance, depression, accusations, and difficulty to speak,' which she 'interprets and connects with the material of the last few days.'

Monday 30 November 1936

Mr B is depressed. He has had many dreams, but remembers particularly one fragment:

> *He saw his brother, who put his foot into his wife's mouth and said, 'That's a nice thing to do.'*

Associating to the dream fragment, Mr B says that,

> *the nails of his feet are still stained from the bogs in the summer. He has tried to get rid of that, but probably it will only grow out. He feels rather uncomfortable about it. He explains to me about bogs, where one finds nice flowers. Bogs, from his associations, contain staining as well as good things. He liked to go barefoot into the bogs, and some people warned him that he could hurt himself. While saying this he hurt his left palm by touching it with the right-hand fingernail. He had scratched this palm on a bush and just touched the sore place. He had had lunch with his father, and felt that he annoyed him by cleaning his nails, i.e., touching one nail with another in order to put the cuticle straight. He knows that his father loathed that, and that he could not tick him off as he did when he was a boy, but Mr B stopped doing this so that he should not annoy him.*

Klein notes Mr B's recent sense of persecution by her too. Particularly, he feels she persecutes him for his sexuality. Nonetheless, she returns to the dream fragment, connecting it to sexual activity between Mr B and his siblings and then to a masturbation phantasy that implies forceful entry into the body.

The foot is standing for the penis. [I connect to] former material where he had said he 'put his foot into it', and recognised that it meant his wife's genital. I remind him of his great anxieties over the anus, his anxiety of being watched from behind, attacked from behind, and other former material, which seems to suggest that his brother had attacked his anus as well as put his penis into his mouth, and also that his brother might have done the same thing to his sister and that Mr B might have done the same to her. I remind him of his phantasies of exploring his aunts' bodies, which were very pleasant. But I suggest that in these phantasies, he must have got into the body in some way. He says he knows exactly the way. It wasn't with his penis, as I suggested before. He was inside, with his whole person, and was climbing up and exploring. There was a large opening between the legs, large enough for him to get in, and that is how he got in. I suggest that here anus and genital are denied, the opening being made so large that the entrance could be made without any violence. Before that he had mentioned a memory (not new) that he had been cutting out figures, he thinks it was a naked figure, for his scrap-book. He was around five or six years of age and had asked his aunt 'should he cut in at the buttocks?', which embarrassed his aunt very much. I suggest that this memory seems to point to his entering the body in an attacking way. [I also remark on] my interpretations having been so much resented recently, representing an attack of the same kind. In the past, because of such phantasies and dangerous faeces, there had been great anxiety concerning experiences with his brother and sister.

Klein returns again to the engine driver dream, connecting anal exploration with the scientific exploration of the engine driver. She interprets,

The wish to explore the anus and to find out all about faeces and the inside of the body, is one root of scientific exploration, and that he might well have meant that the engine driver comes up now when his interest and exploration in these things comes to the fore. In relation to the engine driver dream he had also remarked about the round line which led from the toffee path to the platform, and that he likes the round lines and hates the rectangular lines. I also remind him of the part of the dream where he was delayed at the round bench by his talk with the fat native old woman. That here the round bench also seemed to be the same thing as the bog, and also blackness came in, and he was not sure whether he took from out of his bag scissors and a knife and some third thing which he forgot, or if she did. He stresses (always extremely exact about every detail of the dream – the way it is put, etc) that he is not sure about it, and I agree that this uncertainty proves that both could be true, and also points to an aggressive attack, the bag in former material having been associated with the scrotum.

Tuesday 1 December 1936

Mr B is early and Klein is once more unconvinced when he says he is very depressed. He says, 'whether one is depressed because of external things or because of one's psychological situation is the same for one's feeling.' Klein writes,

After having expanded about his depressed feeling he asks me when I am going on holiday. I answer. Then he is going to get drunk, he says, which he never does. I connect the anxiety of my leaving and his depression with the anal material. His anxiety of parting and being left alone has followed him throughout his whole life, and even recently we discovered that he cannot part at an exhibition from people, he adds 'especially women'. I connect his constant anxiety of death with the anus. Here he remarks on a grammatical point. In English one says, for example if one has met somebody, one says one cannot part from 'them', using 'them' as if it was singular, because one cannot know whether it is him or her. They are mixed up with each other. I interpret that this expresses his feeling that the woman is mixed up with the man and that that is a terrifying situation, because they will attack each other anally, and thus the death of the woman occurs.

Mr B then describes,

that as a boy of five when he had just started to understand the compass, when he was travelling on a train, he could only imagine that the finger of the compass was to be either in the direction of the train or at a right angle; that he knew already that there was north, north-west, south-west, etc., but he did not acknowledge this when he went on the train. He asks me whether I can explain this, and seems pleased when I say that I cannot. He says then that he thinks it was as if he had to carry the map or the country in a box which had to fit exactly with the train. But then at this time he seemed to have liked the right angle. He hates and dislikes it now. I ask him how this anxiety and dislike are connected with the anus. He says 'Rectum, rectangular.' He could not understand that it could be but intellectually he knew it. I suggest that also the mixture was not to be acknowledged, it should only be one thing.

Then, Mr B tells Klein,

with low voice and strong feelings that he had felt awful when he told me the dream of the engine driver, and had interpreted that the engine driver was himself and that he felt absolutely sure about it. Then I brought forward the idea that the engine driver was me and half a dozen other people besides; and that it came like a torrent out of my mouth and he had to take this in. Then says he exaggerated. He knows I had not suggested half a dozen people, but at least two. I interpret that even if my interpretation was wrong there was no need for him to be so hurt. If he had been, it meant that he had wanted to drive himself – [expressing the] unity of his personality, and that I, i.e., my interpretations, [instead,] were pushing into him like the thermometer and myself, and I was driving his engine.

One sympathises at times with Mr B's sense that Klein is forcing her way in, though she does acknowledge the impact of her interpretations. Here, she continues to interpret Mr B's anxiety about her being inside, and more generally of having objects inside that he feels come under attack and cannot survive there. She reminds him of,

His remark the day he told me the engine driver dream, that 'he could not stand my hurrying him and driving him quickly'. [He had said that] if I was patient then he could tell me all about it. I suggest that here he is speaking of wanting to have no object inside him but himself, and that I, through the anus, was pushing myself into him, connecting this again with the attacks on the anus of the day before. Also, his constant wish to save the mother inside [meant that he was extremely alarmed] that the thermometer was broken into so many bits. Mother and I are then mixed up with the thermometer, and are injured and killed inside him, and [this accounts for] his constant anxiety of losing the external mother, because he could not keep the internal one. I remind him of yesterday's material [his masturbation phantasy of bodily exploration], [and the] denial of the anus and the vagina; … the memory of cutting, and especially of his own tearing up phantasies.

Klein's interpretation enrages Mr B, who 'becomes very threatening.' Klein writes that this is unusual. Mr B may be often angry and full of reproach, but not with this threatening tone of voice.

And now he warns me to be careful with my words. Was I telling him that his own phantasies had been tearing, he asks? Had he said one word about tearing? How can I put my own phantasies into him? I explain that he had not used the word tearing, but that the scissor memory and the denial together seemed to me to suggest violent phantasies of entering the body, together with anal material, violent entrance into the anus. He then in the same way accuses me that I have used the word 'violence' where he has not said it. In between, he agreed that he himself could not know his unconscious phantasies, and that I had to find them through the material, but finishes by leaving me in anger because I put my phantasies into him.

Wednesday 2 December 1936

Mr B is miserable, but 'not angry as he had felt the day before.' Klein says that in his anger, Mr B,

had left me, as it were, without making up, reminding him of a situation [in childhood in which] he goes to sleep without having made up with mother or nurse, which he agrees to. He has read that in the zoo two cranes which had not been successfully nesting had adopted a goose and were walking about in the zoo with the goose. I interpret that he suggests that I should adopt him, that he is not my son, but that I should be more motherly, not leave him alone. He says that it is quite likely that he wishes that, though of course it is difficult for him to admit. I interpret that his need for mother and for always having her with him, is stimulated by anxieties of the kind we have just in these last days analysed, and with attacks on the anus, through cutting, etc and therefore anxiety of death. [This all contributes to his] continuous need for a real object.

Klein again goes back to the engine driver dream, in which Mr B talked to an elderly foreign woman and took three things from a bag, possibly hers, including scissors and a knife. She reminds Mr B, *of former material of his mother's work case where there was father's dissecting knife, and the connection with father's penis inside mother. Whether the penis is injuring the woman or she has the injuring penis inside her seems one of the most obscure parts of this dream.*

Thursday 3 December 1936

Mr B is very silent and depressed, 'guilty, not angry.' He 'cannot make himself speak.' He says that,

I shall understand that he cannot speak after the material. I may be right, he says, but it is impossible to stand it. He hates my rectitude.

Klein notes Mr B's use of the word 'rectitude,' and points to earlier material about right angles, which Mr B had said he now hates. He had connected this hatred to the word 'rectangle' and then to 'rectum' and so evidently, Klein remarks, to anal material. Mr B agrees that this must come into what he is saying now about Klein's rectitude. Klein interprets that,

silence and misery connect both with my attack but also with my being strict, finding out, blaming him.

Friday 4 December 1936

Mr B is about half an hour late. He is silent, and has no thoughts to share. He is terrified of Klein and feels he must give up coming. It is unfair, he says, that he does not give Klein 'chances to work.' Klein interprets that,

he [feels he must] must stop the communication between us because of the dangerous anal attacks which speech means. Also, because I should be saved from the sexual attack.

Monday 7 December 1936

Mr B is not so late but is still very silent. Again he 'complains he cannot talk.' Finally, he says,

How could one talk and not talk at the same time? I say something about 'talking alternatively'. Mr B corrects that – I mean alternately, and he goes into detail to make this quite clear to me. His voice has changed. He is friendly and quite in contact with me. I interpret this change and say that now his talk is felt to be constructive because he is teaching me something. That speech is now not an anal attack and that allows him to speak fluently.

Klein says that Mr B feels,

less dangerous and full of bad anal things if he can be good to me. Mr B, again with a changed voice, says that it is terrible how all the time I am bloody well with him and quotes the psalm 'Thou art on my path and about my bed'. He feels very guilty and reproaches himself about not cooperating with me.

Klein notes that,

The internalised me, the me linked up with him, bloody, is the same as his own bloody reproaches – pointing out the super-ego. Mr B says 'of course on my path and about my bed means always.'

Before reporting his dream of the previous night, Mr B tells Klein that,

One of the people on the Board, Mr X, whom he was expecting to support him, is rather hostile. Recently he answered one of Mr B's questions with a Latin quotation which was wrong and at the same time hostile. Mr B then repeats to me the story of Bophocles. One of the students at his College – a very silly person – had a whole essay written by another person, and was reading it out, reading the name of Sophocles as Bophocles. The Don corrected him and the student gave the whole show away by saying, 'He said Bophocles.'

Then in his dream,

Mr B was telling the story of Bophocles to Mr X who should have course have understood it because he was at public school, but in the dream he did not in the least understand it. I was behind Mr B but closer than usual, more at his side. I understood perfectly the story, though I knew less Latin than Mr X should know. But Mr B and I understood each other perfectly.

Mr B says,

He thinks it amazing that we should be in such a good understanding in his dream while he suffers so much under the bad relations with me in the daytime, but it is true that in the dream he had such confidence in me.

Klein interprets that,

again the little sister who knew so much less than the grown-ups, even not having complete language, at times was felt to be such a good mate and there was such a good relation between them.

There is a long silence. Before leaving Mr B says with difficulty that,

last night he tore his sheet which had never happened before and seems to confirm important interpretations about tearing. I interpret that the bed seems to be mother, the sheet, one part of her. I ask also whether this was an old sheet. Mr B laughs, saying that that is a remark which he should not have made – as if blaming me for putting so much on the external factor. Then says that the sheet was not old – and not quite new – it was all right when he went to sleep, and he did it when he was turning over to his right side.

Tuesday 8 December 1936

Mr B is early, 'but does not speak for ages.' Again, he says that he wastes Klein's time, and she draws attention to his 'repeated guilt' about this. He then complains about wasting his money. He says that,

> *if he has to tell dreams he feels better because we agree that these are a production of the unconscious.*

He does then report a dream:

> *He was shooting grouse. Great point to make clear where the grouse came from. They came from the left and then they also came from the right, coming out from behind a large dark obstacle, or (he says) should he say 'object'? Of course, the whole position where they came from does not seem to matter so much because he was shooting them and they were in front of him when they got up from the ground. (His voice now more anxious.) Mentions again they were coming from the left and from the right and then says, 'Don't kill me for having said that.'*

Klein notes that in Mr B's analysis, birds have so often stood for children, hence his lifelong ambivalence concerning shooting. She writes,

> *I cite the strong feeling he had when he had first been shooting with his father and Mr B agrees that he actually never quite got over this feeling, though he does shoot. I then interpret the large dark obstacle on his right as myself, and his sudden anxiety of me killing him as the fact that he was killing my children coming out from behind me. Mr B says that he knew while he said it that the large dark obstacle is me.*

Klein makes a connection now to Mr B's sister:

> *I stress the way he said that he shoots the bird when it gets up from the ground and suggest as a possible interpretation, not terribly well grounded, that this seemed to be the little sister when she was just getting up from the floor to walk. I remind Mr B of his father asking him with tears in his eyes to be careful when he shot with the soldiers not to injure his little sister – a memory he had mentioned for some time. Mr B says that before this interpretation he had thought of this himself, after I had suggested that birds were children.*

Mr B continues,

> *He speaks of grouse as nice birds and also peculiarly English – one could not translate the word 'grouse' because they exist only in England; and then a story of a schoolmaster who*

said when some manoeuvres were intended in Scotland, that one could not do that because of the grouse. There are some associations about a possible war between Heligoland, which he saw when he went to Germany, the nice island, and Scotland …

Klein interprets that,

the war between Scotland and the nice island is the parents' destruction, them destroying each other, and then that the babies, the grouse, which one likes so much in England, are comparatively unimportant. I suggest he might have studied the little baby sister with these mixed feelings and anxiety, and thought she is only so tiny, like a bird, and would she matter so much?

Mr B's associates to a photograph in the Times which shows several people who are shooting, looking happy. Klein interprets,

that sexuality, represented through shooting, could be enjoyed or was enjoyed by them as children, but that everything has turned to unhappiness. Also, Mr B is wondering whether or not his parents perhaps enjoyed sexuality, and that it is not identical with blowing each other up. I stressed his mother's unhappy disposition and attitude towards sexuality, which must have so much confirmed all his anxious feelings.

Mr B responds angrily,

saying that that is nonsense and bilge and rubbish, and that of course only the child is bad and foul, and that there was a time when he hoped that one could put him right, but now he is quite hopeless. I interpret that this is partly his anger about his parents having behaved as they did, and also recognition that it was his own destructive tendencies and phantasies which made things so bad for him.

Wednesday 9 December 1936

Mr B begins with complaints about his wife. He feels very depressed. His wife 'won't be put right.' She,

Is nothing but a repressed child. He complains about her lack of insight, her child-like behaviour. He was reading Ovid's love songs, but could not make her interested in them. Of course, she does not need love and sexuality. She has asked him to invite her brother for Christmas, with whom she is perfectly happy – they are like two children in a nursery. That is her ideal. Mr B feels insulted by this kind of happiness with her brother – it is so un-grown up.

Klein interprets,

that these associations are continued where the last hour finished, viz complaints about a little sister who cannot share Mr B's sexuality. I suggest that his wife's brother stands for himself in relation to his sister in the past. There are two aspects of this relationship, happy and with good understanding and then expressing a denial of sexuality, and anxiety in this connection.

Mr B objects, to begin with, protesting that,

He had not spoken about a child but about his wife. Do I translate simply wife into sister? I point out that he had stressed his wife was a repressed child with childish features in the whole relation. I then emphasise that he cannot keep enough as a possession the happy relation.

Mr B is then more reflective, and in response says,

that there is only one analytic hour in which he felt that it was perfect – that it was flowing out of him and that we were in full contact. I highlight his difficulty also to keep in mind the happy memories of mother, which he also partly acknowledged but cannot enjoy, and as it were make his own. I suggest that the reason for that is that when he was in a perfect happy relation to the sister then she might have done what the little Princess did in his dream – she might have been exciting him sexually, bringing her face (genital) close to his face, and therefore good understanding and a pleasant relation with me, mother and sister are too much linked up with sexual desires, which are felt to be bad and dangerous.

Klein notes that this is first time she has stressed this connection; that the reason for not allowing himself friendly and happy relationships is because it could lead to sexual relations. She writes that,

Mr B has in between agreed he has very happy memories with his sister, with great pleasure in teaching her and enjoying seeing her progress, and that she was devoted to him. There is also a reference to willows – and the weeping willow. Then there was an association to Desdemona who died because the weeping willow had pushed her into the water. It was, he thought, the fault of the weeping willow. He was the weeping willow, I interpret, in connection with his recognition that he was sad – weeping because he had pushed her into the water.

Mr B responds to this interpretation by saying that,

He had had the pond drained where the willows grow, so that the water has become running water. How pleasant it is to see this water trickling away and how essential it is for the willows that the water should be running. Mr B speaks with great feeling about the beauty of a well coming out from the earth in spring. He recalls the place where his grandparents lived in his early childhood, where he remembers one well where one sees it coming out from the earth. He says that this is probably the most beautiful place in the world.

Klein interprets that,

> *the feeling that he can make the willow grow indicates the good and creative penis; the clear water, also the place it links up with, the grandparents, and very pleasant early memories, points to the clear water of the well – standing for mother's breast … Recent interpretations which have shown why he cannot remember pleasant things, have led to strong feelings about the earliest and happy relation to his mother – to being fed by her.*

Mr B weeps in response to this interpretation, and says he thinks so. There is then some discussion about work done in the analysis. Mr B,

> *talks about his actual worry about his wife and the unlikely prospect of her ever getting right and also about his worries about his children. When I remark on his not having implied that analysis is hopeless, rather that he has only stressed his wife's being cured as hopeless, he says that he must admit that his insight about his part in his difficulty has grown – that he sees what is going on, etc. Implies that he knows that work is being done and that he values it, though it has not produced the effect which means cure. Klein remarks on this very great division which is in him between great hope and persistence in this hope, – the willows and his wish to put his wife right, and his determination to put his children right, etc. – and the despair that the two things are not to come together, like the good memories with the bad sexuality. After this talk Mr B says his wife is certainly nice and helpful too. He had asked her to look through all the letters which he had to answer and to tell him which is urgent, and she did so.*

Then, Mr B tells Klein that he,

> *Has taken an acquaintance to lunch whom he found in very poor state, without shoelaces and very neglected – and asked him after lunch how his financial situation was. He said that he has no money at all. Mr B was embarrassed to offer him money and says something about starvation. Then he himself feels as if he had got no money (though this is quite untrue) – as if he had empty pockets. I interpret that this feeling of emptiness and about the starved and neglected child, the acquaintance, had come up after my having pointed out the well as the first and most important gratification, and his feeling of being starved because he is deprived of it. I also make a connection with the holidays. Before leaving Mr B asks again for the bill, saying "Aren't you going to make my pockets still more empty?"*

Thursday 10 December 1936

Mr B is once more 'miserable and silent.' He accuses Klein again, 'though less strongly than on recent occasions.' Klein writes,

> *I draw his attention to the fact that in complaining that the treatment had made him worse he ignores the important fact that his mother has very recently died and that he is mourning. That he does not acknowledge the mourning when speaking of his grief and his despair of*

not being able to put right things which are irrevocable. In the last hour he had mentioned that in his first psychological treatment he had cried one day when he thought that his mother had never played with him on the nursery floor. I now remind him of that, saying that this accusation of his mother is only one aspect, the other aspect is that this cannot be altered because she is not alive anymore. Mr B ... quite changed his attitude while I was telling him this and expressed repeatedly his agreement. Says he cannot really stand the grief and also that it isn't as if he had always felt love and is now in despair, but that he and his mother have always got on each other's nerves and that changes the situation.

Friday 11 December 1936

Still, Mr B is 'depressed, but is capable of speaking.' He tells a dream, but 'prefaces it by saying that he and his wife are going to spend an evening with relatives who have rather a hard life, little money.' Mr B also feels that the wife of this couple is not in love enough with her husband. Another couple will also attend. The wife of this couple is 'very nice, shy, and nearly blind.' Mr B then reports his dream:

> *He was at a party and a couple said goodbye to him. To his surprise the woman kissed him to say goodbye and he only got to know them when they said goodbye. This struck him even in the dream as very unusual. The woman's face was the same, colourless, puckered up face as the little Princess's in the earlier dream. When they left, he thought he hoped that the husband would take it in the right way, and get on nicely with her.*

> *In association, Mr B mentions another couple where the man seems quite jovial but the woman is very unstable and neurotic. I interpret that this outgoing couple, whom he only gets to know when they say goodbye, seem to be the parents who died, mother already, father soon, and whom he only got to know through analysis, revising his relations to them.*

Saturday 12 December 1936

Mr B is 'late, silent, in despair.' He begins by speaking again of his wife and her ailments:

> *His wife was to be X-rayed, but did not take the powder which the doctor gave her, so she could not be X-rayed. Mr B speaks sharply about her anxieties of the doctors, who probably give her, in her mind, bad powder or do the wrong thing with her, and therefore she cannot be helped. Before that he mentions that his wife always has dealings with doctors and implies that they are of no use. I ask why she actually was to be X-rayed and Mr B seems to imply that there is always something wrong with her inside, but that actually he doesn't seem to think there is. I interpret that it is not only his wife but also Mr B who has suspicions of the doctors as being of no use; the bad powder being also his conception. That he is also afraid that something is wrong with her inside, and I lead this back to the past when he has been watching every action done with the little sister in the nursery with anxiety; he had been afraid of sister's death and mother's death and that he now is always terrified of his wife's death and his children's deaths. He quietly agrees to these interpretations. He sees himself at his parents' place in the country; in the shrubbery, being unhappy and worried and silent.*

Monday 14 December 1936

Mr B is again very late, and in despair, wanting to give up analysis. Just before leaving, an image comes to his mind:

> He is sawing a piece of wood, the other end of a piece of wood, which is sticking out of a heap of gravel. He adds that this association came quite suddenly and he cannot account for it.

Tuesday 15 December 1936

Klein notes that Mr B,

> had written to me, as often, that he is despairing in his wife's getting right and in his own being cured. He would like to give up analysis but can't. He speaks very bitterly about a letter he wants to write to his wife's doctor. He feels sure that she cannot be cured. I remark that it seems so clear that his despairing about his wife is absolutely identical with his not being cured. Mr B says that, 'if one thinks that there is A and B and A cannot be cured, then of course, intellectually, B could still be cured, but emotionally it is not so. I should not forget that B is so much attached to A'. I interpret that this attachment is more than it seems.

Klein says that Mr B feels he has injured A, that A is damaged, and this is why he believes he cannot be cured. She also says that,

> if goodness inside him dies – in so many ways represented in analysis by the mother inside him – that if that goodness dies, he must also die, and that if I cannot put right the external object, which stands for this internal mother, then it means his death.

There is a long silence. Mr B goes back to the image of a piece of wood sticking out of a pile of gravel. He,

> thinks that this is so obviously a symbol for the male genital that it needs no interpretation. Then, he says that he hates his sexual activity with his wife. She makes him feel so rotten about it, and so did his mother with his father. I interpret that the piece of wood being symbolic of the penis is not the whole explanation, since his next association was to intercourse with his wife. I suggest that the piece of wood is the penis, but that the heap of gravel is also the place in the woman where he puts the penis. Mr B remarks that trenches had been cut through one of his fields to make a sewer. That several inches under the soil there is a sub-soil of gravel, which he thinks is not good at all – no good for anything. I interpret that the gravel seems to stand for the faeces and that intercourse here is really getting into the anus. I remind him of the toffee path, which was like gravel, and that in his phantasy obviously anus and vagina have been quite equated. [I remind Mr B of his] complaints about his wife's neglecting her genital in a way, and making herself unattractive. He very strongly repeats this accusation – also that his mother obviously made herself detestable to his father. I interpret that this attitude of his wife confirms the old phantasy that the woman's genital is dirty like the anus, the contents of the body being dirty and bad, the bad faeces, and also that he himself in his association was sawing off the penis.

Mr B, in a low voice, says, 'because it is no good if she doesn't want it.' Finally, Klein interprets,

> *the anal attacks in recent material, the anxiety of his wife being injured (and sister, mother) and Mr B's overwhelming feelings of guilt with wishes of self-castration because of this act. Mr B says that probably my holidays are also coming into his mood.*

Wednesday 16 December 1936

Mr B, again despairing and hopeless, speaks of a 'nice river going through pleasant villages, with beautiful flowers,' which becomes 'dirty when it goes into a stream; bad dogs, bilge, etc.' It becomes 'dirty through contact with civilisation.' Mr B says that the river is himself. He wants to tell a dream, but he,

> *had got only a fragment of it, or rather the whole dream was only a fragment. It is no use recalling it because it was unintelligible, unfit for the situation. It was like a manuscript with the first pages torn out and each page torn partly. It was like part of a shoe, with the heel missing.*

Klein interprets that Mr B,

> *feels he has nothing positive to give, only bits, these fragments representing both the wife's genital and his own damaged penis. Here the gift of his unconscious, the productions, are identified with the useless penis and the useless genital, and he feels he has nothing to give.*

Thursday 17 December 1936

This is the last session about which Klein makes notes ahead of the Christmas break. According to her diary too, this was the final session in December. Klein notes that Mr B is in fact less despairing than usual. She writes,

> *He was late because the garage people had promised to get his car ready, but didn't do so. He speaks of unreliable Irish people, and also that they don't hear what they don't like to hear. I interpret that he doesn't like to hear interpretations when they are unpleasant, and it's no good having people being friendly but unreliable and telling him things which they don't keep to, in contrast to me who tells the unpleasant things but is reliable.*

Reference

Steiner (2017) *Lectures on Technique by Melanie Klein*. Routledge.

Chapter 5

The relief one gets from tears

The material of this chapter comes from the months of January to April 1937. This is a tumultuous period of the analysis which, as the title of this chapter suggests, is eventually to bring Mr B much relief from suffering. The material Mr B brings enables Klein to understand more fully, and to analyse, his terrifying conception of parental sexuality, phantasies related to which have haunted him throughout his life. The extent of his repression of any knowledge at all of parental sexuality becomes much clearer, and Mr B's inhibitions and anxieties concerning sexuality more generally are linked by Klein to his sense that a dreadfully dangerous parental intercourse is all the time going on inside of him.[1] Material also seems to confirm a sexual attack from behind by Mr B's brother and points to a possible early seduction by an aunt, though neither event is ever confirmed by Mr B. The damaging effects of such sexual activity, even if these did occur at the level of phantasy, are devastating and far reaching. Indeed, Mr B's belief that he had very early on 'swallowed the bad penis' contributes to feelings of depression, worthlessness, and hopelessness from which he feels he will never recover.

That said, and perhaps following her very thorough analysis of the foregoing, Klein continues to feel that Mr B is unconvincing in his claim that he is 'so depressed.' In fact, there is evidence that he sees significant improvement in himself following work in the analysis. For example, he acknowledges a definite increase in affectionate feelings towards Klein, which leave him regretting his earlier criticism and hostility towards her. This seems to go hand in hand with mourning for his mother, which is really now underway, and which sees a raft of loving feelings emerge. Mr B also despairs about Klein's possible death, of which he dreams, which she connects to the death of his mother and to his sense of responsibility for this, his having failed, to his mind, to sufficiently protect her both from a butchering father inside of him and from his own destructiveness.

Hatred and contempt of Mr B's father in the person of the Chairman also come strongly to the fore, and in fact, this too seems to account for the emergence of more loving feelings towards Mr B's mother and Klein. Klein's strong belief that the analyst must 'give plenty of rope' to the patient's complaints and grievances, because only then will the love that is buried beneath have a chance to see the light of day, seems to be fully borne out in Mr B's case. The emergence

DOI: 10.4324/9781003373414-6

of loving feelings is problematic, however. Mr B can readily feel that Klein 'persecutes him for his sexuality,' and he again turns to accusing her.

Klein proposes that Mr B's overwhelming hatred of his father had previously been strongly repressed (or redirected towards his mother) since he believed it would destroy his father. Yet the impact of this repression was a more general and debilitating inhibition of ambition. As such, significant relief comes as repression lifts, if much anxiety and guilt also emerge. Regretful feelings emerge too, concerning Mr B's feeling that his father never seemed to want to spend time with him or do things with him. Mr B admits himself that this very likely fueled criticism of his father, which has during the analysis emerged so strongly in the transference. Indeed, as this powerful repression of hate is analysed, Mr B becomes 'carried away by murderous hate' towards Klein. Klein firmly withstands this, but one feels she must have been quite shaken by it. Klein also evidently believes that persecuted and hateful feelings are ramped up by Mr B specifically in order to evade grief.

That analysis of so much grief and hate and anxiety bring relief, is abundantly clear. Klein writes that 'relief of anxiety of death brings up life.' But she also notes that 'complaints against parents are more bearable than sexual love for mother and hate/anxiety against father.' The oscillation between love and hate, guilt and aggression, is very dramatic at times. Nonetheless, very movingly, as much warmer feelings about his daughter emerge, Mr B tells Klein with great conviction, 'as long as there is life in somebody, people can be changed and actually there is hope.' Mr B also conveys his belief in the importance of telling his children the truth about all sorts of things, including the facts of life, about which he had been so in the dark. This is so hopeful for the analysis, since it suggests strongly that Mr B wishes to know and understand so much more himself. When Mr B discovers that he feels much less like a jealous child when he hears of the birth of a new baby in a family, he almost can't believe this. This is evidence, Klein tells him, that experiences in the past which were so difficult, and which felt so miserable and irresolvable, can actually be 'revised in the present and mitigated.'

Finally, the problem of internalisation comes into the foreground when Mr B 'forgets' progress made, or understanding recently gained in analysis. The question of how he can take in and keep a good object safe inside when he feels so assailed by his impulses, where his 'internal ground' feels to have been irreversibly poisoned, is absolutely agonising. One comes to feel that Mr B is very courageous to go on with the work of analysis, which Klein is so obviously dedicated to helping him with. Again, very movingly, she will tell him that she feels her task is 'really to help him to find his mother … [to] find his love for her and thus preserve her inside.'

Wednesday 6 January 1937

Mr B returns after a two-week Christmas break, the last few days of which he has spent ill in bed. During this time, he telephones Klein to tell her he is unwell and to ask when they are to resume. Klein's phone was initially engaged, so that she had called Mr B back. This interaction comes into the following material. Klein writes that Mr B 'starts by saying he is depressed,' though she is rather unconvinced of this. He then tells a detailed dream from two nights before:

Somebody rang him up at his home in the country. He could not hear the person well, and did not know who was talking. He said so once or twice, but the person, a man, seemed to insist that Mr B knew him. It was a man called Leonard or Lionel. Mr B gave in, thinking that he should know the man, and the man said that he would come to dinner with a famous German actress. Mr B says he is going to ask his wife whether this would be suitable. His wife, in the dream, makes some protest but agrees in the end. Mr B goes back to the telephone but in the meantime the man has been cut off. After some time, the man rings up again and Mr B says that he will be delighted to have them to dinner. While he is saying this they are again cut off. Mr B is very indignant about his telephone being so indistinct and feels that he must go to another telephone. He crosses the road and walks on but passes the Post Office and cannot find a telephone. The whole geography was as it is in reality but the details were different.

The dream moves to another scene:

Mr B finds himself sitting in a wood with his neighbour, W, a friendly old father figure. Trees are being felled and one tall old dead tree falls to the ground. Mr B heard his favourite little daughter screaming – she had been buried under the falling tree. He goes to dig her out. She is lying with her face towards the ground and seems injured, probably dangerously injured, he doesn't know. No injury is visible but he had an impression that she was injured inside. Mr B refers to the tree again, saying 'Perhaps it was not dead. It gave a lurch when falling – but even that wasn't perhaps a sign that it was alive.'

Klein asks Mr B what 'lurch' means:

Mr B explains it by saying for instance, a man going by underground would suddenly sway if the train makes a sudden movement, or a drunk man would also go with a lurch. I interpret that the old, tall dead tree injuring his little daughter was compared with something going on inside, the man being swayed by his drunkenness inside, and the underground also standing for something internal. I suggest that the old, tall tree stands for an internal father or penis, as former material has shown.

I remind Mr B that when I spoke to him over the telephone during the break, he had remarked on its being very indistinct and also that this being cut off may have to do with his feelings of being cut off from me. I became so distant because of our lack of contact but also because of his anxiety of having lost me through death. Mr B admits that the telephone talk with me had been pleasant to him. First when he rang up and then I rang up … He thought that really, I am nice to him and that he should not be so frightfully critical and aggressive with me. He says that it is awfully embarrassing to him to admit that the telephone talk was pleasant, but it is true.

Mr B returns to his dream:

> *About the actress, [he] adds that her Christian name is the same as his sister's. Acting & the*
> *stage are to him about the same as music; things so far away, and very difficult in his attitude*
> *to them. At the beginning of the hour, he had mentioned that his wife excludes him from her*
> *musical interests, but admitted that he also excludes her from his factual knowledge in many*
> *branches. Mentioning the actress he speaks again in this connection, of music. He then says*
> *that the word to act is used in so many ways. I interpret that the sexual act of the parents*
> *stands for all acting, or rather the other way round, and that the distance of the whole situation*
> *in the dream (the man he didn't know who mentioned that he would bring the actress, whom*
> *Mr B also did not know), all this indicates how far away from his mind by repression had*
> *been the sexual act of the parents. I also link up the unknown foreign actress in the dream with*
> *myself and the mother in the past as well as in the present – her deadness making her distant -*
> *and also with his little sister, through the name in common.*

Klein also interprets that the falling tree that harms Mr B's daughter stands for the
parental intercourse that is felt to be so perilous. She notes that the prospect of the
distant mother (the unknown German actress) and father (the man, Leonard or
Lionel, whom Mr B doesn't know) coming to dine arouses such anxiety because he
feels their coming together to be so dangerous. Klein adds however that,

> *The falling tree ... also stands for the internalized penis of father and brother, as well*
> *as for the internalized parents in intercourse. The tree falling, injuring his little daughter is*
> *Mr B's penis, also containing the father's penis, injuring the sister.*

Thursday 7 January 1937

Mr B expresses 'the usual feeling of depression.' Klein notes again that he does so
'without much conviction.' He is to attend a Board meeting that afternoon, and,

> *speaks with great anger against the Chairman whom he calls a footling despicable person ...*
> *Goes on saying that he has all the time in his life been surrounded by footling weak persons*
> *whom he despised and they were the authorities. He feels like throwing the inkstand against the*
> *Chairman in the afternoon. Laughingly and contemptuously says that the Chairman had done*
> *something entirely ungentlemanly which Mr B could use against him (about selling shares and*
> *so on), but actually he thinks that the Chairman is quite innocent, a charming man in a way,*
> *and obviously Mr B does not feel that the Chairman had bad intentions when he did that.*
> *Still, he wonders whether he is going to use it against the Chairman or not. He is going to have*
> *a little conspirative [sic] luncheon with some shareholders.*

Klein interprets,

> *Mr B's old contempt of his father, whom he must have watched with the greatest care and*
> *sharp criticism, and had felt that his father was in some ways much inferior to himself. But*

he could not allow himself to know of this criticism, because it was so revolutionary and meant to destroy the father, plotting against him with the brother, and therefore he had to repress the criticism in connection with father altogether. He had also to repress the wish to beat the father because it would have been such a dangerous, destructive thing, and for these very reasons, his ambition on many lines, and various activities became inhibited. I refer to Mr B's remarks about writing books, and various things which he obviously was able to do, but cannot even try. Mr B says that this horrible criticism of his father, which I suggest he had wanted his mother to see, and so to make father despicable to her, to make trouble between the parents, that this criticism must be very deeply repressed because he doesn't remember anything of the kind. But he seems to feel that I am right.

Mr B then reports several fragments of a dream, only one of which Klein records:

His wife was conducting a distinguished foreign lady through a kind of ward to a patient, and the patient was Mr B. It wasn't like a hospital.

In association,

Mr B remembers laughingly that when he was ill his wife would discuss him with the doctor in a kind of matron-like way, quite impersonal. But he adds that the foreign distinguished lady was obviously me. I then suggest that Mr B might have wished for me to come and see him when he was ill. Mr B admits that the thought had crossed his mind after the telephone talk. I suggest that he was unconsciously arranging it in such a way that his wife takes me to him. That makes the situation harmless, while underneath it might have been his wish to have me there, to love him or to take care of him …

Returning to his feelings about his father,

Mr B says how painful it was to him when we had found out before in his analysis that his father never seemed to admire him, that he for instance wanted Mr B to learn carpentry, but never did it with him and that he wasn't encouraging in this way. Mr B is not inclined to criticise his father so strongly but thinks that this might have added to his wish to. Says that things would not be so bad in the world if people would only try to get on with each other better. Mentioned he had heard recently that another baby was coming in a family, and also heard of the reactions of the older child to this newcomer. Mr B was astonished to find that he was now so much less strongly identified with the jealous child than he had been in the past, when he heard of such cases, because he had felt so frightfully hurt when his sister was born. I interpret that all this seems to indicate that he believed that though things had been so difficult and insoluble in the past, they can be revised in the present and mitigated.

Between 1 and 14 February 1937

Klein writes that there is 'deep despair prevailing.' Mr B complains repeatedly of 'feeling as though dead.' The analysis, he feels, makes him worse. Sessions often begin 'I cannot stand it any longer.' There are 'long silences and feelings of guilt about not speaking.' In one particular session, towards the end of the hour, Mr B

> *mentions that he had looked at a list the typist had made in his business (a list of amounts paid to insurance companies). On the first page she had put down all of the facts he had given her quite correctly and also in the right order; on the second page, where there were only a few lines she hadn't put the facts in the correct order. Mr B associates to insurance companies - that one [particular fee had] seemed too low and that he should have expected it to be higher. When mentioning the word 'facts' he himself recognizes that this has to do with me, whom he so often had reproached recently - that I am telling things which are not true – not really the facts. He now says that actually all he reproaches me for is that I sometimes don't put the things quite in the right order – also connected with the way I put things. Further, there is appreciation of the value of my work expressed in the reference to the insurance company who asked less than he thought they were entitled to ask.*

On the following day, Mr B makes 'some remark about sexual intercourse with his wife, [which had been] unsatisfactory.'

> *Then a bitter outbreak against me that the next thing I shall say is that it has to do with his sister in the past. That I am telling him things about the past and he doesn't know anything about it and I am accusing him wrongly. Then, with an entirely changed voice, says he must make himself tell me the dream which he had the previous night, which was awful.*

The dream is as follows:

> *My daughter, (about whom he knows nothing but that she is an analyst who is analysing somebody he knows), told him that I was dead. I had been drowned in the river R, which is near his estate. He saw the river the day before & found it swollen and muddy. When he heard that I had died he broke down entirely, 'he was shattered'. He cried and cried & was in despair. He then tried to find some help for my daughter who seemed very cold and seemed to say that she couldn't do anything for him, and would not analyse him, which he seemed to wish. The conclusion was that I was quite irreplaceable. My daughter had reminded him of some unpleasant person. He spoke with great emotion and said that he felt it was not the analysis only, it was losing me, which was so unbearable.*

Klein remarks that the river R, in which she is drowned, is near Mr B's estate. She also

> *remind[s] him of a dream in which his river was nice at its source, going round nice villages, with flowers and so on, but then was dirty, with dead dogs, further on its course. He had interpreted the river as himself being spoiled by education and civilization. I interpret that it is then Mr B who killed me, associating it with his phantasies of bad urine and faeces, and he himself containing bad and dirty and dead objects.*

Klein connects Mr B's despair and grief about her death, to the death of his mother, saying:

> *He has full insight that his reaction is connected with this loss. I interpret that at the beginning of the hour he was sharp and bitter, blaming me for persecuting him about his infantile sexuality, standing for a persecuting mother or nurse, and that this blame was increased in order to get away from the grief – which he clearly sees and acknowledges.*

Mr B then reports a second dream from the same night:

> *He was trying to fix a floating object, probably a boat, to a post from which six chains were hanging down. This reminds him of the Lady of Shallot by Tennyson, drifting down the river. He adds, she is dying. He couldn't tether this floating object because when he touched the chain, he saw that the chains were snakes. He heard the word 'pythoness' and says 'She is God's voice, the mouthpiece of the God, the oracle of Delphi.'*

Klein writes,

> *Mr B was first standing beside the post, which was about his size – then the chains were quite ordinary chains. When he discovered that they were snakes he was up on the post. It was as though his body were hanging over the top of the post. Then the snakes were about up to the waist of the post. I remark that it sounds as if the post was a person. Mr B agrees that the post and himself seem entirely linked up, actually the same. He recognized that the chains were snakes and he had his fingers between their teeth. He was frightened, but not overwhelmingly. Mr B agrees to my suggestion that being so interested in animals and snakes he managed to cover up his anxiety of them and remembers that he had once, as a child of about eight to ten, put a snake into his pocket, believing that it was dead and harmless, while he found afterwards that it was actually alive and an adder, so he confirms this mechanism of denial.*
>
> *I interpret that the dead Mrs Klein of the first dream was to be kept in his inside but she couldn't be fixed because she was drifting down the river. Between her, the pythoness, (the Delphi oracle, repeatedly identified with me and analysis) were the snakes which would not only bite him but also her, taking the whole situation of the post, etc as internal. Also, that the pythoness is not only the priestess of the Gods, the good parents, but also a huge serpent herself, in another sense.*

The following day, Mr B brings another dream:

> *Somebody whose name reminds him of a nursery expression, which has to do with buttocks, is with him and Mr B has got shorts on, and they are so short that they expose his buttocks entirely. The other person, (whom he had only met when he was grown-up, at college) admires his buttocks very much, and Mr B was extremely embarrassed.*

Associating to the dream, Mr B recalls

> *that he had been to this person's house, which was rather grand, and he felt extremely self-conscious. When I ask how old they might have been in the dream Mr B says 'from one onwards'. I interpret that this person connected with the grand house which embarrassed him might have been the older brother, to whom he exposed his buttocks, and as former material has shown, might actually have done something to his buttocks, on the line of pushing the penis in or something of the kind. Mr B bitterly complains how little grown-ups care about small children's feelings in this respect. He remembers an aunt who used to rumple his hair, and he remained quite cheerful but was indignant and furious underneath that grown-ups have a habit of caressing the buttocks of children who may feel very badly about it.*

Klein comments that Mr B 'obviously dislikes my interpretation about his brother, and stressed the part of a grown-up woman having, as it were, seduced him.' Mr B agrees, however,

> *that danger to him is always danger from behind, and he likes to have his back protected. Former material [has suggested a fear of] me attacking him from behind, and whenever he feels that somebody might attack him or watch him, it is from behind. I connect this feeling of danger from behind with the dream and the material of the snakes. I ask for associations to the six chains on the post, and Mr B at once answers with a nursery rhyme in which the line, 'Five, six pick up sticks' appears. I interpret the significance of these sticks as the penis pushed into him and changed inside into snakes.*

On the following day,

> *Mr B mentions, speaking about the company, that though he hasn't succeeded in getting the Chairman out, there is a lot of improvement which is entirely due to his [the Chairman's] suggestions. Actually, they are paying dividends and so on. Mr B is worried that that could make the Chairman believe that everything is all right. If he was asked whether it is all right, Mr B would say, 'Some of it is all right, but other things need being done'. Mr B connects this spontaneously with his analysis, and says that over the weekend he has been openly worried by the thought that Klein might think that he is better than he is and that she could finish the analysis. Mr B agrees that this implies that he believes in definite improvement in himself.*

In the next session, 'the whole situation of hidden grief,' as Klein puts it, is discussed:

> *Mr B complains how children are stopped in being sad, are always cheered up and have to be cheerful and it seems quite familiar to him that he had been sad and worrying about his mother's death. When I agreed to this attitude of people in connection with children's sadness, he starts crying, and goes on crying hard for some time. He also speaks of the relief which one gets from tears.*

On another day from this period, Mr B reports 'an awful dream.' There are three distinct parts, which he tells out of sequence:

He said goodbye to some female acquaintances. One of them gave him a bag and he said that his shoes would fit into the bag. He put them in, taking up his luggage to go for a journey. Returning to the first part of dream, he was with his son and eldest daughter. Mr B notes that recently much grief and worry about his daughter going to school [has been analysed, with Mr B] being identified with her who separates from the home, meaning losing mother altogether through death. But in the present situation, it also means losing his daughter through death when she leaves. In this dream, Mr B's daughter was in a tree, in front of him on a branch. His son had disappeared. Mr B himself felt in the greatest danger because though in the scenery there was actually no precipice, it was at the same time true that he could fall at any time from the branch down a precipice two hundred feet deep. Then he managed to extricate himself somehow from this situation. Then, his daughter had disappeared. He thought the boy might be amongst some children who were happily playing, but he was not among them. He then said he found him and that he had gone to Mr X whom he connects with teaching and rigid principles, etc, and was happily playing with him. In another part of the dream, Mr B was going on a kind of pile of wood which sloped down towards a river. An old woodcutter was making this pile of wood, but used firewood, which could not really fill it up in the right way.

Associating to the dream, Mr B thinks of

an old man, eighty years old, on his estate, a woodcutter, a nice friendly old man with whom he likes to talk. But the man in the dream was fierce and frightening. He did not talk, was very silent but then he moved. Mr B agrees that these descriptions seem to signify that he was dead or dying, and that there is also a connection with his own elderly father whom he feels to be so near to death. In the dream this man did a fruitless thing, because one could not really make a platform out of firewood. There was no stability in it. First of all in connection with the woodcutter, Mr B had spoken of the great amount of wood he has got at his estate - old, dead wood, which is really too old to be burnt; but the young wood is too young to be burnt. Still he has got such a lot he had once had a passing thought of offering me a load of wood.

Klein interprets that

the old, dead wood stands for the dead people inside him. It should be done away with, but one must be careful not to burn at the same time the young growing things, (the willows). The old man, who stands for his father, is also myself, who is trying to make stability which should protect from the river, the muddy, drowning river, but we cannot do it because the father, and me, are so near to death.

Klein says that the dangerous tree also stands for analysis. She writes that while Mr B fears 'falling into the depths of it,' also, 'not having analysis is the danger.'

The following day, Mr B,

> *Speaks of a very unpleasant joke somebody – an Austrian friend he is very fond of – made once in front of the undergraduates, which referred somehow to buttocks. I remind him of his earlier dream connecting with buttocks; also that this Austrian friend who makes this unpleasant remark and whom he values very highly, is standing for me, who gave interpretations about buttocks which he did not want to hear.*

Klein notes that as they are discussing this unpleasant joke, Mr B becomes very annoyed because she had not heard a particular word he said. She writes,

> *He admits that this annoyance is really quite irrational, but that he feels it very deeply if I cannot understand a particular word he says. Obviously, I should know all his thoughts, even without words, and that may have something to do with his silences sometimes. I interpret that the internalized me, who would really know all his thoughts, would cooperate entirely. Mr B says he does not at all know what I mean by that – by my being inside. I point out that this sudden not understanding of something which a few days ago he had seen in the material connects with the anxiety of the bad thing inside him, the snakes, sticks, the bad penis, which makes him deny entirely the possibility of internalization. If it was only the question of my being there as the understanding mother he always would like to have with him, he would understand and take in what I interpret. But it is the anxiety of the snakes which drives him to deny this process. Mr B mentions that he had been dead tired in the morning. It felt like having lead in his veins. He associates to the King in Hamlet, who had been poisoned. I interpret the connection between poison, behind, snakes and penis.*

Klein records that Mr B then falls asleep on the couch briefly and wakes having dreamt:

> *He had seen a word written out, and this word was spelt IOGENISTA. But he saw it in Greek and in Greek capitals. In the dream it was spelt IOOENISTA instead of the other word, but he knew in the dream it should really be spelt the other way. To one part of the word he associates 'Owen', a cousin of his mother's, an Austrian, a very nice person, who died. To another part of the word he associates that it means 'child of Violet', and Violet is his mother's name.*

Klein makes the following comments:

> *The second part of the word is related to 'the family of Ion', that is, the lost child who served Apollo and the pythoness of Delphi, who found his lost mother through them. Also, the word Athens means in Greek, 'Violet ground' so that it all refers to his dead mother, since he is the child of Violet; the lost child. It is also characteristic that he should have this dream in my room because this kind of falling asleep for a minute and then bringing parts of dreams is usually the most direct way of bringing dream material, and has to do with his wish, shown long before in analysis, that he would like to lie on my couch and to be looked after. It is really*

relaxation and trust and so on, so that he in this way really finds his mother. I interpret that I am the pythoness, who is really to help him to find his mother, in the sense that he can revise his relation to his dead mother, find his love for her and thus preserve her inside.

Thursday 18 February 1937

Mr B returns to earlier dream material about the woodcutter who cannot make a stable woodpile:

Especially he wants to make quite clear to me that this wood which the woodcutter put into the gorge, should have been quite straight, but could not be because it wasn't right for this purpose. He also associates to the part of the dream where he got a bag from these female acquaintances, and says he strongly suspects that they were his aunts, of whom he had a number, who were unmarried, and very fond of him when he was a child. He says that one especially, he suspected (as former material showed), of having excited him sexually, or had done something to him. He says that the symbolism of the bag into which he puts his shoes seems very obvious as a seduction.

Klein interprets that Mr B needs

to make her see clearly how the wood should have been put into the gorge, which was identified with the analysis, and the task of putting things inside him straight. The analyst should straighten out the bad penis and people inside him.

In response, Mr B remarks

that recently, on certain occasions, he had the strong feeling that the different feelings and tendencies in him are so little assimilated with each other. On other occasions he said that he feels himself not to be a unity, and once said he had so many people in him. I interpret that the lack of unity he has felt recently is connected with the insight that these pieces of wood, old and young, are the internalized people whom he could not assimilate because first of all he could not at all face the fact that he had internalized them. She explains that without being able to face at all the anxiety of internalized people, there is obviously no possibility of assimilating them better. Mr B is very understanding about it and says 'Why, what else could he do to help towards that?' but concludes that obviously nothing can be done with conscious will, but just by cooperation.

Saturday 20 February 1937

Klein writes that 'there had been a definite improvement and relief after the last few weeks' work' and that Mr B is almost always on time. In this session, he brings a dream:

He met Mrs M in the slightly hilly part of the county where they both live. She lives in another part of the county and these hills are as it were in between. He had mentioned her before repeatedly, a very attractive woman, beautiful, and quite friendly with him but not actually especially interested in him. In one dream (where an old man was poisoned by a young man), he actually made sexual advances to her, and apart from this has had many phantasies about her. He describes this softly undulating part of the county and adds 'my feelings were as pleasantly undulating as this part.' In the dream he was to tighten the girth of a horse, and it was understood that Mrs M also wanted him to do that. He explains to me that of course horses sometimes blow themselves up as soon as one has tightened the girth, then it gets loose again. Probably a little inconvenient for them to have it tight, but if not, the saddle goes up and down and he demonstrates it with gestures, the saddle doesn't hold well. The whole atmosphere of dream was pleasant and satisfactory.

In the second part of the dream,

He was ratting. There might also have been other people, but his dog was definitely with him. Anyhow he was in charge of things. It was a small and empty room and they caught the rat. Then he was ratting in another room which was large and full of junk. There were other people there & they didn't find the rat. There were two rats in this ratting - one was found, the other wasn't found.

Klein writes,

To Mrs M he associates that she has eyes like a deer, and he often compared her with a deer. Then she is like a horse. I interpret that Mrs M herself is the horse on which he tightens the girth and the whole thing stands for intercourse. She also wanted it in the dream and the whole atmosphere expresses satisfaction, apart from the one detail that it is necessary to tighten the girth. This is slightly inconvenient to the horse and seems to show Mr B's belief that the beginning of the intercourse, his inserting his penis must be felt as painful or unpleasant by the woman. Also the undulating feelings and the undulating hills are a reference to the undulations of the woman's body.

Mr B 'becomes restless and angry.' He tells Klein,

He knew that the thing was going to finish in a sermon or in a homily, referring to the Church fathers. I say that while I was interpreting pleasant sexual feelings towards a mother figure (Mrs M is felt to be grand, he is good friends with her husband, and other details speak for her being a mother figure) the anxiety of the father arose. Mr B admits that in dream there was no question of her husband – he wasn't there, and also that their meeting each other meant something especially friendly. I interpret that the expected anxiety of the revenging father appeared in the transference where I am felt as the Church father. (Mr B's father has a strong belief in the Church, and also Mr B once fainted in Church as a child.) I interpret that the killing of the rat which Mr B was alone responsible for, stands for the father's penis.

Mr B leaves Klein in an angry state. She also records that,

> *At the beginning of this hour Mr B had also referred to his daughter and said that of course if he doesn't feel so gloomy then the whole matter of her going to school takes on a different aspect, since it also has its advantages for this child. I remark that analysis of so much grief and anxiety has produced a relief which he can admit. I also connected this with the fact that relief of anxiety in relation to his dead mother brings up sexual feelings in connection with a mother-substitute. Relief of anxiety of death brings up life.*

Monday 22 February 1937

Klein records that Mr B is 'very angry again, and despairing, very much in connection with his wife who can't be improved.' Klein returns to his dream of 20 February, pointing out that,

> *His having given way [in that dream] to sexual phantasies in connection with Mrs M and to feelings of hate towards his father, Mr B turns necessarily to bitterness, both against mother and father (he had connected me very much with the doctor who treats his wife, and accused me of not doing anything for his children).*

Klein expresses strongly the view that

> *complaints against both parents are more bearable than sexual love for mother and hate and anxiety against the father.*

There follow further associations to the dreams of Saturday:

> *The small room where the first rat was killed reminds Mr B of a lavatory. The second room, where the rat couldn't be found, reminds him of the stables in the country which are used for storing all sorts of furniture, pillowcases, etc which he feels go rotten through damp, mice and rats; through the fault of Mr B and his wife.*

Klein interprets that Mr B's dog, which killed the rat, represents his own 'tearing tendencies.' Linking Mr B's association to the lavatory to recent material about attacks from the behind, and on the anus, she interprets that,

> *The dog, his own tearing part of his personality, attacks the behind of the woman, of his mother, to kill there the father's penis, represented through faeces.*

Klein continues,

> *The larger room is the deeper inside of the body containing junk, dirt and many people. The objects and dangerous faeces it is full of, the place where, through the fault of he and his wife, actually of he and his mother, the good objects are destroyed. Here again it is rats and mice,*

bad faeces, and father's penis, the many people, the many foreign bodies he was complaining about some time ago, when he referred to his sudden feeling that he is not a unity.

Klein also points out that Mr B's mother was pleasant and loved when she is represented by Mrs M, but that 'things turned awful as soon as her inside came into question in connection with the intercourse.' Mr B has an association which, he says himself, seems to confirm Klein's interpretation:

He says that he had thought about a quarter of an hour ago something which may be unimportant, but he feels he should say it. While I was interpreting, he thought of the two dreams – and even before I had started to give the detailed interpretation about the rat dream – as an outside and an inside dream. He agrees that this is an unusual way of putting it. He agrees that he should have thought of an out of doors dream and an indoor dream ...

Immediately after Mr B shares this thought, his tone changes dramatically:

He suddenly says, 'One of these days I shall kill you', in quite a special voice. I ask how. He says, 'With the fist I shall bash your brains in.' I ask for his phantasies about it, and Mr B replies, with rather grim laughter, 'I shall tell them to you when I have done it'. 'I shall ask you to analyse them when you are dead.' Mr B describes seeing me as a corpse with a bashed-in head, and he asking me to analyse him. I interpret that Mr B might often have felt I was sitting there as a corpse, whom he had destroyed through poisonous words, associations, etc, but Mr B says very decidedly, 'that was different. Now, that was with the fist'. He leaves me without looking at me at all.

Klein also records that in this hour, Mr B,

had mentioned that a doctor examined him because of a pain in the belly, that he had black faeces, and that there is a suspicion of a gastric ulcer. He tries to argue that this doesn't frighten him at all – that his faeces are being analysed, and that the probability of an ulcer is very little.

Tuesday 23 February 1937

Mr B is late. During the hour he,

mentions that the analysis of the faeces has so far not proven anything, saying bitterly, 'Of course in analysis one wouldn't find anything.' Also mentions that it is very painful to him that he can be so carried away by his hate. He puts this quite generally, and does not connect to me, or his anger in the previous session or to my feelings about it, or to his anxiety of having hurt or frightened me. Judging from former occasions when he had lost his temper with me, which he had felt guilty about, it is obvious that he should feel some guilt or something after saying such an unusual thing. Mr B says that it was because of my sermon, though actually, as I point out to him, he didn't [lose his temper following this]. [Rather, it was] after his mentioning, or rather recognizing, outside and inside, [in connection to the two dreams]. I suggest that Mr B's wish and strong impulse to kill me, was in the transference, to the father, because he was representing the destructive rats inside Mr B's mother's body and his own. Going over the material again, I explain that the actual Oedipus situation (not using this word), and love for mother, including strong death impulses against father, was unbearable, and had resulted in the relation to his mother which he had called on the razor edge between love and hate.

Klein also interprets,

that the bashing in of my head was partly an attack on my body to get hold of the rats, and that I should then actually go on analysing him.

Wednesday 24 February 1937

Klein records,

Coming into my room, Mr B says that he had never yet noticed that I have got such a long hot pipe in my room. Refers to the radiator between the windows. He had noticed the one in the waiting room but not the one in the study. He feels very guilty about the bad relationship with his wife. I interpret his guilt, referring to his wish to bash in my brain some days before, and that he had been sorry for that, though not in connection with me, just saying that he felt afraid of being carried away. Mr B reiterates his feelings in connection with this phantasy. He sees himself as being full of revenge when he had bashed in my brain … Then Mr B says he thought of Jael, the woman of the Bible who enticed a King who had been beaten on the battlefield into her house by offering a bowl of milk and butter, and then when he was asleep hammered a long nail into his head so that he was nailed down on to the ground. When saying so, Mr B clenches his fists and shows strong signs of anxiety. I interpret that the clenching of the fists is the expression of his impulse to bash in my brains, which he had expressed some days ago, and that now we can see that his bashing in my brains had to do with his anxiety of being attacked by me from behind. Mr B says that his head is actually aching and that he actually feels strong anxiety of me. He keeps his fist clenched. I interpret that the long nail is the same thing as the long hot pipe which Mr B had never noticed before in the room, and that is the long penis of the father who had recently played such an important part in the associations. The headache and the anxiety lasted for some time, and then Mr B says that he has never before felt so strongly the impulse to kill; also, never before so strongly the anxiety of me as a dangerous person attacking him.

Friday 26 February 1937

Klein writes that Mr B is now 'very peaceful.' It begins to get dark and she is about to turn on the light. Mr B says however that,

he wouldn't need it, because it is quite peaceful in the dark if somebody is there. I point out that he is speaking of somebody who is a friendly and helpful figure and certainly not as the woman Jael. I then explain the way in which this awful mother-figure came about by projection, through his murderous impulses against me and his father in the night, and in a situation in which they would be helpless and overwhelmed by him. I interpret that Mr B's mother was never for him alone, because she was always connected with the long nail, the hot pipe, and always part of a couple.

Saturday 27 February 1937

Klein writes that Mr B,

Had seen a picture of a bird which was supposed to be a rare bird in this part of the country, and then it had been discovered that it was a shag. In the picture the bird looked as if it had been crucified. Mr B is very indignant about that. He says that the shag is a nasty bird, with very bad habits, but that is no reason why it should be crucified. Also, that people say that the shag is picking out the sheep's eyes, and Mr B is quite certain that is not true. I interpret that the shag is here identified with him, that he feels so bloodthirsty and bad after his phantasied attacks of the last few days. Also, that the sheep, the eyes, which the shag was picking out or picked out, are the other children. Mr B remarks that his own child had once said as a small child that she could pick out the eyes of the others if mother loves them and is paying more attention to the others than to her. Mr B mentions that he had seen the lions in the zoo being fed and noticed that one bar, which had been opened for the reason of having the pieces of meat passed through, had not been shut again, so that there was actual danger. He thinks that the bar should be shut, that is what bars are for.

Klein interprets that,

again, he feels bloodthirsty, like the lion, and that the pieces of meat are the pieces which he would tear out of me and in the past out of his mother and the other children. He feels that I should be on my guard against him, putting bars between him and I because of his phantasy, really a wish for attack. Mr B then mentions that he had seen a picture of seals – the fur seals – and that he thought that of course they would be much used for fur coats and killed in such large numbers, and also speaks of preserving birds against the women who will have their feathers for hats, but actually, why does one eat cattle – cows, all sorts of cattle, who are quite harmless. Then, indignantly, says that he could quite as well walk out of the door if the lion comes and leave the part which he had caught behind him. Had said in this hour as often before, that he feels quite bad, and says now that he could leave the corpse behind on the couch to be analysed by me while the live part would walk out. Certainly, the corpse would not contradict me but would accept everything I say.

Klein interprets,

that this is not only a joke, but very serious. He wants to go out and leave the dead mother behind on the couch, for one thing to get rid of the corpse, and another thing so that I should put the corpse, the dead mother right by analysing her. I interpret that he wants to put the objects inside him right. I spoke of his great joke of some days ago, that he would analyse me when I was a corpse, and I say this was actually also the wish to bring me back to life when he felt that he had killed me through his associations and dangerous attacks.

Mr B turns to speak of his youngest daughter:

He says that her attitude towards him is sane. She seems to have much more confidence in him. I suggest that perhaps Mr B's attitude towards his daughter, whom he formerly wasn't very fond of, has changed. He then mentions a talk with his children about some biological facts, eventually coming back to my suggestion that his attitude towards his daughter might have changed. He says that as long as there is life in somebody people can be changed and actually there is hope.

Later, Mr B,

Speaks about Mendelism, the important biological discovery of the Czech monk which was forgotten and rediscovered later, and very important in biology. He speaks about the live tissue which one can observe under the microscope, and also that there is a way of observing a live tissue. Says he feels guilty that his son had once asked him why one speaks of a female and a male screw, and that he had avoided giving him the explanation of the symbolism. He intends writing to his son or telling him on the next occasion that he did not give him the right answer.

Klein interprets 'the greater hope in all these associations about life and pro-creation.' She notes that Mr B feels,

one should give the child the right information which he himself had never had. Of course, he had deeply repressed [certain knowledge, and curiosity], though he was able to develop a great interest in natural science. Yet he told me most definitely at the beginning of the analysis that he had never had the slightest interest in his parents' sexuality, childbirth, etc – had never known anything about it. He definitely admits the repression, saying that obviously as soon as the knowledge was infringing sexuality, he could not stand it.

Monday 1 March 1937

Klein writes that Mr B,

Had some black faeces and the doctor put him on a special diet. Also, he had had pains in the belly, referred to in former material. He describes the doctor jokingly as having decided to starve him for sheer fun, and that he amused friends who were there to lunch by putting it this way. He says he would rather not talk about these things with me but instead go on amusing me, and says he knows that he can do so if he likes. In between also makes great fun of his partner, who had asked him how he was, whom he had made a fool of, at least in his mind. I interpret that actually he wanted to amuse his mother very much and make a fool of father in his talks with her. Mr B agrees that he could fascinate his mother by his jokes and talk, and that it was only too pleasant for him to do so, but that he would never have wanted to make fun of his father with her. His father he did not try to amuse – he never succeeded in doing so. His father never appreciated this at all.

In the following days, Mr B is in 'great distress and despair,'

to a minor extent also about his analysis, but actually I connect it to his internal anxieties. He had been X-rayed, and did not yet know the result. The analysis of the faeces had been negative, but one could not explain why they had been so black. I connect the external anxieties with internal persecutions and dangerous faeces.

The day before Mr B was to hear the result of the X-ray, he had an 'awful' dream:

He was in a miserable car (all cars are miserable – all mechanical things are, in contrast to flowers and things which grow, and nature). He was in this car on the road that runs past his house, and he was reversing on the wrong side of the road, disorganizing the traffic. In doing so, he ran over two children and killed them. People came to tell him that he had done it. It was near to the police station which is near his house. His wife was not there. She had gone away in the direction of the hospital. In his car there was a man who reminds him of the obliging but unimportant librarian at his club, (who had offered to keep a book for him the evening of the dream.) Still, he feels that he himself was responsible for running over the children. There could be some doubt also about the other man's part in it. He then has to tell his wife that he has run over his children, and that is quite intolerable.

In association, Mr B remarks that a few days before, his wife had gone to their son who was unwell, and Mr B had thought it 'very fussy.' Klein writes that he is 'obviously hating his own anxiety of the child's illness.' Returning to the dream, Mr B notes that 'the other man was not harmless, but felt to be harmful.' Klein interprets that,

He had chosen a picture of an inefficient but friendly father, while he Mr B was full of black faeces and ulcers inside him; and of destruction – running over, and so on. I interpret that the dangerous thing was having to confess to having killed his own children. His wife was standing for his mother and the two children were his brother and sister, to whose backs, behind, he had done something. Mr B gets very angry, saying that what I think is material is none – that I cannot prove these things to him, and that they are my ideas.

Monday 8 March 1937

Klein records that Mr B,

Had had intercourse with his wife, which was pleasant, and which she also enjoyed more. It appears that he had been much more patient about the beginning, which is always

difficult, and if he can get over that, then she can enjoy it. Also, there was some change in her own attitude about it. He also says he has been planting so many willows. In the meantime, he had the result of the X-ray, and there was nothing the matter with him. I interpret that in contrast to his dream of the day before and the interpretation, he felt quite different. His intercourse and his penis had become better, creative, and that altered his own attitude to the intercourse, which of course again was helped by his wife's different attitude. He seems quite willing to accept this. That here, life is contrasted with death, there is greater belief in life. In leaving me, Mr B asked for rearrangement of his hour, and says very emphatically, 'I do want to go on with this job'.

Tuesday 9 March 1937

Mr B brings a dream:

He dreamed that he told his wife, 'I have told her and there is no fuss to be made about that. I am not regretting it, and I was quite right to tell her'. He had told his mother he was in analysis. He associates that though she might have disagreed with this fact, she would have understood that if it gives him comfort and help, that it is right. Mothers, besides all their faults, do have a great lot of advantages and understanding. As so much recently, he recognized how much deeper his appreciation and love for his mother actually are, as well as for the analysis, which he quite frankly admits now. He thinks that he should not keep it a secret from everyone, as he does. That being in analysis and the results of analysis means childhood, old feelings, and so on, coming up and the whole revision of his relation to his mother. He had partly associated this, partly I had interpreted it.

The tone shifts, however, as,

Mr B suddenly objects to [my] talk, feeling at the same time that it is awful that he should shut me up. [He feels] so ungrateful. But he hates talk in general. Association about a car accident he had some time ago in the wilds, when his car caught fire. He got out of it and some Indians came and helped him. He couldn't talk with them, but he made them entirely understand that this was his car, and they were most helpful. Why should they? They are only treated with contempt, spat upon, did not get any money for that and yet were kind and helpful. He thanked them profusely, but they might not have understood. I interpret that the Indian is myself, the foreigner, and that he feels that he has treated and treats me badly. I point out that the Indians help without speaking, and that analysis is so awful, which he always felt, because so much is done by speech. He always is worried if I have not understood things, and I remind him of the dangerous quality of words, we had seen so far, - stones thrown at his head, caterpillars, being eaten, dangerous explosion, the burning excreta; but also that speech was a way of confessing; of telling his mother the truth; Also speech of the grown-ups, for his feeling was always [that he would be] blamed for all the bad things which he felt he had done from the beginning.

Wednesday 10 March 1937

Mr B comes in rage and despair.

> *He had written a very unfriendly letter to the Chairman and not had a reply, and later on agrees that this also contributed to his anxiety. I interpret in connection with his great admission of the last few days and the co-operation, that this has stirred the well-known anxiety of fondness and all the conflicts and anxieties with regard to father. He then speaks to me in a rather frightened voice – a very deep voice I had never heard him use – in a very sharp and bitter way, and warning about my interpretation. I interpret that this seems to be the frightening father himself who with his deep voice was frightening Mr B – he had reversed the situation. He then suddenly says in his natural voice that he has got some pains in his penis inside. Then speaks of cellars, and that he had always been frightened in dark closed-in places. Then especially of the cellar in his parents' house. Then associates an entirely different scene. When he was with his family in Scotland and while he was fishing or doing something near water, he saw suddenly that his mother had left him – had gone away – and he felt awful despair and anxiety at this. His father and brother were shooting. Mr B remarks on the fact that this is entirely opposite to enclosed places. I interpret that the shooting father seems to be one link and that being left alone with his mother meant the dangerous father was to shoot him. That the pain inside the penis has to do with castration and that the anxiety was of being shot by father, castrated by him, and left by mother. The dark places are also standing for the woman's genital, and that he is afraid of meeting this dangerous father inside her. That the connection in the transference situation is that having been on such good terms with me raises the anxiety of the castrating father, whom he felt would interfere.*

Mr B says that he has had many dreams, but 'stresses that they are his dreams, [that he] does not want to tell them to [Klein], not even to himself, because they may be shattered, like breaking an egg if looking into it.' He does however report one of the dreams:

> *He was on a mountain. It was very early, [dawn]; he recognized that the place … was very dangerous; He was glad to see the footsteps scratched on the rocks of people who had been there before. On the mountain side there was a house, and when he discovered that it was so dangerous to be there in the [dawn] and in the mountains he tried to get in through the window. [He] felt that he was using the wrong entrances. He felt like a burglar.*

> *[He is] very silent, [giving] no associations. [I] interpret … the wrong entrance as the anus, and his activities with sister, and his brother's activities with him. (Before I gave this interpretation Mr B had mentioned that he had seen his brother, whom he had not met for many months, and there was some feeling about his brother in the dream). In the morning at breakfast, he had suddenly had a thought that actually he had been very tyrannical with his sister, as far as her mental development went; that he had not allowed her any mental independence, and he had felt sorry for that. I interpret the wrong entrances, etc, as what his brother did to him and what he did to his sister; the forcing … his physically forcing her. In*

the transference situation his thorough dislike about my conduct ... of the analysis, of my convictions about analysis, about his tendency, which he so often feels guilty about, to want to conduct the analysis, etc. I am standing here for the sister; and also his anal attacks on me; which he thoroughly denies as monstrous ... I also refer to the dreams – the broken egg as castration, the whole scene [on the mountain being related] to experiences in the early morning, but also to phantasies of having mother to himself. The footsteps of his predecessor being the friendly traces of the father's penis, which indicate that mother's inside is not bad.

Klein notes that recently she had had to cancel Mr B's session, which had not happened before. In this connection,

He remarks that he had thought ... a catastrophe must have happened to somebody else ... that I had had to [attend to] something important – a patient being very ill, or something of the kind. Then Mr B asks what was the matter, and when I say I was unwell, he seems rather struck, and said he would not have thought that. Expresses being sorry etc. Obviously the whole hour is influenced by this remark, because very little aggression was to be seen. [Mr B is] going to see his father for the weekend, and says his wife is not going with him. It will be the first time that he is in the house alone with his father. On former occasions his mother was always there, or a nurse, or somebody else. He admits that he feels very uneasy at this thought.

Tuesday 23 March 1937

Mr B begins,

With violent accusations against women. His wife was invited to go somewhere and he heard her say over the telephone that she would love to go, but would like to be present if her little girl's hand is taken out of the plaster. She had broken a bone ... Mr B is indignant, and rages about the anxiety of his wife; [her needing] to be present at that. Women who always do the wrong thing over their children, and fuss over them, and actually their love means sucking the blood out of them. Wild accusation against me because of his son not being analysed.

He then reports a nightmare which he had had when staying at his father's house:

Two hands (he demonstrates this very vividly) were put round his waist, holding him tightly; but he was a baby, he felt it quite definitely. It was an awful nightmare.

Mr B 'refuses any associations to that for some time.' He is silent for a time, and then,

thinks of a bull and of the bulrush plant. Actually, it should not be called bulrush because it looks exactly like the penis of the bull. As a child he was amused about the saying that the spring is dangerous because the hedges are shooting and the bull rushes out. I interpret his rage against women as the well-known wish to escape from the anxiety of the father. The fact that the little girl had broken [a bone] in her hand, which he had minimized ... expresses anxiety of what had happened to his sister; and again the mother's anxiety and care has stirred his own, and rage is covering up anxiety.

Klein reiterates,

But in fact, the rage against the woman is an escape from anxiety of father. It was in his father's house, [when Mr B was] alone with him, that the bull, the penis of the father, was rushing on him. [His dream represents a] violation, and he suggests that actually the brother, three years older and representing a grown-up person when he was a tiny baby, is standing for the father, and violated him. ([Earlier] material about his brother's sleep-walking, his actual anxiety that his brother might attack his penis; [his association to] Hamlet: "It was a brother's hand", etc) ... Mr B had [earlier] said, what is the good of interpreting if it does not help ... if he feels suffocated it cannot help if I interprets this. I ... connect the feeling of suffocation with this early violation.

Wednesday 24 March 1937

Mr B brings another dream:

He walked on a tight rope with another fellow, a very nice man who reminds him of ... one of his employees.

Associating to the dream, Mr B says that the employee's name

reminds Mr B of his toothpaste, which he had looked at in the morning. He had found this toothpaste open when he arrived at his father's house, and asked the butler to try to find the top. It was messy because it had come undone. But the butler did not find it. His associations show that the man is felt by him as a servant, supposed to do what Mr B tells him.

Thursday 25 March 1937

This is the final session before a short Easter break. Mr B complains that his wife has a bad throat. He then tells Klein another dream:

He was to take some earth by car to the doctor. The earth was round the school, or his old home, or something of the kind. It seemed an entirely impossible task to do this. Then he went first to the left and made a detour, before he did this, and fell in with some unknown boys on the street. He was also a boy apparently. One took him up a very high tower. There was an iron erection, onto which he was holding, and when he saw that the iron staircase was bending, he declined to go further and did not do so. He never arrived to take the earth to the doctor.

Mr B remarks that,

> *He felt less anxiety in this dream than he had the night before, because he felt that he could decline [to go on] where it became dangerous. [I interpret] that when he was alone with his father (for the first time, Mr B says, in his life) homosexual desires had come up ... in a very frightening way, though it was a servant person who did what he wanted and not the frightening father. The next night's dream is less frightening, I suggest, because of my having interpreted some of the anxiety with regard to homosexuality the day before. His falling in with the boys, the iron erection to which he was holding [on] the bending staircase, [I] interpret on the line of sexual activities with his brother. Sexual desires [were] transferred from father to brother, and in this way made apparently less harmful. Anxiety of the brother [is] denied by covering up, putting him in an inferior position. [The] dream of the second night, I suggest, means that he could not take the earth to the doctor, which was the home, school, etc standing for mother, because he had made this detour – had gone to the left (which often before has meant doing something wrong). That through homosexuality he has spoiled his relation to his mother; ... the doctor comes in because he did not stop at the right moment, because he had taken in the penis, which made him ill. The earth is himself, which he should take to the doctor, but also his buried mother whom father took to the doctor to cure her; ... he accuses himself that because of his having the bad penis inside him he cannot help his mother inside him.*

Wednesday 31 March 1937

During the brief break from analysis Klein notes, Mr B's wife continued suffer with a sore throat. Mr B,

> *Begins with the greatest despair, wants to stop treatment, cannot talk, hates me. He then associates to lions. He had read a story of East Africa, of the times when Uganda was not so civilized as now, where a lion came in through an open door of a train, taking out one of the passengers and jumping out with the passenger, and only his feet were left. Mr B had never until then realized that lions can be so dangerous. I interpret that his admiration for the lion, whom he had so often before connected with himself ... was a denial ... of the dangerousness of the lion, because he knew all the time that lions can be dangerous, and it is the same relation with the brother and the father ... When he said he hated me and then associated to lions, I was standing for the father and brother, whom he really thinks are] dangerous, like lions.*

Klein's notes on Mr B's treatment aren't so regular going forward, though the material from 10 April is clearly a continuation of that recorded in the above session, from 31 March. Unfortunately, the only diary that exists for 1937 is blank, so there is no way of checking when Klein did see Mr B in this year. In other years, her diaries are much fuller.

Saturday 10 April 1937

Mr B now complains of a bad throat himself and says that he 'feels so ill, but cannot describe why.' He says he has no pain in swallowing and no other pain at all. He speaks again,

> with the greatest hate against women again, that of course they make men miserable, and do not want the man, and interfere … I interpret that his anxiety of having swallowed the lion's penis, expressed now by his bad throat, gives him these feelings of being so ill, which he cannot describe and also cannot explain. He had felt with his mother, when he looked at her in the morning that she also had swallowed the lion during the night … He admits that he always felt bad when he saw his mother in bed in the same way that he … has an unpleasant feeling when he sees his wife in bed, even in the morning; and his anxiety and hatred against his father he could not deal with other than by emphasizing the badness of mother and by covering up his anxiety and hate against the father, as well as his attraction to him.

Monday 26 April 1937

Mr B reminds Klein, 'in that certain way in which he always tells … material which he knows to be important,' that 'there had been material about the throat in connection with homosexual activities in childhood.' He then begins by speaking,

> about the moat and his clearing it up, felling trees with the axe, generally clearing it up, etc' … He says, if you see a little twig standing out of the water [referring to clearing the moat] and want to pull it out, then you cannot, because there is a branch underneath, and under the branch there is a tree, forty feet high. Of course, you can't pull that out.

Klein interprets, bringing this

> into connection with the homosexual material, anxiety about the throat, and a former important dream about the moat, in which Mr B saw a relative – a man, then his wife and then his own child, and all were dead, but came to life when they were taken out of the water … Mr B had felt very guilty about being an unsatisfactory patient, and not associating when he should. In between he says he had seen a bat in the sunshine over the water. It belongs to a very rare species. I remind him that his feeling that he is so unsatisfactory and that he is so terrified of me, which he so often says, connects with this ·bat, since in a dream (which I can give him all the details of), he could not stand any longer listening to the accusing voice of the bat and had to crush it in some receptacle … I show him … that this bat was internal. Mr B did not remember the dream but had a feeling I must be right. He did not deny it.

Tuesday 27 April 1937

> Again, Mr B tells me in a certain way at the very moment when he comes in (fully on time and without first saying that he is in despair, etc), that … while sitting in the car very near

to my house, he suddenly realized that something which he had dreamt many years ago was only a dream and was not real. In this dream he had not done his school prep in Latin or maths, and had gone ... on and on doing this and nobody knew, and he knew, and thought it would all be awful in the end. It is impossible to say what a relief he felt when he realized that; he had not realized it before.

Mr B then tells 'an awful nightmare:'

Somebody who has been dead for years appeared, a doctor, (a friend of his, an extremely gentle, unselfish person, who actually died from septicaemia in the service of humanity. This friend had had a withered hand.) Actually in the dream Mr B saw him exactly as he had looked and also the withered hand, only that he looked very pale. Mr B stretched out his hand and caught this friend's hand, telling him how glad he was that he had come. Then Mr X, Mr B's partner, (as Mr B describes him, a worldly and selfish person,) appeared and did not see the dead man, and Mr B knew that he would come in between them, and that if the contact was disturbed, the friend would disappear. He did not know how to stop him doing that, and felt that in the next moment the contact would be broken.

Returning to his sudden realisation that he had only dreamt he had not done his Latin or maths prep and feeling enormous relief about it, Mr B says,

'If this is due to your work then it actually has given me the relief which I (Mr B) had had once in the matter with X'. ([X was a] definite father figure, to whom Mr B had once confessed a few things he felt guilty about and experienced relief that lasted for years.) But he adds that actually he never experienced it so strongly ... with me as on this occasion. I point out that this [relief] seems to come in smaller doses [in analysis] and remind him of the memory which had come up about a fortnight ago which ... connects with his wife's illness of her throat which he was in despair about, and his feeling that she wasn't well looked after. He had spoken repeatedly as if his wife was a baby. She behaved like a baby. She did not take any notice of the people in the hotel where they had gone for a change of air; and that he was worried when they had come back to London ... The memory was that he saw himself sitting in the nursery eating his food while his baby sister was crying and nobody, neither mother nor nurse, was looking after her (for reasons of regime); and he went through agonies because he had to sit and eat his food while nobody looked after the baby.

Another disturbing memory comes to Mr B's mind:

somebody had told him that when driving in Kent he saw a bundle on the street and coming near he found that it was a dying woman. [This person] took her to the hospital and she died on the way.

Klein interprets

> *that he expected his sister to die and felt something awful was going on inside her and that nobody would look after her and help her. When Mr B had told this memory, which had come up during the analysis, he was sitting up and crying bitterly. I reminded him of that, and that repeatedly in the last few months where he cried, relief had been afforded in smaller doses.*

Mr B agrees to this interpretation, though says 'he wished I would not bring it in connection with my work.' Returning to his nightmare, he says that,

> *when he woke up out of [it, he had] sat up on the side of the bed and was interpreting the dream. He felt he had put in a kind figure [in the shape of his doctor friend] instead of an extremely frightening one, and asked if I agreed. I do agree, of course, and point out all the work in recent times about the kind father covering up his anxiety of the bad one. Also, that this figure stands for his dead mother, and the withered hand for the female genital, and that he must have had feelings of the kind when he first saw his sister's genital – that she was injured and castrated. Before I give this interpretation, however, Mr B had said ... that he is really terrified of doctors ... And that what he is terrified of is that thing which he never can remember the term for and which he always thinks of in terms of castration – and that is circumcision. He feels that his anxiety of doctors boils down to this anxiety ... Mr B then speaks about his wife fussing about their son because he had a corn on his toe and that there is a very simple way of dealing with that, and he told her; and she looked so worried and frightened, and this is all wrong, and women will be frightened and they have a bad attitude towards the male genital; and he complains generally about women, including me. I interpret that he is now doing what he has said in the dream. He has himself without realizing it spoken about the woman's attitude to the genital when he spoke about the corn on his son's toe that stands for the circumcised penis. He felt his mother's attitude and worry as a confirmation of his having been castrated, but that he [emphasised] the less frightening figure, the mother, instead of the castrating father ... I remind Mr B that the people he was afraid of seeing him in the street were men, and that his greater persecutor is the man and not the woman. He first denies my interpretation, but then suddenly says 'I think you are entirely right'.*

Wednesday 28 April 1937

Mr B refers to Klein's interpretation of his nightmare in the previous session. He thinks that 'a lot was missing, which should be interpreted.' Thinking of his dead doctor friend in the dream, he recalls,

> *a man of a similar name, somebody who had said that he has got a lot of Jewish blood in him, and also another man, a famous man, who has done a lot for an old castle in England, and who has also spoken in favour of the Jews. Some more associations of the kind. Mr B says that it seems to be a Jewish day today. Before that he had twice said a German word, and not been able to admit that he knew that actually German is my mother*

language. Speaking of the Jews he says that he definitely associates me with Jews and thinks that I am a Jewess. I interpret that the Jewish man is connected with the dead man and that now it appears that this unselfish doctor who died for the sake of humanity is me. I remind him of his repeated remark that his words are poisonous, his feelings of guilt … that he is an unsatisfactory patient, and so on. Mr B admits that he often thinks that he must be awful to me. I interpret the anxiety of my death and that Mr B is holding me by my hand so that the contact between us should not be lost; that the anxiety of the holidays therefore is not only that some harm will come to Mr B, but that some harm will come to me – that I might die and that he might lose me.

Returning to Mr B's complaints about women of the previous day, Klein tells Mr B,

that his blaming the woman was again an escape from the anxiety of the dangerous, castrating man, and that he actually always starts to blame her, putting in, as he had said about the dream, a less frightening figure for a more frightening one. Mr B agrees to this, and says that women are not so bad and not so dangerous, but they are useless. He remembers the night when he had woken as a child out of a nightmare, feeling that a dog was biting off his penis, and calling out for help. His mother did not come and comfort him. I interpret that he felt his mother to be also powerless, because she herself was dominated and injured by the dangerous and bad penis.

Klein writes that Mr B seems to understand that his dream really refers,

to the anxiety of my death and of his wife's death, but especially to my death. He mentions also how awful it was to him when Mrs X^2 who loved him, died. He always feels that he could have done things differently and helped her, and perhaps she wouldn't have committed suicide. I interpret that he had never gone fully through the pain and sorrow about this death, though he was feeling very guilty and upset about it … I then hear for the first time from him that he had actually spoken to Mrs X of making love to her, understanding that he would go to bed with her, and that she said that she would never do that because her vow to her husband binds her. It was, of course, only because her husband was his friend.

Thursday 29 April 1937

Mr B is late. He tells Klein that he is depressed and then that his family has moved into their new house. He then reports a dream:

They were moving from one hotel to another … and back again; there was a sense of moving in the dream. He had lost his overcoat and was trying to find it, and was therefore separating himself from his wife. Then he was in the hotel and went into the room where there was a woman in bed. She didn't seem to mind his coming into the room, only she minded that she had some cream on her face and was cleaning her face behind the pillow. First, she was at the other side of the room (he points at the part where my other divan stands) then she was in this part of the room (pointing at the consulting room), the part where the divan is on which he is lying. He definitely says that it was my consulting room – it looked different, but he felt it was this couch on which she was lying, my couch. He had been properly dressed when he came into the room, 'as I am now', he said, but then he was suddenly in his pyjama-suit, only in the jacket of his pyjamas, and he intended to go to bed with her. He thought of doing it gradually and was sitting on the side of her bed, touching her thigh with his thigh. Then he suddenly had an emission and ran out of the room, went into a kind of bathroom and cleaned himself and came back into the room. The woman must have been there, though he did not see her … because in the meantime a woman cousin of his whom he liked, a very nice woman, who speaks rather loudly and gaily, and a lot of other women, were in this room.

Associating to the dream,

Mr B says that while the woman was at the other end of the room, near the other settee, her hair was … not light, but then, when she was in the consulting room part her hair was conspicuously fair. This reminds Mr B of a friend of his who recently married, quite a nice woman, a friendly woman. I remind Mr B that for some time he had been lying on the other settee in my consulting room, because he had been frightened of the corner of the room which he couldn't see, and then I was sitting behind him; and then we again moved to the actual consulting room where we were working now. I also suggest that the conspicuously fair hair seems to indicate something to the contrary, and that this fair and young woman seems to stand for me, which Mr B doesn't deny at all. I point out that he was able to bring a sexual dream in connection with me after we had done some analysis of the anxiety of my death. That at the beginning of his analysis he had many more sexual dreams, in which I came in, but that this stopped when we came nearer to the analysis of his anxieties of … destructive and dangerous intercourse.

Klein's notes end suddenly here. The next notes, which the following chapter opens with, are from January 1938.

Notes

1 Mr B's guilt concerning his failure to protect his mother from his father, readers will remember, is evident in the early 'bull dream' which sees Mr B 'saving himself' and abandoning his mother to her fate. This guilt was greatly obstructive of mourning, initially.
2 Mrs X, who commits suicide and was in love with Mr B, Klein later calls Mrs D (page 137).

Chapter 6

Reproaches, depression, the old picture

The clinical notes presented in this chapter are mainly from January to March 1938. There is therefore a nine-month gap between the last notes of chapter 5, which are from April 1937, and the first notes of this chapter. The reasons for this gap aren't known to me. Klein's 1938 diary actually shows that she saw Mr B until mid-June of that year, but I have yet to unearth any clinical notes for April to June. Her diary is then blank for the remainder of 1938, and until September 1939. We know however that Klein saw Mr B during the months of May to July, 1939, because some clinical notes survive from those months, and these also appear in this chapter.

The Second World War broke out on 1 September 1939. In that month, Klein moved temporarily to Cambridge where she continued to see a number of patients who could travel to see her there. Her diary shows that Mr B attended two-hour long sessions, once a week, until the end of June 1940 when Klein moved to Pitlochry. There then followed quite a long gap in their work, so far as I can tell, and I shall return to this in the following chapter.

As the title of this chapter suggests, in the material that follows readers will see Mr B once more retreating from more loving and affectionate feelings towards Klein, into depression and familiar accusations. Upon returning after the Christmas break, he conveys powerfully a feeling of 'deep exhaustion.' Klein feels that very early experiences are being relived in the transference; specifically, a terribly distressing and unsatisfactory early feeding situation. Mr B has again had to wait too long, and Klein has once more become the depriving mother of his earliest experience. He then feels she cannot possibly understand or sympathise with the frustrated baby at the breast. Such a revival of early feelings is further seen when Mr B is for long periods unable to speak, feeling he has no words, and is utterly helpless.

Dreams continue to reveal a very mixed set of feelings about Klein. She is, for example, the vulgar, castrating mother who shoves breast-interpretations at Mr B, as well as an analyst who can on occasion sympathise deeply with his suffering as an infant and later child. What also becomes clearer is that whilst Mr B often feels his two castrating parents to be united against him, his father is often pushed more into the background, along with Mr B's anxiety and fear of him, whilst his mother is

DOI: 10.4324/9781003373414-7

typically felt to be responsible for all of Mr B's deprivations and suffering, and is hated as such. This accounts for the frequent resurgence of a very negative transference. Indeed, the 'difficulty of going on peacefully' with Klein is thrown more into relief as she analyses Mr B's terrible difficulty in maintaining a better, more constructive relationship with her. Good, cooperative feelings are felt to be so dangerously close to sexual feelings, that these must be strongly guarded against, lest some disaster unfold.

Despite the foregoing, there is also increasing evidence that Mr B is managing to install a good mother inside of him, and alongside this, there is some diminution of reactions against the treatment. Where more loving and sexual feelings and phantasies can be allowed, depression also reduces. Mr B, no longer wanting to accuse his mother, whom he is mourning and towards whom he is much more loving, directs his hatred towards Klein. Having said this, feelings of gratitude for her help are also evidently felt much more strongly.

In September 1939, Klein records that Mr B has been called up for military service. Though his anxieties concerning the war aren't so thoroughly explored in the record we have of his analysis, primitive anxieties concerning survival and about badness inside prevail, and must surely be connected to the war. These anxieties can perhaps be seen most clearly in Mr B's increasing distress and concern about the state of his wife's health. This has always been a source of significant worry for him, if it remains unclear quite what is wrong with her. Concerns however undoubtedly increase around this time, with Mr B feeling that an operation may be necessary, and that even if this takes place, his wife may never be cured.

Awareness of how close to death his father is, Klein interprets, translates into Mr B having a bad taste in his mouth. Klein sees this as revealing his experience of having a dead or dying father inside, who is in this state because of Mr B's hateful attacks. Jealousy and hatred of the father have had a devastating effect on him inside Mr B, and 'thus the fear of death had controlled his whole life.' One particular form this takes, Klein interprets, is that earlier death wishes against his father have made it impossible for Mr B to enjoy success in life, or to develop in a number of possible ways.

Finally, in an important moment in the analysis, Mr B accuses Klein of always having minimised the impact on him of the unhappy relations he has described between his parents. She has, he accuses, always emphasised his particular reactions to his experiences, rather than the more general impact of such experiences. Klein is eventually quite direct with Mr B about this, saying that of course she understands the interconnecting aspects of his experience and his reactions and impulses towards them, but that in analysis the emphasis simply is more on impulses. And in any case, she remarks, 'others have had worse histories.' She cites, for example, the awful experience of poverty, which Mr B has never known. She tells him, 'Analysis cannot undo what [your] mother did, but can have effect by clearing up early feelings.' This is why, she says, she often emphasises the latter. This appears less a giving into frustration on Klein's part, or a retaliation against Mr B's familiar accusatory attacks, than an attempt to help him understand something further. Klein does acknowledge responding to her sympathy for Mr B, who was so rarely given answers as a child, and instead felt so often in the dark and alone. At this point therefore, there is a sense of his desperately wanting to understand the impact of his history as well as his own responses to it, and of Klein wanting to help him to understand. It is a fascinating exchange which shows Klein to be very much in touch with her patient and his needs.

January 1938

Before she records specific sessional material, Klein makes some very interesting general points about Mr B's difficulties and his analysis which will serve as a helpful reminder to the reader. She writes,

> *In this analysis the early feeding situation has come up over and over again. Strong feelings always accompany these associations. Mr B even feels strongly that his difficulties could not be put right because they are rooted in early frustrations which could not be undone. He had remarked repeatedly about the inadequate ways of his mother which were so inadequate to help the baby in the right way. We had understood his liking for milk, which made him drink a glass of milk at a very smart party at a hotel, and it seems that milk was always a great relief when given to him. He had spoken generally of his having had a bad feeding time, assuming that he had not had enough. The sadism connected with this frustration had been to a certain extent analysed. In the transference situation, time and again he pointed out the frustration. His wish to lie down and be looked after by me for 24 hours a day was also brought into connection with the baby's feeding situation, and so on.*

Monday 3 January 1938

Klein writes that,

> *As usual, Mr B complains about depression. He wishes to die. Life is intolerable. The holidays are terrible, but even if there were no holidays what is the good of the analysis, which doesn't help him anyhow. He complains about exhaustion, and feels as though paralysed. He gives details of all that he can't do, and should do.*

Mr B reports a dream towards the beginning of the hour:

> *A young, attractive woman, Mrs S, asked him to come with her and he could not do that because he had to go to Mrs Klein.*

> *Since he had very much stressed the attractiveness of the young woman, I point out that it seems to imply that I am also attractive to him. That may show that there are sexual phantasies about me which are repressed and which are so very difficult for him to admit. He then says that he should be quite inclined to agree with this interpretation, that he may often have been afraid of having this analysed. He reminds me that in the first part of his analysis he had been afraid of being attracted by me sexually.*

Klein notes that many times during the analysis when she had interpreted Mr B's erotic feelings towards her, 'it led to a crisis.' She continues,

When he complained about deep exhaustion (so often the difficulty of getting up in the morning in this connection), I suggest it connects with frustration in the holidays. I suggested that this feeling seems to be like an inertia, and I wondered how we could connect such an inertia with all these difficulties in feeding which we have so often discussed. Mr B says it is more than inertia. 'It is like half death, and you know that I so often feel as if dead.' But then Mr B reacted strongly to my suggestion that he might have felt this way as a baby at the breast, telling me that I know that he always feels that if I struck this chord, it is the right one. [There is then a] reproach that I do not exhaust this topic enough and that he could go on talking and talking about this for ever. My interpretation (not given at the time because he was not to be stopped, but brought in later on) is that this of course is the reproach, that I do not give him enough of this early situation, i.e., that I am the frustrating mother at the breast.

Klein's interpretation stirs a memory in Mr B. Suddenly, he says that,

history relates that he had been fed by his mother for one month and after that when his Nanny came after the monthly nurse, she found that he had been starved, or was starving, and he was put to the bottle. This nurse is the good figure in his life. She stayed with the family for many years – he was quite a big boy when she left because she was the nurse of his younger sister. Mr B always speaks of her with love and though she is likened in reproaches to awful females who castrate boys and do the wrong thing, she is on the whole a good figure.

Klein notes that once he has relayed this history, Mr B is willing for her to interpret and connect some facts. She says that,

getting too little from the breast, which filled him with anger and dismay, had the effect of making him turn away from the breast with disappointment and at the same time with craving. Mr B says that he has always been thin and is still thin, and that he is moderate in his eating – no greed. He should be very greedy.

Klein refers at this point to 'the difficulty of the baby which might be held in a clumsy way by his mother, and the difficulties for the child which are increased by this fact.'

Mr B at once connects this with his rather rigid and awkward way of holding himself; he says, one shoulder a little higher – something rigid and he can so well imagine how clumsily his mother held him towards the breast. He has an objective judgement here from his wife, who suggested that Mr B's mother held her grandchildren, though she was very fond of them, like a horse. So he can imagine how she must have done so with her own children. Mr B had often told me before about his mother not being able to hold a child. He had seen this with his sister – she never seemed to be at ease with the baby. He feels very strongly about the picture I gave him of the baby which cannot get easily to the breast because it is not held well, gets too little, wants the breast and at the same time is unsatisfied with it and the inertia which may result.

Tuesday 4 January 1938

The work of the previous day seems to have made quite an impact on Mr B:

He says he has a pain in the chest which he had never had before and seems to link this up somehow with material of yesterday, stressing the fact that he had never had this feeling before. He had thought a great deal about what we had discussed and felt very strongly about it. He could imagine his mother having all sorts of trouble when she had to feed a child. Even his wife, who in so many ways is an excellent mother (a thing which he had never so distinctly told me before) and who loves feeding, managed to get some pain in her breast always when she was feeding – though she did it perfectly and had gallons of milk. He speaks about women who are good mothers and others who are like flat fish. Goes on telling me a lot about the flat fish.

Klein refers in her notes to an interpretation she gives a few days later concerning the flat fish, namely,

that this fish has the two eyes in the wrong place, and this awkward position of the eyes means that the baby could not get well from one breast to another, and seems again to signify the whole awkwardness and clumsiness of the feeding process.

Klein notes that, 'it meant a great deal to Mr B that I should have been so understanding and sympathetic yesterday.' Nonetheless,

He has somewhere a deep conviction which is very difficult to shake, that I am in favour of not giving children enough milk – of frustrating them, and so on. (This accusation had appeared innumerable times during analysis, and every time something seems to show that I am not this kind of woman he seems quite surprised.) He yesterday had the feeling that I really fully understand what the baby at the breast suffers if frustrated.

Wednesday 5 January 1938

Mr B explains that,

Mrs R and her husband had dinner with them and he talked very pleasantly with her. She is a very nice and very honest woman. Then he dreamt about her, but just that he was talking to her. He is in a much more diffident mood. He seems to have been very much occupied with recent material, and tells me that at the same time he would like me not to blame his mother and that it is painful to speak about that. In contrast with this is his continuous accusation of his mother in the past in analysis. It is true that in recent months the sorrow and mourning for her and the love for her had much increased. Reluctantly he says that this Mrs R has been standing for mother or for me, and gives various grounds for this conclusion.

Mr B then brings two more dreams. The first,

was about a Mr C, one of the members of the greatest firms in the City, who had appreciated one suggestion which Mr B had once made to him, though it was quite amateurish and just a thing which had gone through his mind, and this man should have known so much better than he. This man had been very useful to his firm (by some financial details). This man's father originally came from Whitechapel and was a Jew who had made his way.

In the second dream,

Mr B was at some party and a friend told him that he, Mr B, had not got a tie. So he left the party in great confusion and embarrassment and went into a shop, a very poor shop, where a woman at once jumped at him with a tie, a bloody, shop-soiled, faded and second-hand tie, wanting him to accept this. A very unpleasant woman. There was another woman as well and in the background a man.

During this hour he had said that he is very suspicious of me, that he doesn't really believe in me being really sympathetic with his sufferings as a baby, that there will be a trick in it, and this trick will soon show. He is reluctant to give any associations to this trick. I interpret the dream, that the little Jew who has made such a position, highly appreciated by Mr B, is me who always in his dreams is a Jew. That it refers to my having appreciated his material about the feeding situation; that this is the amateurish thing he suggested to this expert. I cite Mr B's humiliation in the analytic situation, that he cannot be led by me, he must teach me, and so on. At the same time he often will say, 'Well after all you should know better than I,' and he is always very impressed and grateful if something he has said in analysis proves useful.

Mr B returns to the dream of the tie, explaining,

that the woman who jumps at him is me, with my interpretations. That I am terrible and irrepressible, and that it is awful to listen to me, and that he cannot stand it, and how did I know that he needed the tie? I wait for a long time and then in a break suggest that my words are so terrible and so clumsily presented, just as the breast which fed him. We have had before so much material of my words being the poisoned and bad food, but now I add that it is the breast which is so clumsily presented and probably pushed into his mouth, stopping him from breathing or something of the kind, and therefore so intolerable. I interpret [that Mr C of the first dream, who had been useful to Mr B's company] represents a mixture of man and woman, the two good parents. In the second dream there is a horrible vulgar woman who jumps at him, and there is also a man in the background – again a union of parents – bad castrating parents.

Klein writes,

> *Lots of times in Mr B's analysis he had mentioned his circumcision as something which he feels has influenced him for ever. He knows that all his horrible fears at the dentist and other things of the kind are connected with a fear of castration. He never can remember the word 'circumcision' and I have always to help him with it. He knows he was a few months old, probably 3 or 4 months old, when he was circumcised. I remind him of all our work on this line and now connect the fact that this woman, and in the background a man, assaulted him with this tie, which he had called a bloody tie. In this hour, four or five times the word bloody had come in – as an accusation in connection with his circumcision. The mother who did not feed him was also the mother who circumcised him or attacked him, who is already mixed up with father. Father is kept in background, though it was a man who circumcised him.*

Klein writes that she speaks to Mr B, 'about the connection between his feeding difficulties and his relation to both parents, and also the influence which the circumcision had on him as a distressed and frightened and unhappy baby.' Mr B then again recalls the second-hand tie. Klein notes,

> *This was the point which made him so furious. Everything he got from his mother was second-hand, he says. In between he rages against me, my voice, my speech, my jumping at him and so on, with much hatred and with great strength. It is also quite clear that he feels disgust about my speech. He makes the remark that here the sexual thing comes in and when I ask what he refers to, he says, 'Of course the circumcision is sexual, isn't it?' He then repeats that he knew there would be a catch in my sympathy. I suggest the catch may be that I cannot leave it simply at the situation at the breast, but have to connect it with Mr B's further development. His dreams have already shown how jealousy – the second-hand comment, hatred and suspicion of both parents, how soon everything he could receive from his mother became bad and how the anxiety and fear of the father are pushed into the background – a mechanism which is easily known to us. It seems that it would be easier for him if it could be kept at the breast situation, and though I fully acknowledge the importance of the breast situation, it is quite obvious it cannot be the explanation of everything. Mr B is furious and suggests that I think he is an idiot, and that he wants to keep it all at one situation, when he knows quite well that this is not true. Leaves me a few minutes before time.*

Thursday 6 January 1938

'In between outbursts of hatred and rage against Klein,' Mr B conveys 'deep depression' and helplessness. Klein writes,

> *Repeatedly, as in last days, says he has no words. He cannot speak. He remains silent until I remark that these early feelings which we are analysing go with an incapacity to speak, and that he reactivates and revives this early situation now in his feelings towards me. Also, that the conflict of not wanting to accuse his mother whom he loves and whom he*

mourns is partly solved by turning his hatred against me and thus keeping mother safe. Mr B seems very impressed and says of course it is true that he reactivates here things which he had felt, being speechless at the time.

Perhaps following her interpretation about this re-direction of hatred towards her, away from mother, a warmer, more grateful attitude becomes evident. Klein writes that,

Mr B had [in an earlier session] suggested that this hour is now a little inconvenient – a little late for him. It makes him so late, since he is not staying at home. He suggests that he could go a quarter of an hour or 10 minutes early, that it does not make any difference if one has done good work in the time [one does have], and that one may quite well lose some minutes without harm. I interpret that if the breast feeding is satisfactory the child may feel that he can do with less, or that he need not be so greedy and possessive and that his wanting to take less time with me is also giving me a present, and trying not to exhaust me. He tells me that when he came home on Tuesday he drank a glass of milk, and only later on connected this with our work.

Along similar lines, Klein records that Mr B also,

Mentioned that there would be a children's evening, and that cook may be a little worried how she should serve at the same time for the children and for the grown-ups. Mr B suggested that the children should only get soup and some bread and butter and jam so that the cook should not have to cook two complete meals. After all it does not matter. The children will have plenty again the next day, and there is no need to be so worried if the children have once less because they have plenty anyhow. This conversation had taken place between he and his wife, whom he thought was worried how to arrange this evening.

Friday 7 January 1938

Despite the work of the previous day, Mr B 'starts again with distrust, hatred, despair.' Klein notes that this leads to 'so much anxiety.' Though he has, in Klein's words, 'very much mellowed down' by the end of the session, he again becomes furious when he feels Klein that implies she can help him through analysing him.

Mr B was to come on Saturday, but gives excuses for not being able to. He is however in very great doubt and guilt about it. He says, 'Well in any case will you keep this hour for me, and I can do what I like about it. It will still belong to me. Is this reasonable?' I say that since we could not help arranging one hour on a Saturday, I had made it clear to him that the Saturday hour would always be optional, so that in case he could not take it there are no fees for it. Mr B says he doesn't want to hear about this at all, though he knew it quite well. He says he wants to have this hour kept for him – to keep open the possibility that he can use it, which means that he has use of it. I am to charge him for this. We had also arranged, since it was an early hour, that before he leaves the place where he is now he would ring up before he is coming – which means I am not disturbed. It is obviously a present, and probably also an expression of gratitude following the very unpleasant feelings of hate and discontent and disgust he expressed in recent/days.

Klein takes up Mr B's oscillating feelings towards her. She interprets that, 'this one attitude of turning away from the breast in hatred and frustration is only one aspect, because no doubt at the same time he had built up a very strong bond to his mother as a good mother.' Both aspects then get displaced onto Klein. Mr B then,

parts from me in an extremely friendly way and doesn't come on Saturday. I thought he knew quite well that he would not come. He repeatedly referred to Tuesday as a special point where our relation became disturbed. He had felt up to this point that I must have been very good for understanding all that. I had brought in nurse who, when she fed him right away and with less trouble with the bottle, took the place of the good mother, but did not do away with his suspicions. Here was a point to which he feels relations were good, and then became bad.

Klein records that she also, during this session,

came back to the flat fish and interpreted it. Mr B was very struck by it, and said that he never knew why this association of the flat fish had come up and he could very vividly picture himself trying to find the breast which was held in such a way that one could not get at it, and the trouble of being put from one breast to the other when one was hungry.

Monday 10 January 1938

There is some worry about Mr B's son, Klein records, though no details are given. Mr B does however 'speak of Abraham sacrificing his son to God,' and what 'children sacrifice for their parents.' Klein refers to,

circumcision and hatred against father in this connection. Recently in a dream it was the woman who was standing in the foreground with the second hand, bloody tie. But now he can see that it is really father whom he hates in connection with circumcision – or rather castration. After a long break he says 'awful weekend.' I suggest that his arrangement, possibly to come on Saturday and for me to keep this hour for him, was deliberate and that he probably knew quite well that he couldn't come, but wanted to be friendly to me and to give me a present. He agrees. I then link up a few facts of last week – his mentioning that he could forgo 15 minutes of his session – that it doesn't matter if one really works well during the hour. The same thing applied to the baby drinking. Then Friday's remark about the children's meal which need not be so much because they have plenty anyhow. Then again, his great friendliness in leaving me on Friday and trying to keep the hour even though he wasn't there, which was at the same time making me a gift. I point out that these details show a different attitude from the one of severe complaints about the clumsy and frustrating mother. It seems to show that here he wants his mother or also the nurse, and wants to give back when he feels he has taken too much, and his mother has been exhausted, and he wants to repair.

Klein notes that Mr B's more affectionate feelings show, 'another aspect of his relation to his mother and may perhaps derive from a little later period than the one where he is full of accusation and hate.' Mr B is furious at this, however. He,

says that I push him into a mess, that he can't get out, he does not know what to do. He is not going to listen to me, doesn't want to hear my voice ...

Klein writes that,

After a long break Mr B speaks again quietly. He is distressed about his wife, feeling that she suffers and that he can't help her. He is worried about her worry. Then complains how awful she was. There was an evening party for children and grown-ups, a lot of people were to come, and he wanted the guest list and she hadn't got it. He went on asking her and then in the end found it out from another person with whom the party was given jointly.

Klein writes that after a break in Mr B's speech, she says she'd like to make an interpretation, and 'he agrees to listen.'

I point out that the appearance of the little sister woke up all his early feelings. He got worried over her worries when she cried and when he thought she was suffering from the same frustration and same distress that he had been suffering from. Then I interpret that his anger about his wife's not giving him the list of guests refers to his mother not telling him that his sister was going to be born. He remembers well all the grievance and the hatred connected with this fact. I suggest that different stages of development are all connected with the old grievance. That we can see that this part where he complains about mother not telling him [that his sister was to be born] – all this was the renewal of the old pain and distress, and that as life went on there were more and more complaints and experiences added to this old experience.

Klein writes that there follows, 'an outburst of rage in Mr B against my ways of speaking.' She acknowledges that she 'had probably hurried [things],' being so keen to make this interpretation. She notes,

He complains that he cannot follow what I am saying; that it is terribly upsetting that he is not left alone, etc. Then he quietens down. He wishes that he had had a placid mother, where there was no speech, nothing but just pleasant milk, and good feeding. He must have his own way of being fed, and he speaks now as if he would get angry with me in any case and blame me however I would speak because it isn't the way he wants to be fed.

Mr B says,

> *that in recent weeks he has come so much to hate clocks. He always hated them but recently it has become stronger. His mother shouldn't have clocks at all. Mothers should lie in bed with the baby at the breast and feed it whenever it wants and there should be no nurses, no doctor, no rules, and everything would be all right. He is sure there would be plenty of milk and he repeats again that he doesn't doubt that there would be plenty of milk, obviously to deny that his mother had actually very little. Then tells me that I must know that even when he rages against me, that he would want to stay with me for 24 hours a day, as he has often said in former times in his analysis. He emphasises that he wishes this even when he is quite furious with me; that even when he wants to go away, he would also like to stay the whole 24 hours with me. But it is impossible.*

Tuesday 11 January 1938

Mr B 'feels so miserable, [he] doesn't know what to do.' He,

> *Dreamt he had a very bad taste in his mouth and woke up to find … that he actually had a bad taste, perhaps through keeping his dentures in through the night. The whole world is so unpleasant. I interpret that the bad taste in the mouth seems to be connected with the feeling of the bad milk given him by the bad nipple. Mr B says after a long break that he doesn't tell me his thoughts as they come because he doesn't know which to select. He notes the death of the father of a friend, a little older than his own father. Then agrees that his father's death is very much in his mind, as often discussed before. Says that everything is mouldy and miserable around and he quotes the hymn, 'Death, decay is all around us.' I interpret that the bad taste in the mouth connects also with the rot and decay inside, that he takes his dying father into his inside and that has a part in his feeling that everything is so terrible. Mr B again reflects on his not being able to select the thoughts for me, and about his being incapable of answering letters, an old inhibition of his. He speaks of the hold-up of the traffic, meaning the hold-up of thoughts and associations coming out. He says that traffic is like a stream of water also consisting of little bits of water. Perhaps he could think of a river in Scotland and perhaps he could swim down this river and catch the salmon in this way. I interpret that the stream of water, the traffic hold-up, is the urine and faeces inside him, and his being afraid of giving them out. He cannot give them out in the right way because the other stream, the milk-stream, hasn't been able to get in in the right way. Both streams are disturbed – taking in and giving out.*

Klein tells Mr B that the bad taste he is so disturbed by, 'is the bad object in his mouth.' She speaks again of his father, saying that,

> *Hatred and jealousy of the father soon made him also into a dying object, and that the fear of death has controlled his whole life. After a long break Mr B says that he really feels it hateful to have his mother blamed for her ways of feeding him. I draw attention to the fact that he has been able to complain so much about his mother and now he feels strongly about*

these early experiences because together with the hatred and the early frustration, also the feeling of love has increased and he is much more mourning for his mother.

In response, Mr B tells Klein that,

he will now temporarily be the acting Chairman of the company, the Chairman being away. That has been so much his wish, but it does not give him any pleasure now. I refer to Mr B's earlier Hamlet associations, his hatred and death wishes against his father, and that therefore no enjoyment of success is possible.

Wednesday 12 January 1938

Mr B is again in despair. He tells Klein that 'nobody can stick him.' There is trouble with an employee and with his business partner. Mr B adds that he is, 'impossible to live with.' Klein writes,

Repeatedly through this hour he says how miserable he feels in connection with unworthiness. Analysis is useless, I put him into a mess – how am I going to help him out? Here he is furious and stamps with his feet before quietening down. His wife and he had forgotten to go to a family wedding, and he felt very sorry about this. This branch of the family are especially admired and esteemed. In childhood Mr B was great friends with some of these cousins. It's all his fault because when they see him, they like him, but if he feels like a worm of course nobody would pay attention. His wife is twice as shy as he and behaves the same way. He speaks with great feeling about these lost opportunities – family branches – partly because he actually feels he has missed much. They impress him so much as being grand (though he criticises some of them as being very dull). He is crying. In between he begs my help – says I needn't be silent if I think I should speak. He goes on, 'speak, or be silent, give me some food or drink, whichever helps.'

Klein connects Mr B's pain concerning the loss of a relationship with these relatives, to,

the child's inability to get into the same class as the older brother, or more in connection with the parents. They also seemed pleased when they saw him, but he was sent to the nursery and kept there. I remind Mr B of his ambitions as a child, his wanting to catch up intellectually with his older brother and his finally beating his brother. He feels guilty and sad, in repetition of the early situation when he and his sister (now his wife for whose shyness he is so often sorry) could attain the company of, and equality with grown-ups.

Klein records that she had earlier asked Mr B to change the time of a session. He refers to this now, and,

in a very friendly way asked whether it wouldn't be more convenient if he came still earlier. I interpreted that it is also my company that he feels he can't have (the wish for 24 hours with me); that I have often appeared as quite grand, if on other occasions as very low, poor, etc. That his being friendly now is the repetition of his attempts in childhood to win the love of the people around him.

Thursday 13 January 1938

Again in despair, Mr B,

Complains that he cannot do anything for anybody, neither family, nor father and sister. Says with strong feeling that really his mother was never a support to him. He could never get help or understanding when he needed it (there are also memories of the contrary kind). Then asks whether I have something to say. I remark that it is now quite clear to me how, so quickly after the material of the frustrated baby, followed the material of the seducing and vulgar mother [the woman running at him with a bloody tie]. I suggest that among Mr B's early experiences (circumcision having been clearly expressed), may be one of his having been seduced as he always felt he was by an aunt (cover memory was her pulling his hair). I mention the contrast between [his sense of a] helpless, inhibited and neurotic mother and his so strong fear of her seducing him, which goes through his whole analysis. I suggest that his frustrated oral desires were so quickly followed by genital ones and the whole Oedipus situation. Under these conditions, more or less seductive handling of the genital, in the process of cleaning, etc., would create the seducing woman.

After a pause, Mr B,

mentions … his wife having been to see Mr and Mrs X. Mrs X was rather attacking towards her husband, though not in a hostile way. Mr B said that the fact that there were children from the first marriage and none of her own would make a wife dissatisfied. He had thought but did not say to his wife that she may still be a virgin. When I ask, does he mean that he thinks Mr X might be impotent, Mr B is angry about the use of this word; he comments at length how useless this word and all words are, what do I mean by that since he had had two children before? But comes in the end to the result that if she happened to be a virgin it must be his failing to do something about it. Thinks Mr X must be unable to satisfy her sexually. Before that he had said how sad he is that his wife doesn't want any more children.

Klein interprets,

the curiosity and ignorance of the child, that the intercourse of the parents, which he wishes and then fears to be dangerous, is taking place always when he doesn't see them and then again, he may feel that father is castrated, mother frigid, or that mother is unsatisfied sexually because father is impotent. The reparative tendencies of the boy would fasten on this feeling that he should have intercourse with mother, give sexual gratification and babies. I remind him of his dream of curative intercourse, which he remembers. These tendencies and feelings are carried over into later life [and are transferred] to his wife or other substitutes and may, if things go happily, greatly add to sexual gratification and happiness.

Klein writes that there is a 'great outbreak.' Mr B is furious and accuses her:

So I seem to believe that things could ever go out happily. That there is goodness and love and that one could use them. He maintains that I have never told him that before in respect to him; I always discarded the effect of the unhappy relation between parents and the influence of this on him. That I allowed for this but never said that he is the product of these experiences and influences. At any answer I make Mr B repeats, that there is 'No need for me to justify myself.' I explain that he feels that he attacks me and therefore expects justification. Again, I show the two interconnecting aspects of experiences and his own impulses and that it is impossible to give the percentage of each: of course, I have always stressed both aspects. Mr B implies that under the circumstances he had to be what he is. I reply that that is true, but though I fully acknowledge the difficulties in his way, there are worse histories than his, which do not lead to the same effect. Mr B is frightfully struck by this remark (since I never compare him with other patients). Says he is aware of that, but seems to ask what this could be. I mention, among other things, the awful effects of poverty, which he never knew. Mr B says he cannot hear any more without breaking down, but parts in a friendly way and says 'stress what you think right.'

I had said before that I cannot always bring in all aspects at once and that therapeutically the study of his reactions, feelings, impulses, (in connection with his experiences) is the main point. Analysis cannot undo what his mother did, but can have effect by clearing up his early feelings and that is why I may stress at times more the latter. Mr B is very friendly – quite reasonable and fully understanding.

This exchange between Klein and Mr B about the relative influence of nature and nurture is quite unusual. Klein herself clearly feels it to merit some explanation. She comments on what might have motivated her to enter into such a discussion:

This is the only discussion of the kind I remember in Mr B's analysis; not actually on the line of an interpretation, and yet effective, but I wonder what the after-effect is going to be. When I mentioned the connection between Mr X, impotence and early curiosity and scruples, Mr B says, very convinced, that of course he would never have believed that his father could give sexual pleasure to mother and that she could enjoy it; an admission which he had never made before. In respect to this explanation, which was unusual, I think I was led by the whole situation in which the patient was the ignorant child who could not understand about the grown-ups' sexuality, motives for behaviours, etc., and at the same time was burning for plausible explanations. If this explanation had had a good effect, I think I must in the transference situation have taken up at the very urgent moment the part of the mother who really explains and also shows that she understands and does not blame him.

Friday 14 January 1938

Mr B is, most unusually, ten minutes early for his session. He comments that he 'had been extremely interested in yesterday's conversation at the end of the hour,' and returns to this:

> *He makes clear that he had not thought his history is the worst of all because actually his parents were good people, never struck them, did a lot for them and looked after them, yet he finds that he is the result of all that he has experienced, and so on. He finds that I must, through some remark, have given ground to his assumption that I did not stress happy possibilities of development in connection with him as well as I did yesterday. In the end says that he finds all that I explain quite reasonable and that he himself could not have put it otherwise. The main points were that every child, even under very happy circumstances, still feels impulses which again rouse anxiety, and so on. But that no doubt had he grown up under happier, cheerful circumstances, he would have been entirely different. Then I appeal also to his knowledge that his four children are all different, and react in different ways to their environment, to which he agrees. I interpret why this conversation had this effect on him, connecting it with his early wish for understanding the mode of behaviour of the grown-ups. He then tells of the burning desire to hear the fascinating talks of the grown-ups and really to understand them. In this connection he also cites his great interest in observing people round him.*

Mr B continues to speak about the impact of recent work. He remarks that,

> *when he left yesterday he felt that he would like to go on talking, that a great deal of things were still to be said. But then when driving up to the country he felt very ill and he had thought of ringing me up and telling me that. He also felt angry again with me. In the evening he felt well and went to a party, to relatives, and since his wife didn't feel like going, he went without her, without being angry or distressed, and enjoyed himself thoroughly. His description of the great pleasure he had includes his feeling that a definite change must have gone on with him and he had been able to enjoy himself, knowing that his wife, for reasons of anxiety or shyness, does not share in it. (He expressed this even to his wife, saying that when he would be quite analysed he would feel at ease in any company, which made his wife tease him and say that probably he is thinking of Buckingham Palace.) He speaks all the time in a quiet and peaceful way and says 'that is of course a consolation, that I have definitely admitted a change.' I ask, 'A consolation for whom?' and he suggests probably for both of us.*

Mr B continues,

> *if he could really detach himself both from his wife in some ways, though he wants to look after her and love her, and if he could look at the children through less neurotic glasses, he would find everything different. He says, quite hopefully without showing anxiety about it, that the 'psychological what-not' of the last weeks has brought comfort and relief.*

He mentioned that he met a few old girlfriends of his, whom he had not seen for ages and who now have grey hair. He felt at ease with them and liked them. I interpret the transference situation and his wish to be on easy terms with me. Near the end of the hour, Mr B asks for the time, and says that the hour was very long and shows a wish to go, for which he cannot give reasons. Before going, he says that it was an unusual hour, a peaceful hour, and also [expresses some surprise that] that he has been able to say what he told me. He said, why shouldn't he have been able to tell me that? Why should there be this reaction?

Klein writes,

In connection with all the material of the week, I emphasise his feeling of being very bad and therefore of not being able to stand that a grown-up should really take him in. That he is also afraid that if he [suggests he] is better I will believe him, [regard him as] the good boy which in this connection means being cured. He had described how fascinated he was when at the party he discussed with a cousin which relatives were there or not and how interesting it is to him to see the people meet. I interpret the nursery situation, the interest in watching mother, the relation between mother and nurse, between the staff, in connection with the situation of the child and the servants, who in some ways are superior and in others inferior. He agrees, saying that he had been passionately interested in all these things, in every department of the staff, gardeners, and butlers.

Klein records that Mr B 'repeatedly emphasised' that he was free associating 'without any hesitation.' He also notes once more the 'peaceful character of the whole hour,' which is certainly unusual. He asks what the reaction to such an hour will be. Klein writes that she thinks he has taken into account her earlier suggestion that a bad hour seems to follow from his feeling happy or satisfied. Some curiosity follows about Klein:

He thinks about the piano which is played next door. He wonders how the room could be made soundproof, and remembers that I had had it done some time ago and mentioned it to him. He wonders whether I know the people next door, or perhaps they know about me from the telephone book, that I am in the telephone book as a psychoanalyst and altogether of the relations between me and other people! If he were in my position he would have a consulting room at a separate place – a professional place separated from the private place. He doesn't know why it should be so but says that probably his association was due to his having to keep things separate from each other. He was always angry when his father asked about what he is doing in the City.

Klein interprets this lively interest in her, saying,

that this goes back to his interest in early times in observing the grown-ups, finding out, curiosity, and so on. Also, I interpret that his thought that my private life should be separate from my professional work is the resistance against his great curiosity concerning my private life. Also, the question of walls being soundproof, connects with his curiosity about what parents do in the bedroom.

Saturday 15 January 1938

Mr B is friendly, Klein remarks, 'and does not complain in the beginning.' He is however 'in an entirely different mood from the day before. The peacefulness has gone, though he doesn't complain or reproach.' He reports two dreams. First, he dreamt,

> *about Mrs D, a woman who was a good friend of his who committed suicide. Mr B connects her suicide with her having been in love with him. (That has been a great thing in his life and from time to time he thinks about it with great regret and guilt, thinking he might have been able to help her better had he known before.) Now, in his dream, Mrs D appears, and shows great devotion to him. He felt very much embarrassed.*

In the second dream,

> *He and another man are climbing mountains, probably in Scotland. Mr B had explained that he likes to climb mountains but does not really like it when it is too rough, that he is then inclined to feel lonely. The other man in the dream disappears. Mr B himself is going along a path which goes across the rocks [and is in danger of] slipping off. Also, big rocks might fall down on him. If rocks fall, he associates to being pinned down by the legs, lying on his back and the rocks falling on top of him. He also associates to the stones a tombstone. Another association that he had was to a part of the fireplace which had been burnt out, renewed. An expert said that this old piece was iron, though it was stone.*

> *I interpret that mountain climbing represents analysis, and intercourse; that his path crumbling down, and he himself being buried or injured in front, represents castration and death. Mr B gives another association – the memory of he and his mother at some lake. He played, and his mother walked off and he broke down in loneliness and despair. I connect this danger of being left by her, of her death and of his castration and death, with going on peacefully in analysis, being at peace with me and being cured.*

Mr B violently objects to this interpretation, with its reference to castration. Klein suggests that Mr B experiences her, behind him, as,

> *Attacking him with a steamroller and on other occasion as the woman, Jael, who stabs him through and through with a long nail. On leaving the room he remarks about the door handle (which is actually faulty), saying, 'this handle seems to get worse and worse.'*

Klein makes a note of the,

> *great resistance which a few days ago arose in the discussion about impotence. He had then questioned me the next day that I would call him impotent because he hasn't had children*

for some years and then had various gloomy associations about his sexuality deteriorating because of his wife's lack of response.

Monday 17 January 1938

Klein writes, 'Again reproaches, depression, the old picture.' Mr B,

Falls asleep, and dreams of a little Arab girl. Pretty face, but her skin looked uglier and became worse when he looked closely. He did some good office to her like tying a bonnet round her head. I remind him of the old dream of the Queen's child who sat on his lap, whose face turned out to be the woman's genital. Mr B reminds me of his dislike of his wife's genital, not when in intercourse, but otherwise. I interpret the girl's face as the genital and the young girl as his sister, the good offices, the bonnet applied, as some sexual act. Mr B is angry, but remembers suddenly his dream of last night: He saw his younger sister-in-law coming towards him in a dressing gown which opened, so that he could see a patch of hair, i.e., her genital. He seems to understand that this is confirmation of my interpretation. In the same hour, he expresses great anger against Mr X. I interpret the castration fear of father in connection with what he had done to his sister and in phantasy to his mother, and say that all these fears are in the way of a peaceful relation to me, as in the past with his mother.

Wednesday 19 January 1938

Mr B is friendly, and there is 'no complaint about depression.' Before reporting a dream, he shares some thoughts 'which gave a much clearer picture of the castration fear' that Klein has highlighted in the last few days, He recalls a quotation:

'Out of strength comes weakness,' [there is then a reference to the Bible and a lion]. He goes on, 'Out of the weakness comes bloodiness.' I interpret that bloodiness makes weakness, and is connected with the lion which castrates him and then to the memory of circumcision, [which] makes him weak. When I connect this material with former material, Mr B says that he agrees; also to the castration fear that I had interpreted some days before.

Mr B then tells Klein a dream he had had several days earlier, on the night following 'the unusually peaceful and happy day in analysis': '*The Hebrides had come nearer.*'

In association, he remarks that the Hebrides are,

not far from where he has been in the summer, but his wife, of course, didn't want to go there because of the crossing. He had been there before he was married – a lovely place, romantic, wonderful birds, interesting creatures. Speaks of it with longing. His mother did not want to go there with him either. After a break, Mr B says some people mispronounce it He-brides. He seems to point to his mother as his bride. If she can't go there, the Hebrides come nearer to him.

Klein notes that shortly before leaving, Mr B tells her about a skin complaint which, though it may have been discussed before, has not previously been mentioned in the notes:

> *He says that the psoriasis he had had for many years, although it had actually disappeared during his analysis, now, recently, has reappeared. Mr B indicates that this may have a relation with the material of the last time. I interpret that he obviously points to a connection with the castration fear, which Mr B doesn't deny. I add that the skin illness seems to show the worry he may have had about his penis and about it being wrong.*

Thursday 20 January 1938

Mr B is 'again quite friendly and peaceful.' He reports a dream:

> *An expert shows him the corpse of a dead song-thrush. This bird is musical, Mr B especially stresses. He looks at this thrush and explains the reason why it couldn't be a Continental thrush or a thrush from the Hebrides, but is a British thrush. He explains the difference between them. He feels quite at ease and feels that he knows quite as much about the thrush as the expert. The expert reminds him of somebody who is a complete bore who knows quite a lot about his own subject but is quite uninteresting otherwise. The way Mr B describes his conversation with the expert, [he seems to feel] equal to or rather superior to this man. Mr B recalls that his brother-in-law once said that a thrush had flown against his windscreen and had been killed, and Mr B was sorry that he didn't bring the dead bird to him so that he could have skinned and preserved it.*

In another part of the dream, Mr B,

> *pulled the feathers of the thrush, actually the tail feathers, out of his mouth. He says, 'I must have eaten it.' Otherwise it wouldn't have come into his mouth. He doesn't know when he had eaten it. It may have been after the expert explained about it, he doesn't know. I say that the Continental thrush stands for me, and the Hebrides for his mother. Mr B agrees fully, he knows this himself. I also interpret that he, knowing as much about the Continental thrush as the Hebridean one actually tells father that not only does he know more about mother, or as much as father, but that he actually possesses her – knowledge meaning here possessing, and that this applies to his relation to me; and that Mr B's knowledge of psychoanalysis and myself may be greater than many experts who may feel superior to him.*

Friday 21 January 1938

Mr B reports that after leaving his session the previous day, whilst running to catch his train at the station, he had slipped and fell on his back.

> *He says it hurt him and he felt quite shaken, but implies that it may also have had a psychological connection with yesterday's material. I remind him of the dream about the*

rock which fell on him; that the position in which he was lying indicated he was on his back. Mr B seems doubtful about that, he would rather think that I had not understood that he was lying on his face and that the rock fell on his back.

Klein returns to the thrush dream of the previous day. She,

Takes up the part of the dream where he pulls the feathers of the bird, especially the tail feathers, out of his mouth. I remind him that he had said he must have eaten it because he pulled the feathers out of his mouth, adding that it was very unpleasant material ...

She interprets, 'that it was unpleasant material because he expects an unpleasant interpretation from me.'

Mr B responds, 'well it is actually unpleasant material, because feathers in one's mouth are very unpleasant – they are like dust.' Klein continues,

Suggesting whether dust isn't connected with dust and ashes, with the bird all in bits, and Mr B agrees with this suggestion. When I ask what interpretation he thought I would give to this material, he says that he thought that I would interpret the tail as the penis which he had swallowed. He is not willing to admit that this is his own interpretation, but says that it could also be the breast. I say that the nice bird, whom he loves so well, does represent, as he himself said, the mother and her breast, and I suggest it is mixed up with the good penis, reminding him of so much material which showed that the parents in his mind were mixed up as bad people, and noting that in this case, they are mixed up as pleasant ones.

Klein then cites Mr B's 'eating tendencies' as she has previously called them, connecting these to the inhibition of his mourning:

I interpret how the mother in this case was meant to become his possession by eating her up, leading it back to the earliest situation at breast. Mr B's way of describing how he knew the thrush so well and how he could explain it all to the expert, all seemed to show that he really not only possesses knowledge and understanding about the thrush, but [also possesses] the thrush itself. I suggest that by eating up the thrush, the wish was also fulfilled to get possession of his mother and keep her safely inside, so that he could never be robbed of her again. This feeling of possession of course is counteracted by the fear of having destroyed [mother inside]. Her coming nearer means that he can revise the relation with her, because the distress, despair and guilt that had inhibited his mourning had lessened; he is able to mourn her at the same time as he is able to re-establish her memory and his relation to her, so that she really becomes his possession.

Klein writes that today, unlike in recent days, Mr B listens patiently to her 'expansive' interpretations. He responds by saying that,

he could tell me so much more about the thrush, which interests him; and then he goes on speaking with feeling and satisfaction of the various kinds of thrush, and then also about the way the Hebrides is spelt. The Celtic language spoken there is a very strong language, has lasted centuries, while the Danish language has died out and has not even been able to stay for 100 years. Mr B speaks of the Kings which have governed the country, especially mentioning the Danish one. Language in his mind connects more with women than with men. In families, idioms are propagated by the women. Of course, he says, of course, it is the mother from whom the child first learns to speak. He agrees that the strong language which is lasting and will not die out is equated with the country, and that the strong mother really is his possession inside which he feels now will last. Then tells me that he had thought of the Inner Hebrides and of the Outer Hebrides, that he had thought this yesterday. He agrees that this seems to confirm the mother inside and the mother outside.

Before leaving, Mr B says, 'If I may remark, the movement you just made with your hand reminded me of the thrush.'

Saturday 22 January 1938

Klein writes that Mr B 'has recently admitted favourable changes without having to take this back.' He has also pleaded with her to 'cure him' on several occasions. Regarding his psoriasis however, he says,

he was not at all concerned about it. He mentioned it himself in connection with the castration fear and understood, or rather drew my attention to, the connection with the reappearance of this skin trouble. After that he said jokingly, 'Well, cure me at least of the psoriasis.'

Klein notes,

This fact is remarkable, since it shows a fundamental alteration in his negative therapeutic reaction. The thought of being cured becomes a direct wish, without reaction against it afterwards.

Mr B continues to speak quite freely and in detail, 'about various real things on his mind.' He then describes to Klein,

how he is reorganising his whole library. He had the paint on the doors taken off and the nice old wood reappeared. Walls stripped of lots and lots of paper right back to the very last paint which goes back about 100 years. He had gone through all the books and sorted them out, catalogued them, etc., and says he was much more careful about the old books his wife possesses – and of course his own – than she. Says that now all the paint is taken off, the window-frames are a different wood from the shelves, but he doesn't mind this – it's nice wood and should show as it is. During this report he thought how like this procedure is the analysis. Getting at the bottom of things and seeing them as they are. Mr B understands how much this procedure pertains to his inside, and to his mind.

Klein reminds Mr B of his dream of the Hebrides,

> *and the different words fitting together, the parents – the good parents in union. He says that he never had a special interest in architectural things, though of course a love of old things ([such as] archaeology) always existed. Mr B agrees about the [importance of the] change; that he should be interested in rearranging the rooms, etc., and adds that he wanted a room for himself where nobody will disturb him if he likes to be there by himself. He connects this with a change recently mentioned about his greater capacity to detach himself from his wife and everybody.*

Monday 24 January 1938

Despite Klein's comments above about 'a fundamental alteration in the negative therapeutic reaction,' after the weekend Mr B again complains that he can't stand the treatment. He tells Klein that,

> *His wife is going away for a fortnight, which he wants for her health, but her ways and difficulties before going make him miserable. His associations are much more difficult. He repeatedly goes to sleep which he so often did, usually waking up with a bit of a dream which was always good material. Then he says, 'It wasn't the words which frightened the birds,' and tells me the whole Limerick, which begins 'There was a man of Boulogne.' It includes a double entendre (pronounced to rhyme with Boulogne). Mr B speaks about the English mispronouncing foreign languages. Before that, he had used in his associations the expression 'I am giving tongue to that thought.' Then, [in connection to the] double entendre and the word tongue, says he has the feeling it meant something sexual. I connect the words 'not frightening the birds' with material about the thrush, [standing for his] mother, wife and I, and sister; the birds not really being words, but the tongue which frightened; 'double entendre' standing for the parents in intercourse. Mr B's not being able to associate today derived from a fear that his words, tongue, penis, would hurt me. That the peaceful and friendly relations of last few days bring the fear at once of sexual desires which would be most dangerous. Hypothetical experience with his little sister and her anxiety on such an occasion (often shown in material but never confirmed by him), would have strengthened the conception of his bad penis. Mr B, depressed, says it is terrible if it is true and it is terrible if it isn't.*

Though there are no notes for the following day, Klein remarks that on that day, Mr B is 'again accessible, and quieter.'

Thursday 27 January 1938

Mr B is late, having been out shooting.

> *He recalls pleasant memories of the house where his grandfather lived in connection with shooting there, and of his very kind and good aunt who pleaded with him once that he should free a bat which he had caught and kept in a cage. She was actually a great-aunt*

and very kind, though 'a dried-up spinster,' as he described her. He says that he was very embarrassed because she had treated him like an equal, and was very kindly, but the bat had solved the problem for itself by escaping from the cage.

Regarding shooting, Klein notes that,

Mr B always has conflicts in connection with shooting. Though now they are not very apparent, they come up from time to time. As a young fellow he burst into tears, the first time he had been out shooting with his father, when he looked at the dead bird. He likes it, though there is conflict. Mr B comments that it is not reasonable to be a conscientious objector to shooting or hunting, because one does eat the game and birds, therefore one couldn't object if people killed them. As sometimes before, I connect these thoughts and doubts with the material about the thrush. Since birds, as we have often seen in other material, do represent babies, children, mother, wife and me, we can see the reason for this conflict. The question comes up why he shoots nevertheless, and he agrees with me that if he had deep conflicts about having attacked or eaten up these women for whom the birds stand, he might have to shoot birds to show that he hasn't really injured them, and that he doesn't really mind shooting, and so on. Mr B's admission is, of course, very reluctant, but he cannot get away from the fact that the doubts and conflict have now come up after the whole material of the birds, and that is what they were standing for.

Friday 28 January 1938

Yesterday, Mr B had reported to Klein that he had shot two rabbits. Then, in a dream,

He was shooting a third rabbit. He was on a destroyer. The rabbit was in a tube which he described as a torpedo tube. Another man was with him. Mr B poked inside the tube with his stick. The rabbit then came out, looking awful, partly skinned and smashed up and was lying on its back, torpedoing himself, as he described it, forwards – a thing which of course the rabbit could not do. Mr B felt awful in the dream about the rabbit. The object in which the rabbit was, Mr B first called a gadget – but in between once called it a torpedo tube. He is very uncertain what it really was like and that no doubt it was not simply a tube because that would have been so easy to catch the rabbit, but a much more complicated thing. He is in one moment angry when I call it a tube, though he himself had called it a tube.

Associating to the rabbit, Mr B says,

That it reminds him of the penis. He had started the hour by saying that he is very depressed. He repeats it during associations and interpretations repeatedly. I interpret that the dream followed analysis of his doubts and conflicts over shooting birds, which I connected with the thrush material. Mr B seems to see that there is not a great difference between the thrush and the rabbit here, and that my suggestion is right: that here rabbit stands not only for the penis but also for the baby and for the whole person; for grown-up people like Mr B, his mother and his sister. I interpret that his depression becomes stronger again in connection with his feeling that he cannot keep his mother alive if there is such a strong desire to destroy, which is expressed in his wish for shooting. These shot and injured objects then were the same mother whom he was now to keep, to preserve, as an inner possession.

Saturday 29 January 1938

Mr B is very late, Klein records, though he says there is no special reason for this. He reports,

That he had great difficulty in getting up. After, he says that he was obviously a long time in coming to me. He is very depressed. He feels that I do not quite understand the difference between rabbiting and shooting. His explanation followed. Rabbiting is a thing he loves to do with his dog. It is a rather rough occupation. Rough farmers do it and of course it isn't shooting, or to be compared with shooting. It is also quite a different thing, for it is more connected with underground – finding a rabbit in its hole, digging it out of there – all more sexual than shooting. It appears that the thirsting for the rabbit is one of the pleasures in it. Mr B also says that it is the practice to find the rabbit in a comfortable place it has made, and to get it out from there. Ratting is something of the same kind.

Continuing to talk of rabbiting and ratting, Mr B says,

that his rabbiting instinct was always very strong; also when he described the dream yesterday he started by saying that he knew that there was a rabbit on the destroyer, in this gadget or object, and that at once his rabbiting instinct woke up. He adds that it is something to do with the woman's genital. I ask him why he thinks it is more sexual than other things. He points to the ground, the hole and all that reminds him of the woman. I now interpret that he has said one of the attractions is to get the rabbit out of this convenient place which he has got into. Then I also remind him that one association to the dream was that the rabbit was like a penis. Mr B gets angry with me because I seem, he suggests, to think that it is a simple tube while it is quite clear from the material, that he is absolutely uncertain what the inner part of this object was like. I interpret that that seems to be his ignorance as a boy, about mother's genital, or rather about the inside of her body and the genital. Connecting all these things, I suggest that the rabbit is the father's penis inside mother.

Rabbiting is also represented by Mr B's dog, Klein remarks, to which he is very attached and which was always his companion in shooting. She then interprets Mr B's,

desire to dig out and to injure and mutilate the skin and castrate the father, and to find him out in this convenient place inside; also that he managed to make the persecuting father always a vague figure in the background. In connection with this, I cite material from the last few weeks – the man on the mountain who was with Mr B and disappeared; this man in the rabbiting dream was also a vague figure; the man who was in the background while the woman came at him with the bloody tie. This man was also standing for father, and that one thing about this vagueness is that he had, as it were, to put all his fears of persecution on to the penis inside mother while he tried to think of his real father and of real men in a friendly way. Nevertheless, he didn't entirely succeed. I remind him that very often he is afraid of somebody coming behind him, that his fear became awfully strong in connection with coming to see me, being afraid that somebody would be behind him on my doorstep; and that when I asked him who this somebody could be, it was always a man. Mr B agreed to this, but says rather slowly that he hasn't had this fear for quite a long time.

Klein continues to interpret the rabbiting material, connecting it to Mr B's interest in the female body, and to an early masturbation phantasy. She tells Mr B that his,

wish for me to know so definitely about the details of rabbiting is also expressing the reversal, namely, his ignorance about the woman's genital and his wish to find out more from me. I remind him also of his masturbation phantasies when he was about eight years old which he remembers, in which he was exploring the inside of the woman's body, always thinking of one of his aunts on such occasions. It was pleasurable; he was inside climbing up to the top. When I ask how he got inside, which opening, he said that that never came into it – it was simply large enough to get in and an opening didn't play any part. I now connect with the fact that the dread of a woman's genital containing the father's penis and the fear of the anus containing the dangerous faeces, had led Mr B to eliminate these associations from his masturbation phantasies. Mr B agrees that doing away with any entrance to the body in his phantasies is a sign of repression. This repression, I suggest, has extended to the parents' sexuality as a whole, as well as to his own genital desires towards his mother.

Thursday 10 February 1938

Mr B reports what he calls, 'a most important dream,' which he feels 'would show all his difficulties.' Klein writes,

He speaks of this dream, as so often, with tenderness, love and admiration, as the most precious thing. He cannot decide to tell it to for fear I will spoil it and injure it. He gives an association before telling the dream: that his wife showed him an antique bowl, saying couldn't he make a handle for it. Mr B said he could, and reminded her that he had already made a handle for it once that was so exact that you could not see the difference. It must have got broken again and she had forgotten the whole incident; i.e., had forgotten his helpfulness and his production. He complains about his wife's general destructiveness – carpets which are torn, sinks broken, etc. Then with more care and reluctance, he tells the dream:

He said to a man – a friendly man, one of those dim and vague figures, that he thought an Englishman should live in Greece to make the Greeks understand England, and also to understand the Greeks himself better. It was to bring England and Greece together. The man said that he would introduce him to the King of Italy, and wants him to discuss this plan with King of Italy. So it happened. The King asked him to sit beside him and listened in a friendly manner, full of attention to his plan. While speaking with the King, a lady arrived and brought the King letters which had arrived for him. The King asked, would Mr B just look at his correspondence, and so Mr B did. One letter had a kind of flag, which reminds Mr B of the flag of Portugal, which he drew for his children, who were writing out the various flags for school homework. The second letter reminds him of a letter which he has written to the Council about some cottages for policemen which were being built in front of his house, spoiling the view, giving an excellent reason against it. He is feeling that he will carry through this matter. Only there is a little hitch in that, though he is right in this reason he gave, [he is not right] altogether, but the others cannot know it because they don't understand. There is no association to the third letter, but I remind him that two days ago I returned to him a letter which he had written to Mr X and his reply, which he had given me to read some time ago. When I returned it, Mr B did not seem pleased, and made a remark to the effect that 'I would rather not know about this letter.'

Klein writes that Mr B listens 'with tension and anxiety' to her remarks, though the dream is hardly analysed during this session. Though he expects Klein to spoil it, before leaving, Mr B says, 'Well you haven't really done any harm to the dream, though I must say I don't like your last interpretation' (about Klein returning his letter to him).

Saturday 11 February 1938

Klein writes that Mr B is very late and extremely aggressive.

He demands to know whether I am going to help him or not. He says 'you should say at once. If you are, then you should at once start to do so.' I remind him of the dream [of the previous session, which] has not been by any means fully analysed. He says 'Do it.' I make a few suggestions based on former material. Greece, through the Classics, is very much connected with his mother, and often standing for her. Pacification between father and mother [is meant by the bringing together of] Britain and Greece. Mr B had explained how much Greek culture is still in Italy, and how much the Greeks had colonized Italy. It is not strange that the King of Italy should be interested in his plans for Greece. He still agrees, however, that it is an anomalous situation that he should discuss Greek plans with the Italian King.

Klein reminds Mr B that he had said that this dream 'would show up all his difficulties if we could analyse it.' He had added however, that that wouldn't be possible, for he is 'frightened of my touching it.' In association to,

the King of Italy, Mr B had in the first place said, 'He is a puppet of this terrible creature Mussolini,' and then, he had said that the King reminded him of a doctor whom he hates because he advised his wife badly. I point out the striking fact that there is the most peaceful atmosphere in dream. During this session, Mr B twice used the word 'bloody' – once speaking of my 'bloody interpretation' – 'go on with your bloody interpretation'; and once of 'bloody rubbish.' I refer back to the breaking of the handle [of the antique bowl] – equated with my interpretation of the dream as castration fear – the precious dream as his penis, his productions in general, babies, etc. That somewhere there is a terrible creature, Mussolini, who will show behind the friendly King, who actually reminds him of a very hated person. Mr B is furious and absolutely against these interpretations. 'Castration, Freud's dogma – your favourite topic, shibboleth,' he says.

Klein suggests that Mr B's,

fear of me derives from his identifying me with the terrible Mussolini – the frightening father phantasy, father of the night anxieties, etc. while the real father, supposed to be friendly and full of interest, though a friendly man in many ways – was never actually so much with Mr B, who never got much appreciation from his real father. Mr B leaves me in great distress, depression and antagonism, but the same evening sent a few lines in which he only complains about his feeling that I try to make him accept this castration interpretation, which is very painful.

'Between the Saturday 19 and Friday 25 March 1938'

Mr B tells Klein a dream:

He had an immovable object under his tongue. They were black spots and couldn't be removed. This was very strongly stressed.

His first association,

is 'my wife, my children and myself,' and after a little break 'and the distrust of you.' He thinks of the round little bit of red paper which is put on a document – one has to put one's finger on it and to swear, to take an oath. In the end it is not really necessary to say the oath – to say the words – but it still means the same thing. Then he goes back to the black – blacks of the nose, he says, and tells me – he had said so before, but now makes it more clear to me – that he used to pick his nose very much, and that he used to eat the blacks from his nose; that even when he was still at public school he used to pick his nose very much. He had been much reprimanded for this and for eating the blacks as a smaller child, and it had been a great source of anxiety to him because he simply couldn't give it up.

Klein interprets that the people in Mr B's life, his wife and children, are actually in his mouth, Mr B having eaten them. She says,

they are at the same time equated with the blacks from the nose, which gave so much ground for anxiety. I now suggest that the blacks of the nose have also something to do with faeces.

> *Here, Mr B gets very cross. He does not want to hear anything more about it, has a great outbreak of anger in which he tells me the most unpleasant things, and then leaves.*

After the weekend, Mr B reports two dreams. Klein writes that 'The analysis of these dreams and what I am saying now extends over several days.' The first dream is as follows:

> *Mr B was going down a street and came into a curiosity shop. He entered the shop and was looking round. He saw a very nice bowl of a kind that peasants have, and he saw also a mark on the bowl which is a nice thing – that is the way pottery should be made. It shows that it is hand made, and that the finish comes on top of the mark, and that anyhow this bowl represented a good thing to him. He saw also very nice china, but pieces of that. He says it wouldn't have mattered if it had been all in bits because he likes, and has done so repeatedly, to put these little bits back together, so they will make a whole; but these were pieces of china, really, as he says, quite useless though they had been nice or good. He went further down the street and a woman assaulted him. She grabbed at his trousers and dragged his penis out. There are not many details about the woman. She was youngish, perhaps 30 years old and he had no other associations. Terrible feeling for Mr B, he felt it absolutely like a nightmare.*

In the second dream:

> *Mr B said he murdered a man, but it was like suicide, because he felt this man to actually be one part of himself. This man came towards him, brandishing a burning ember in his hand, and Mr B knocks him down and kills him this way. He cannot explain any more why he should have felt that this was part of himself, but that is what he felt.*

Klein notes that before telling her the dream,

> *Mr B had been friendly and very quiet. He says he felt very bad about not being at peace with me, and says 'Let's wash out this Saturday dream [about the immovable objects/ blacks in the mouth], and not think about it anymore.' I precede my interpretation by saying that of course we cannot simply wipe the dream of Saturday out because the material contained in it does reappear again. Of course, Mr B interprets this by saying he is not an idiot and he knows he can't wipe it out, he says it was only his way of putting it …*

Klein interprets,

> *that in the most recent dream, a person, who is a persecutor and who is attacking him, is part of himself. I link up to the dream of Saturday where I had suggested that he actually had the people inside him, not only inside his mouth [as immovable objects under the tongue], but inside him, and that they were not removable. That was the point which was most important – he could not shift them, Mr B added. Now, I say that obviously the man who was part of himself became part of himself by having been eaten like these other objects.*

I also link this up with the interpretation which had so much aroused Mr B's anger, and that was my equating blacks of the nose with faeces. Mr B is now ready to take this interpretation in. I continue that the black spots, the people and the dangerous man inside, are equated with faeces which one tries to get rid of. Here, Mr B says that actually his whole constipation, which had been there as long as he remembers, had altered during the analysis, and that there is now no trouble of the kind.

Klein writes that 'it is characteristic' that Mr B had not told her previously about this improvement. She returns to the curiosity shop, which she says, also stands for the analytic procedure. She writes,

Mr B discovers there a nice bowl which is all right, though it is marked, and another nice thing which is in pieces but which can't be repaired. The pieces stand for the destroyed me, Mrs Klein, the destroyed good mother, whom Mr B feels he has attacked, especially having felt guilty on Saturday for his very great anger and what he told me. I also suggest that in spite of his anger, obviously some part of his anxiety has been resolved through Saturday's work about the black spots; and that also the analysis is felt to be something better – the curiosity shop. I also stressed that actually, as we have often seen, but which is not often admitted by Mr B, there is a great pleasure in the discovery through analysis – his meeting his own unconscious and things of the kind – that this is a pleasure which he doesn't want to show because it does connect so very much with pleasant or friendly feelings towards me. Mr B again speaks of the woman who assaulted him. He says the next association of course would be that it is me; that this connected with the former dream where the vulgar woman was jumping at him with a second-hand tie, and in his associations that was connected with castration as well as with my interpretation. Mr B says that after all, I do through my interpretations, drag things out of the unconscious into the conscious, similarly as the woman dragged the penis out. I of course interpret the fact that interpretations are felt as a real, serious, and physical attack.

Klein's notes from 1938 end here, and there is then a long gap until they resume in May 1939.

Tuesday 23 May 1939

Mr B reports a dream, dreamt the night after he had apparently decided not to return to his analysis, 'owing to a most complicated external situation connected with his wife.' Exactly what this situation is, is unclear, though later Klein reports that Mr B's wife is severely ill. Klein writes,

Mr B dreamt that he was in bed with a man and he inserted his penis into him. It was a female genital, but then in going on with the dream in further associations he decided it must have been an anus. Then two elderly women came into the room. To one of them he associates a distant relative whom he had only met a long time before and did not recognize her. He said he did not remember her name, but remembered her. Through their coming into the room this sexual activity was interfered with. There was no special anxiety in the dream, no special affect or pleasure in connection with the activity, it seemed rather matter-of-fact. The women were not specially felt to be hostile.

Mr B's first association to the dream is that,

he was about to break off his relation with Mr J, who at the time played a most important part in the whole situation; also his wish to break off the analysis with me. The dream led me to interpret his complicated relation not only with Mr J but also going back to his father. He had decided to come back to me after the telephone call I made two days later; and he suggested that he was only able to dream such a dream because he thought he would not see me. On the other hand, he obviously had the dream partly to do work.

In another dream,

He dreamt that he was flying with a woman pilot, young and attractive, in an aeroplane. They were close to, or over water, and were in danger of colliding with a ship and also with a piece of rock, something concrete which he describes as circular, like a manhole. He saw the danger, but the pilot did not see it, even as they had got past it, and he drew the attention of the pilot to the things they had passed. But he patted her breast to comfort her because he thought that when they have to die they may at least die happily. Mr B stresses that though she was definitely the pilot she was unaware of the danger which he saw, and it was as if it could not be prevented and that they just happened to have escaped it.

Mr B shares some associations. Thinking of the ship leads him to recall the name of,

an important father figure, and the profession of his father. There were nails sticking out from the ship. I only drew his attention to the manhole, which struck me. Mr B notes that his brother as a man fell into a manhole and hurt his sides very much. The relation to the pilot is obviously a very friendly and tender one. He did not blame her at all for not having seen the danger, and spontaneously says that obviously the pilot is a vision of myself as a young person. Mr B himself interprets the depth as the unconscious, the whole thing as the analysis. He is aware that the whole thing means also a sexual experience with the pilot. The dream is in great contrast to the avowed disbelief in me, mentioned just days before. Despair and depression had very much increased through the enormous difficulties of the real situation at the time. On the next day I gave two interpretations, both of which he thoroughly disliked; the danger of sexual intercourse, which he himself had admitted when he said it referred to a sexual situation, his father inside the vagina, inside the woman … I connect this with the dream about the man in[to] whom he inserted his penis, and a female genital was there; and I referred to this mixture between man and woman in that dream and in the present dream – the other way round – the man inside the woman, connecting it with the danger his brother had through falling into the manhole. The second interpretation is a transference interpretation: that I am unaware of the danger for myself of falling in love with him, a danger he always is aware of, or thinks exists, when he is fond of a woman or when women get fond of him.

July 1939

Klein writes,

There had been a great improvement in which Mr B's sexual desire in connection with other women had come up, and at the same time a great lessening of depression. The situation with his wife had been terribly tense because of her severe illness. Important decisions had to be taken. His being called up for military service brought anxieties which had made the whole situation again very difficult. The sexual fears and desires seemed very much stimulated by this situation. At the end of June there had been the following dream. A cousin of his who very often took the place of his brother in his mind had just finished his meal, and Mr B ate something which the cousin had left. He at once said that it must have something to do with sexual matters – that was his interpretation. The thing which was left by the cousin and which Mr B ate, had qualities like brain or something of the kind, and then he thinks about a vegetable, an onion.

Klein remarks that Mr B's reference to sexual matters means,

the fellatio which he might have done with his brother, though nothing of the kind had been admitted by him. This interpretation rouses a store of hatred, fear, and so on, and I interpret that he now feels found out by his mother in the thing that he always wanted so much to hide from her. There are many references to actual fear in him about his brother as far as his genital goes – the memory of his being terrified at night that the brother was walking towards him, and connecting it with some attack on his genital, and so on. It is especially acute because the fears about the penis inside him correlate with the terrifying external situation – war danger – and at the same time his wife's illness, about whom he feels quite hopeless because the change which has been made implies to him that she may not be cured. That means that he is terrified of the bad object inside her and inside himself. I try to link this together, but it is terribly difficult to bring it home to Mr B because his anxiety is so very acute.

Two days after the above dream, Mr B has the following dream:

He was communicating through secret messages with a person who was under water. He was invisible and Mr B could not see him. The repeated messages he sent to him were on 'lavatory paper.'

Klein writes that, 'altogether associations were terribly difficult,' and that Mr B had in fact told her the dream with great reluctance. One thing was quite definite, however. Mr B says, *it was not salt water, but fresh water. Fresh water seemed to him so much better because of course the water in a pond or in a lake could not be so deep either. There is obviously deep concern in Mr B about the state of things under water. When speaking about the fresh water and the better condition, he urged 'When I come to think of it, it isn't a great help because a pond or a lake might also be very deep. He recognises that the fresh water conception is one way of diminishing his anxiety about the fate of this [man he is communicating with]. When I ask what was the position of the man who was swimming in the water – was he lying, standing? Mr B said indignantly, 'he wasn't lying, he was quite truthful'. I linked this up with the dream two days before, which I could not go on interpreting because Mr B had got in such a rage about the interpretation that the onion might represent the penis – saying that his penis never has such a shape, and accusing me of dishonesty. I refer to this remark, saying that now the truthful man may also stand for me; interpreting that the man is underneath the water, invisible, but just in communication with the patient. This is his internal object, represented now by me.*

Klein further suggests that Mr B's fear of salt water corresponds to a fear that his internal object, which he has imprisoned inside himself, is also at risk because of 'the dangerous quality of the urine,' which is the salt water. She writes, 'for this we have had much material before.' Klein's notes become somewhat difficult to follow at this point. It is clear however that her interpretations bring a psychosomatic effect, which she notes. Mr B says,

He has got such an awful headache and cannot stand it. He has very often mentioned the psychological reasons for his headaches, calling them psychological headaches. Now, I remind him that he had told me a theory of one of his schoolfellows that faeces go up into the head and that causes headaches. He got very depressed when I was interpreting, but told me about his interest in chemistry and physics when he was about 13 years old, that he always connected with creating, scientifically, sunbeams, which were not alive and which he felt were very uncanny and frightening. And then he speaks about ghosts, and his great terror of ghosts – that he always dreaded ghosts when he was by himself at night in the nursery, and it does appear that he is still, not rationally, very frightened of ghosts.

Klein connects Mr B's fear of ghosts with the man under the water, with whom he was communicating, which she says is an internal object. She refers to his feeling, expressed many times in the analysis, that he is full of different people, which are also his internal objects, of which he is afraid. Her notes continue,

That was on a Saturday. On Monday he comes in an entirely different frame of mind. He had been able to come to terms in a matter where he had reasonably to change relation to a man. He was able to do so apparently without hostility and following rational considerations; but after a few days the anxiety about having a father who wasn't helpful enough appeared again and led to awful tempers with me and with his wife, as if he had to prove that I am also wrong: because if the father isn't helpful, then I cannot be helpful. In spite of his wife being ill, and actually injured by his tempers, he rages at her, and goes on doing so in the same way in my room. While running up and down in my room in his temper, he looks at the bookcase, and singling out one author, saying, 'he is also here.' I interpret that he is not raging at me, but at the author he dislikes, and says that he does the same thing in connection with his wife, when he must show her that he isn't improving, which really makes her worse.

Klein acknowledges that Mr B has not said that his raging makes his wife worse, but that 'that could be concluded from his own associations and his feelings of guilt about the row he had with her.' She continues,

I interpret that when he is raging and feels that his wife should do something to help herself, he behaves as he did when he felt that he must explain things to his parents when they were in bed, [that he must] make them sit up and look. He could never explain what he really meant them to listen to, but I interpret that at the time he had felt that he could not really look at his mother when he saw her in the morning in bed because he so much disliked the look of her bed, and that he also felt that he could not look at his wife sitting in bed. Now referring to all that I say that he felt that his parents were injuring each other. That mother does take in the dangerous penis of the father, contains it, and that they should listen to him.

Klein tells Mr B that 'his raging at his wife in tempers which he cannot control and which he is awfully sorry for afterwards is also to make her sit up and listen.' She speaks of his feeling that his wife contains an 'awful creature,' a dangerous object inside, as did his mother, and as does he. She tells him 'he is raging at her in order to get this awful creature out of her, to get this internal dangerous object out of her, or to destroy it.' Klein continues,

I interpret that Mr B wants to warn his wife continually about what she contains; in this way as it were, not allowing her to hope for improvement because he is so terrified that his hope may be wrong. She does not realise the danger inside herself, as his mother did not when he wanted her to sit up in bed and listen to him. It appears to me after the interpretations given to Mr B that these kinds of rages and tempers are quite similar to the tempers of children – that in his state of mind no reason and no sense of reality prevail. That in his shouting and raging at me he does not see me as I am. Rather, he is in a delusional state, and that he is really talking to an object that is not visible but that he feels to be inside me. This is the parents mixed up together in sexual intercourse; and the same thing applies to his own inside. He is raging at the man inside me, and he is also raging at the man inside himself. But, he really was also in sympathy with the internalised object, his father, the drowned father, the injured father, and also the dangerous father – the dangerous father he is addressing himself to when shouting at me and shouting at his wife.

Klein's notes for July 1939 end here. There is no mention of her plan to continue seeing Mr B given the precarious relations between England and Germany and the likelihood of war breaking out. We do however know that Klein moved away London, to Cambridge, in September 1939. Her diaries show that Mr B travelled there once a week for the duration of her stay there, but there are no surviving notes from these sessions. The next chapter contains notes which Klein presumably made for teaching, some of which are undated, and clinical notes from the years 1940, 1943, 1948, and 1949.

Chapter 7

No longer so much in the depths

It seems likely that much of the material presented in this chapter was used for teaching, since Klein organised it under headings that suggest it was to illustrate various theoretical points. There are notes for a handful sessions from 1940 and from 1943. Another handful of sessions are dated 1948, and finally there is a dream from 1949. It is possible that this later material comes from an earlier period, and that Klein was merely drawing upon it for teaching given in the years 1948 and 1949. As I wrote in my Introduction, unfortunately Klein's diaries end in 1946, so it isn't possible to triangulate the clinical notes that are dated after 1946 with the diary entries, or to know when she finally stopped seeing Mr B.

Among the material presented in this final chapter, there is much analysis of anality, which is connected by Klein to sexual activity that may have occurred between Mr B and his siblings. We can of course never know whether such activity took place in external reality, or only at the level of phantasy. Klein seems to suspect the former, though as has been seen, Mr is often furious at any such suggestion. Nonetheless, his guilt at having destroyed his sister, this 'vision of delight' as he felt her to be, does emerge and he is seemingly overcome by this. Anxiety regarding the war also features, and Mr B's own painful sense of being unable to protect his family from all that is going on in the world comes to the fore. This frightening reality notwithstanding, overall one can see that Mr B is much more in touch with his difficulties; with his guilt, and paranoid, accusing tendencies. He does easily revert to accusing Klein, and is still depressed to some extent, but he is far less hopeless and much more loving than at the beginning of the treatment. He also longs for his mother. His fear of and inhibitions regarding sexual intercourse are diminished as Klein continues to analyse them. For example, in the pages that follow the reader will see Klein interpreting Mr B's dread of encountering his father's bad and dangerous penis inside his mother, or in representatives of her, which had led to significant restriction of his loving, affectionate, and sexual feelings. An example of this is his rather concrete anxiety concerning his wife's polyps, which seem unconsciously to stand for the dangerous penis inside, which he fears she will not survive.

Analysis, the 'unconventional food' as Klein calls it, also uncovers after many years Mr B's wish for his objects only to be interested in him; that he was not so

DOI: 10.4324/9781003373414-8

much interested in them in their own right or for their own sake. Mr B feels this highlights his enormous greed, that he had earlier denied, and very great feelings of unworthiness and depression emerge. Predictably, in response, Mr B fiercely accuses Klein of only bringing out the bad aspects of him. There is also further evidence that Mr B's relations to men, which had been so disturbed by his jealous, poisonous attacks on his father, are externally much improved, and he is now much more able to stand up to superiors, and to give orders. Mr B's father is still alive, but as the end of his life looms, there is continuing anxiety about not being able to keep a father alive inside. Finally, an important dream seems to evidence Mr B's stronger belief that his internal parents are united in a better, even curative intercourse, and indeed have perhaps long been united, despite his enormous anxieties to the contrary. His own sense of his constructive and reparative capacities, glimmers of which have been seen throughout the analysis, is also, hearteningly, much more in evidence.

The first material I am presenting here is undated, but comes first in archive file B.68. It is similar to earlier anal material and refers once more to possible sexual activity between Mr B and his siblings. Klein's notes are headed,

> *Material showing clearly the internalised objects, and the connection with anal activities.*

Klein presents a dream, reported by Mr B:

> *He was driving a little girl, which he thinks was his favourite daughter, and took a way to the left. An old woman came out from a house when he passed by. He came into a very muddy part, but later on saw an exhibition of nice paintings, jewellery, and so on.*

Klein interprets the dream, as much material before,

> *as something anal, muddy; something being done to the little girl whom he drove. His daughter – in the past his sister. The old woman who sees him stood for the analyst, whose interpretations on this line had always raised the greatest storms.*

Klein writes that, 'Mr B resented this interpretation terribly, and refused to give any more material, and nothing more was done about the dream'. Shortly following this, he reports a nightmare:

> *There was a colourless, inert, ill-formed mess, which he felt on top of him.*

In association, Mr B comments that,

> *his eiderdown was heavy, and waking up he felt that this was his mother stopping him in sexual intercourse. A string of adjectives he told me remind him of the definition of 'camel' in the Oxford English Dictionary. There is an association about someone who collected the dung of camels. Mr B complains about the heat, the eiderdown, which he wanted to get rid*

of, and about his wife who does not understand him. Later on, [he complains that] I don't understand the dream. He then resented my not making enough out of it. He says I do not understand him because I mistook the word 'hump' for 'hunch', connecting this with hunchback. I had also mentioned the word 'hunch', meaning having a hunch to do something, or a hunch that a thing is so.

Klein points out that,

the camel, as I suggested, also stood for mother, and so the hunch did not seem out of place.

Continuing to associate to his dream, Mr B says,

there is also a depression between the two humps of the camel. I remind him that the depression between two humps points to the two breasts, which he agrees to. He complains in the course of the hour about constipation, and it appears that his constipation, which had been very strong and usual in former times, had very much decreased in the last year or so.

Klein interprets,

that this strong feeling that his mother inhibited his sexual intercourse is connected with me as a forbidding figure, not understanding him. At the same time the associations about constipation and the dung of the camel, and also his description of the colourless, ill-shaped, ill-formed, inert mass, point to faeces inside him. That seems confirmation of many interpretations of mine that this is an internal mess, an internal mother, who stops his sexual activities. Mr B is reluctant to give any more associations to 'camel', and especially to quadruped. I point out that this quadruped, the four feet, two humps, also points to the mixed up parents in sexual intercourse.

Klein notes that this material was followed by 'clear anal material' in the form of a dream:

Mr B is sliding down a sliding staircase. From there, something points to the right. At the bottom of this staircase there is an indistinct woman. Mr B's next association is that he had the feeling that it is anal, after having mentioned 'at the bottom'.

'About a week later', Mr B brings another dream:

He had an accident on the road. He felt this accident had come about because of his indecision, because he had not clearly shown which way he was going. He collided with a cyclist, probably a motor cyclist. His car ran into the cyclist from behind. In the dream he did not know, but he feels the man is dead. He felt responsible and ran to fetch the police. The direction in which he ran was felt to be near the home where his father and sister live. The house into which he went was not like the one near his father's, and he

did not know the people, and they did not know him. There had been a gay party.
He did not find the police.

'With great decision', Klein notes, Mr B says,

> *that it was a male car. That reminds him of a mail cart in the nursery. This connected*
> *with very pleasant memories. He spoke of transport and then of transports of delight,*
> *mentioning somebody, a young girl whom he had seen in his youth, who was a 'vision of*
> *delight'. The fellow who was run over, the cyclist, he associates to a nice chap, like himself.*
> *He feels it was himself. In between there had been an association to a cousin, his senior in*
> *age and position, who took some advice from him, put himself, as it were, under the*
> *patient's command.*

Klein, in her interpretation, returns to,

> *much material in which the brother had done something sexual to the patient; to Mr B's*
> *conscious fear that the brother might come over from his bed and do something to the front of*
> *his body. I connect the accident from behind, due to his own indecision, to an anal attack by*
> *his brother. Mr B had always felt conscious of anybody behind – much material of the*
> *kind, which meant deterioration and death. Then there is the other part, in which, I suggest,*
> *he made a similar attack on his sister (after the vision of delight – this beautiful girl – I*
> *asked him what he felt about his sister, and he said that he had had her picture with him*
> *when he went to school, he thought she was most exquisite.) He was doing to his sister*
> *what his brother had done to him, and in this way destroying this beautiful picture; and*
> *this had something to do with the absolute loneliness he felt when he looked at this picture of*
> *the sister, and felt that she was so beautiful. It was the feeling that he had destroyed this*
> *vision of delight. Mr B had mentioned that the expression 'transports of delight' seems to*
> *indicate sexual gratification. Also, that in the dream he had been running in the direction of*
> *his father's and sister's house, expecting to find police there somewhere. The early fear of*
> *being found out by this terrifying father in connection with such an act with his sister – fear*
> *of his father having become more and more conscious in relation to various people recently.*
> *Mr B reminds me that the whole thing had taken place in Clifton Hill.*

Klein writes that following her interpretations,

> *there was a great relief, much less resentment about interpretation, and a great wish to*
> *cooperate. Mr B himself drew my attention to the fact that I had not enough interpreted this*
> *or that of this anal material, and recognized that it was impossible for him to go through*
> *this material without having the painful and unpleasant feelings which it roused. At the*
> *same time his attitude towards men again altered, less anxiety in connection with superior*
> *figures, more able to stand up to them, and also to give orders, and so on.*

The following material is dated April 1940. It too seems to have been selected for
teaching purposes, for it is headed,

Another instance for the connection between sexual potency and depressive position. Technique.

Friday 12 April 1940

Mr B is very depressed about a sexual failure, and a feeling that he could not find his way in. He reluctantly admits that there was something wrong with the erection, also obviously he had a premature emission. There are accusations against analysis and great depression. Denial that it has anything to do with the war, but great despair about his wife's very bad health. His first association sounds partly like a decision to have an operation performed on his wife. This is entirely his own idea, because there is no ground whatever to do that. He is feeling that that might give her the feeling that she is very ill and thus improve her desire to get well again. There is an association about having a brain operation performed on her. Then as the hour goes on, with great accusations and depression, he mentions the fact of this sexual failure. In between, references to Dr X, whom he always accuses in connection with his wife, his having failed her.

Mr B also mentions a dream:

In the dream he had lost the instrument which is so necessary for his tooth. He demonstrates it by showing me what it is. He has a tooth which should have been pulled out long ago, only a shell, and he cannot submit to having it taken out. He explains that in order to keep this tooth going he puts cotton wool into it before every meal and has an instrument, a little needle with some little pink part (but the pink part had gone), and afterwards cleans it with this little needle which has a sort of little brush on it. This instrument came to him in the following way. When he was at the dentist's the dentist must have dropped this needle on his coat and it stuck there. Mr B found it afterwards and never gave it back to the dentist but kept it, and now treats himself in this way. How precious this needle is to him is shown by the way he keeps it with him always and uses it to preserve the tooth.

Klein interprets Mr B's,

ambivalent attitude towards Dr X, whom he always wants to get back to cure his wife, though he feels he won't do this. His despair about his having failed his wife, at the same time his great hatred about it, [motivates] his desire to have (entirely irrationally) his wife operated on, identifying himself with her internal fears. The taking out from her the dangerous penis; at the same time, she must be put right by the doctor (father).

In this connection, Klein remarks that for the first time, Mr B has said 'that his father was not a good husband to his mother'. Klein interprets his longing,

to reunite the parents before his father dies, to preserve the dead mother and the dying father, [which explains why he is] unable to give up his feelings about Dr X. At the same time, he is terrified of his mother as a bad external, and still more internal, object. I suggest that the cavity of the tooth stands for his mother. Material about half dilapidated castles, and so on, also stands for the mother. Also, that he recently felt quite suddenly that the way his mouth is drawn is as his mother's was. The cavity he tends with such care and love and feels he could never separate from, since it stands for the mother. He himself had associated to the pink part of the instrument that it is the penis. I interpret the good penis of the father who is to restore mother and with whom he wants her to unite. His fear of the dentist, with whom he is on quite good terms, is only one reason why he cannot allow him to pull out the tooth (much material about castration fear, etc). That would mean to him the loss of the internal mother and that she must be restored by the good penis of the father to make harmony between them and himself and to keep them both.

Klein writes that 'Mr B has become peaceful and does not object to these interpretations'. Not unusually, he then falls asleep for a few minutes, and awakes having dreamt:

A man popped out his head from a dug-out and said 'This dug-out is a farm.'

Associating to 'dug-outs', Mr B expresses,

concern about there being no underneath shelters for his workmen. Discussions over that have been so far unsuccessful. At his farm, he was very annoyed with his foreman for having arranged to pay too much for the use of part of a field on an adjoining little farm, paying more for the use of this field than for the rent of the farm. About this there were again discussions for some months. The man who puts his head out of the dug-out is somebody who wanted him to help him into some position in connection with the war, which Mr B could have taken but did not think he deserved.

Klein takes this dream as confirmation of some former interpretations. She says,

The dug-out, the tooth, the mother's inside, her genital, contains a hostile man. In sexual intercourse he would meet him inside the woman. The farm shows that this inside of the mother ... is overrated; that there is no need to put so much value on this vagina or on the inside of the woman. I also interpret the cavity as Mr B's own penis containing the good penis of the father, or the bad one, and to preserve his own potency he must keep the penis inside, but then he is terrified of the bad penis inside him, his own. Operating on his wife means taking the bad man out of her and also, in identification, from his own penis. Feelings of loss and sorrow about losing the good penis out of himself and out of her, contribute to these conflicting feelings about sexual activities, but extend from the genitals to the whole person. It is the fear of loss of the good parents if he frees himself (through castrating or injuring the penis of the father).

Klein notes that 'great relief followed these interpretations'.

'Middle of May 1940'

Again, material was presumably intended to be used in teaching since it is headed,

> *Reactions to acute anxiety stirred by real situation.*

Mr B is, Klein notes,

> *depressed, but not angry or uncooperative. He had indigestion the night before. He had a woman friend to dinner and instead of the simpler thing he had ordered they were given mushrooms with the dish. The friend mentioned that she had once been very ill after mushrooms, and that years ago when she went again to stay with the same friends she found herself in the bathroom suddenly quite ill, near to fainting, without having eaten mushrooms this time, repeating the experience of years ago. Mr B adds a theory that probably faeces can be thought to be so unpleasant because from the physiological point of view they are unnecessary things inside and are to be discarded. In between he had complained about his wife's state. I interpret, referring to former material, his fears about poisoning faeces, (recalling a dream of his defaecation making the world artificially green.)*

Mr B then reports another dream:

> *He defaecates, and somebody falls down dead.*

Klein says,

> *that this phantasy may help explain the feeling of the child when it has pain and discomfort that he actually produces poisonous explosive faeces.*

Returning to the first dream he reported, Mr B,

> *speaks of phantasies of sexual intercourse with this friend, whom he thinks is still inexperienced. He has ideas of giving pleasure to her, mentioning various reasons in her life [that cause her] to be dissatisfied and unhappy. He had bought on the same day in an antique shop a very nice piece of marble, and associations show that he actually wanted to show it to me, even more to give me a present. I interpret that the friend, standing for the sister, reminds him of much material of anal activities, which were dangerous to the sister, and yet, as I now suggest, pleasure giving. One problem is, whether his faeces are bad or good. His desire is to have them as good, productive things, like the marble, but he distrusts his own good products, because as soon as hatred comes up, they change into explosive and poisonous things. I remind him of the expression 'poisonous hatred', which he recently used in connection with an authority, a man. [There was also a] connection to his mother, and also to the transference situation, which I could show him in this hour. He was attacking*

father because of jealousy with explosive faeces, poisonous faeces, and [there followed a] disturbance in relations to men for these reasons.

Mr B refers to the fact that his relations to men, externally, are much improved. He cites,

Difficulties which he really overcomes quite easily and which would have given ground for great trouble in the past. He then reluctantly associates to the present situation, to latest war news, dangers, prospects of the war, fears, and so on. I now link all that with the fear of having given a bad meal, poisonous material, to somebody he is fond of. Regarding analysis – his wrong associations, his fear of not doing the right work with me, his wife in the past, his sister and mother. His incapacity to protect them all against the actual war danger, and his guilt that he has really done it all. Therefore, real anxiety is so much increased by guilt that he has to get away from the real anxiety and can only mention it after we had analysed some of the earlier anxieties. The interesting point is that he is in a position of authority, and that it is all the more striking that such news as we had recently should give rise to such material so far away from the actual danger situation. I forgot to mention that when he said that he had indigestion he also mentioned the dream of the night before.

The dream was as follows:

Someone died of a stomach ache – someone in a slightly inferior position to his; but in other ways somehow superior, through social position and in other ways. Associations show clearly that this man is a typical brother figure, and in some relations, a father figure. At the same time, he stands for Mr B himself. Mr B quite definitely says that his own stomach ache and the stomach ache of this man were obviously the same thing, and that he was partly represented in the dream by this man. I could show that his death through the stomach ache implies the destruction of all these people, women, inside him, the internal mother, and that he is guilty for that because he produced these dangerous faeces. In external and internal relations there was an association reluctantly given that the mushroom itself has similarities with faeces, and that he understood his friend's report that she found herself in the bathroom nearly fainting actually as her sitting on the lavatory when she felt ill. Her faeces are interpreted as poisoned food which he wanted to put into people anally and orally, and the poisonous faeces inside himself destroying him internally. The parachutists had come up before in this hour, in connection with anal intruders, cunning, secret and only to be prevented by similar methods, which increased the whole anxiety about internal destruction.

There is now a significant gap in Klein's notes of her treatment of Mr B. As we know, she left Cambridge for Pitlochry in June 1940, but it is apparent from her diaries that she saw Mr B a handful of times even while in Pitlochry (presumably he travelled to see her there). Regular sessions began again on Klein's return to London in September 1941, and continued for the rest of that year and through 1942. Klein's clinical notes on Mr B, however, only resume in January 1943.

Klein records below that she is seeing Mr B while he is on occasional leave from the War. We don't know what position he held during the War, or where he was stationed. There is no preamble at all to these notes, so we are also in the dark about other external events or situations, such as the state of Mr B's wife's health. From the first entry below however, it would seem that Mr B has developed some insight into his difficulties and is much less depressed and hopeless, if he intermittently returns to blaming.

Tuesday 5 January 1943

Klein writes,

> *In this hour, Mr B showed a great understanding of his own feelings of guilt, and of his paranoid and accusing tendencies. It appears [to him,] that he is really the cause of all this evil. He complains about the way in which he complained of his mother, complains to me in analysis; his own difficulties and his own guilt come very clearly to the fore. All this he said without reluctance, though he at once lapsed into an attitude of accusing me and mother, and everybody for his deficiencies.*

Nonetheless, Klein continues,

> *Mr B is so much more open to understanding his own feelings of guilt, (the result of many months of work, particularly about his anal fears.) While he is so much more able to do this, he is less guilty, and though depressed, is not in such a state of deep despair and hopelessness. This hour was characterized, as I said, by understanding, by severe feelings of guilt, longing for his mother, depression and greed, together with a certain amount of love. He also expressed gratitude for my having arranged to see him on his occasional leave, and for seeing him on this particular day; and also arranging several hours for the following week.*

Wednesday 6 January 1943

Mr B reports a dream. With some reluctance he admits that 'before going to sleep he had had flatus'. He also mentions that 'he still smelt the soap which he had used in the house of a friend, with whom he had been staying, a soap which was scented'. The dream is as follows:

> *He saw a place where bees were making honey, and he smelt the pleasant smell of the honey. Somebody remarked that this is the very pleasant smell of bees and of honey. Another point of view seemed to be, or perhaps another person said – uncertain – that this is the foul smell of a dog. This led him to associate to his own family, not the immediate ones, but the family of his parents, of whom he had less pleasant things to say; they were socially not quite as good as the ones he had mentioned before. The second part of the dream was about a place now on the outskirts of a town, having as he said, all the disadvantages of the country and of a town.*

In the dream, there is,

> *a heap of broken up things, bedroom furniture, dirty, placed in an untidy way, not put straight one beside the other, but strewn about, full of lavatory water. The whole thing was characterized by a lavatory atmosphere. There was a man there, a man who belonged to – as he calls it – a regiment of the mucker, and Mr B remarked that there isn't such a regiment, and it makes him think of muck. The man had a black hat on, and seemed to be ready to be shot. There must have been others about too, but Mr B did not see them. In between Mr B had mentioned that he was in a boat somewhere.*

Klein encourages Mr B to think about the contents of the dream. She writes,

> *I could not get any associations to the two people – or the two views – about the smell being pleasant, or unpleasant. When I reminded him that he had begun by speaking of his flatus, and introduced this as something very unpleasant, he said, well, that isn't the only view I have about it – it could also be called pleasant. He told me of a scent which experienced women use to attract men, produced from a flower. While he was telling me that, (it was the end of the hour), he had put his glasses on, and put them over his hankie, which he very often does, which he had tied over his eyes. When he did so he said, 'Now do I want not to see, or do I want to see?'*

Klein notes that Mr B tries to prevent her from interpreting during the session. However, at the end of the hour, she manages to say,

> *that both pleasant and unpleasant smells are illustrated by this dream – but he insists so much on the beauty of the honey and the good smell, because he wants to cover up the fear of the unpleasant smell which he produces. I also agreed that he might also have thought of his own smells as pleasant; as we have seen on many occasions, and much material has shown in the last year. I also referred to his placing his glasses over the hankie, and his own comment: doesn't he want to see, or does he? I pointed out that there was the obvious fear of allowing me to analyse this dream because he is also afraid that it isn't the good bees that are making the honey, but something very bad. I forgot to say that he had been speaking with a friendly and grateful feeling about the bees, calling them the good bees who work so well for us and make the honey. I also interpreted that obviously the smell part of the dream was his flatus. The bees are equated to faeces, and the whole thing is about his childhood.*

Friday 8 January 1943

Mr B begins by saying,

> *'I am battered, I am finished'. He goes on to speak about his unhappy relation with his wife. She was in an awful state; she had just had flu, and apparently was very depressed. He gives various details – how difficult she was, that he can be of no use to her. In his report the word 'battered' reappeared twice. This is particularly interesting because it is one which I have hardly ever heard him use before. Particular anxiety attaches to the fact that*

his wife will disregard the doctor's opinion; particularly also that she had missed her analysis. He rang her analyst, and it was reassuring to him to hear that the analysis[1] ... Mr B mentions that the doctor said that the polypus [sic] might recede, [but] altogether he does seem to be hopeless.

Mr B reports that he,

had been out shooting. He speaks about the cruelty of shooting and the unnecessary pain inflicted on the birds by shooting them, particularly if, as happened yesterday, one wasn't quite dead. He tells me about one bird which he found still half alive, which he killed. When he came home, he found that the bird was not dead, but had been alive all the time. He appears to be horrified about that. There are earlier memories of the kind. The patient remembered a dream which he had told me in his analysis, in which he killed a rabbit, or it was supposed to be killed, but actually was found long afterwards still alive and in a suffering state. The material at the time showed clearly that the rabbit was standing for a child – an unborn child or a baby. I also referred to the earliest memory of shooting when Mr B was out with his father and broke into tears.

Klein notes that 'The whole mood in this hour is, as it had been in the former one, predominantly that of guilt, and constant accusations about the harm he has done'. Then,

after some silence Mr B says that he often felt, not just at the moment, as if he would break up my whole furniture, push his foot through my chest of drawers, (which stands just opposite to the couch,) and break it all up. When I suggest that this must mean an attack on me, he agrees with that. The expression that he is battered, that he is injured, reappears. I point out that here, this guilt because he felt that he had injured me, his wife, the mother, is very closely connected with his fears about his wife being so injured, and that must have a bearing on his guilt.

Klein learns at the end of the hour that Mr B's wife wants to have an operation, even though her doctor has said her polyps may recede. She writes,

At first I understand that Mr B's wife is actually bleeding. He did not hear from his wife that she intends to have the operation, but heard a remark from the nurse, whom he himself thinks is very stupid and must have misunderstood the whole matter; but he thinks his wife thought of having the operation done unnecessarily, and that as it turns out was the main thing in his fears. At the end of this hour, it turned out that the patient is incapable of telling me the actual event or thing which stirred his anxiety, and he keeps this back till the last moment.

Instead, during the session there is some further analysis of Mr B's dream of two days earlier:

Mr B was trying to squeeze through these various heaped-up objects to get into the open country, and he didn't know whether he succeeded or not. I asked him for more associations

to the second part of the dream, the heap of unpleasant bits of furniture, etc, muck, and so on. He repeated part of these associations, but added that there were unmentionable objects about. When I asked him, 'do you mean chamber pots?', he said, yes that was what he meant. He told me that he tried to make his way into the open country, but had to get through these tanks filled with lavatory water, and it would have landed him into a country with small holes, apparently with the danger of being shot at. He does not think that he ever got out into the open country. In between, he tells me the dream of the night before.

The dream is as follows:

He heard birds overhead, but they did not come near enough for him to shoot, so he did not shoot. Part of the dream was that from an island or from a boat he fell back into mud, or would have fallen back – he did not remember anything more.

I interpret these unpleasant things, debris, bedroom things, as the presentation of the inside, very much connected with the many parts, the part where the unpleasant bees, the bad faeces, the foul dogs and internal people, appear. The relatives, people who are inside himself, we have had much material for. I now connect this with the associations to the foul dogs, following the question of smells, and following the question of his own flatus. He was well aware of the whole lavatory atmosphere of these things, the lavatory wall-paper, pink, the unmentionable objects, the chamber pots; the whole thing connected with bedrooms, which I suggested was also connected with his parents' bedroom; and I suggest that this was not only a presentation of his own body but also of his mother's body.

Klein comments once more that only at the end of the hour does Mr B discuss his fear that his wife will have an operation. He also refers to her continued bleeding, and 'his horror of what was going on in his wife's inside'.

Saturday 9 January 1943

Klein writes,

On this day I could connect the material of the dream with this fact which he had only mentioned at the end of the hour; and now came also the analysis of a part of the dream which he had told me later. Mr B saw his wife making love to him in the presence of the doctor, and in this connection he twice or three times used the word 'shameless'. Also, in this part of the dream she was not fully dressed and turned her behind towards him.

Klein asks,

whether or not it was unpleasant to him. I pointed out that the way he told it seemed to indicate that he did not like it. I drew his attention to the fact that his complaints had always been on the line of his wife's not liking his sexual love, of withdrawing from that or making difficulties. He says that his wife is more developing on these lines, which could have been taken as a problem on his part. I pointed out that there must be something in this love-making which does not seem to appeal to him so very much. He replied that of course if she would do it in the presence of a stranger he would feel it shameless; but did agree after a little pause that actually he is not so very keen on her becoming so interested in love-making. He pointed out to me that for a long time he had told her – years ago – that if he were married to Venus he wouldn't be happier either. As often before, he accused analysis of having made him less interested in sex.

Klein tries to bring together the material of these various dreams with Mr B's concerns about his wife's health. She writes,

I pointed out that his feelings about sexual intercourse and his penis were horrid; [they are signified by] a place, full of bedroom things, faeces, urine; where he would either be shot – that is the country into which he would climb - or where he would shoot the mucker, the soldier, [who would be] damaged by the penis of the father inside mother; this conflict would either mean being destroyed inside the mother, or destroying the father inside. This would contribute to his fear about sexual intercourse, would work as an inhibition towards liking sexual intercourse. He denies the fact that he gets much pleasure out of sexual intercourse but says that his anxiety increases if he has reasons to be frightened of his wife's inside being a danger, and full of something which he seemed to think a dangerous object, the polypus [sic]. Then the early fears of his mother's body, the early fears of sexual intercourse, would be reinforced and revived; at the same time all these unpleasant things which he assumes inside his wife's body were also part of his whole inside. He had been injured and battered because that was what would happen to his wife's inside in the operation. As often before I could show him that he carried his wife in his mind inside him and shared every symptom, every bit of pain or distress which she felt. That is what he did not wish to see when he first covered his glasses up.

The following material is repeated twice in file B.98. First, it appears in note form, immediately following the above entry, dated 9 January 1943. This note-like material, which itself undated, is however followed by a tidied-up version of the same material which is dated 9 February 1948.[2] The material is headed,

Material to illustrate how unconscious material expresses internalisation.

Klein writes,

After the usual complaints about his frustrating domestic situation, Mr B remarks on the wonderful poultry shop at the bus stop near my house. An extraordinary collection of game – one of his great interests. When he was a boy of between seven and nine, when he went for walks with his governess, how terribly bored, how completely hopeless he felt. The one good thing was when they passed a shop with game. This was one of his great interests in childhood and since. Mr B wonders whether I ever look at this shop and has the idea that he would like to explain to me the various kinds of game. At least I am bound to see it when I get onto the bus.

He then reports a dream:

He saw his car. It looked quite different from his car, but he knew it was his car. In the car some people were sitting – he did not know how they got in. Then this vanished. Instead of it he saw a stone wall. On this wall there were various kinds of game hanging which fascinated him. Then a piece of corrugated iron 'apparatus' like a roof came down over the wall, and the next change in scene was that both the corrugated iron and the game had gone, but he knew in the dream definitely that the game was there – it was inside the wall.

After a silence, Mr B adds,

that his good dog had taught him how to find rabbits which got between stones or in holes. They might have felt quite secure there, but his dog showed him where they were and he pulled the rabbits out. That was quite a kind of sport which he developed. The wall was primitive but made of good stone – this reminds Mr B of Scotland – a visit to relatives. One of the associations to this town in Scotland was that I also stayed there for a time, (which he knew from a letter from me.) Again, he speaks about game, and his interests and of what it meant to him that his mother shared his interests so much, which he feels his wife does not. This is a constant source of complaint. After some other associations, this was the interpretation I gave of the dream: His loved objects – the game, birds, the same as moths (another of his interests) are all killed by him. I cite a memory of his crying when he first went out shooting with his father, and shot a black-cock.

Klein remarks that Mr B has brought many dreams,

showing how game and birds stood for people. To mention one, he was chasing a pink-footed goose in Clifton Hill – the goose being a good and particularly attractive object. He wondered what would he do with the goose? He could either put it into a cage or eat it. The dream showed that the two things amounted to the same. By eating it (in this case me [which the pink-footed goose in Clifton Hill stood for]) he would really encage it in his insides.

Klein speaks to Mr B of,

The destruction of his loved objects – first of all mother – by eating. The first dream when his car was unrecognizable but he knows it is his, is an expression of a feeling expressed in many ways during analysis that he does not know who he is, because he is not himself, he is full of other tendencies and forces which make him do at once this and at once that – who is he? Right or left? – 'One is a bag full of people', Mr B had once said. The car thus represents himself and not himself because it is not him, because it is full of people, and he does not know how they got into him. The second part of dream shows how – because he ate them. The corrugated iron is in contrast to the game, which in a way seems something alive, something interesting, the iron being to him the epitome of everything ugly and horrid and dead and mechanical. I also point out that the fear of eating and thus destroying his loved objects goes further. It refers to the situation inside [and the question of whether] he can keep his objects inside him alive if he keeps on using them, eating them, taking advantage of them?

Klein now reports an earlier exchange in which it had seemed to dawn on Mr B that he wants his objects to be entirely a reflection of him; that he is not concerned with their independent existence at all. The first 'complaining' material is very familiar:

Mr B had been complaining about the lack of interest his wife has for him and similar complaints in past about not being understood, etc. He spoke of some interest his wife has, and it appears he does not share it at all. That seems the usual persecutory complaint that she will develop or have interests which he cannot share.

However, when Klein puts to him the question, 'is he then not interested in what his wife was telling him about?' Mr B suddenly says,

No, I only want her to be a mirror of my thoughts, I only want her to be interested in what I am doing, she is not to be anything else.

Klein writes,

It had taken a long analysis for him to be able to realise this attitude, and I could then point out to him that he has the same attitude towards me, being often unable until quite recently to express any concern about me, though it is quite obvious that he also has such feelings, but everything is centred on the fact that I am to be there for him, entirely at his disposal, being in a sense denied the right to be a person on my own. (This is exaggerated but represents one essential aspect of his attitude.) The recognition of how much this attitude towards his wife and children influences his domestic life was extremely painful and was soon followed by strong depression, feelings of worthlessness and the accusation that I and analysis stress, or bring out, the bad sides in him.

Klein draws this material together, showing Mr B 'how it fits into the whole dream'. She says,

Here is his loved game – but what is he doing with it? He eats it. I point out how his early attitude towards mother and her breast and her love was maintained at the level of she being his food. The guilt about that increased the persecutory accusations that others wronged him, did not give him enough, frustrated him.

Mr B returns to his dream:

He recalls the rabbit. The rabbit, he thinks, had also disappeared into the wall. It was his doing. Why did he get in there and feel secure? I say that that would imply that his object

trusted him when it got into him, but that he could not preserve it there. I cite the pulling and tearing out of the mother, the good or desired food, father's penis and babies (I make reference to former rabbit associations and dreams when once the rabbits were the number of children in the family and one of them was tiny, representing baby sister). But also looking, as it were, into the inside – both mother's and his own – to see in what state the object is – i.e., the dream is a representation of an internal situation. The object then trusted him and felt secure inside him but it was not, because he felt that the eating of the object by which he got it into him was continued in the internal situation.

Mr B reports another dream from a few weeks earlier:

Salmon, mangy after mating – as they often are – going down river. Mr B is looking down on and watching with dismay the look of the salmon and also the place into which the salmon had got. It was muddy, dirty, quite the wrong place for salmon to be in (sewers).

Mr B's associations and interpretations showed,

that the mangy salmon, the old and decaying father, could not be preserved because it had got into the sewer – part of himself. His interest in salmon fishing as well as salmon as a particularly good food. Again, many dreams and material have shown the salmon he fishes to be the father's good penis and the father, and the conclusion of this dream was that his fears about his father's death linked with the fear of not being able to preserve him internally, in this case because he has got mixed up with bad faeces.

Klein therefore suggests that there are two dangers to the internalised object:

The bad faeces inside and the continued greed which exploits the internal object, which I connect with Mr B's recent recognition that this is the attitude he uses towards loved objects at present, and in the past also towards analysis and me who are only used as internal food while the personal feelings and consideration of object as such are denied.

Mr B makes some associations to the wall in his dream:

It was really meant to be a very nice wall, stone, reminding of Scotland, something very real and good and alive, in strong contrast to the corrugated iron which was bad. The game which appeared on this wall was not as good as that in the shop [near to Clifton Hill] because it was all higgledy-piggledy – bits and pieces. In association to the wall, Mr B thinks of Pirimus and Thisbe, where there was a wall between them. They were on two sides, the wall being represented by a person who put himself in between – which is so funny for an onlooker – but in a sense this wall was a very tragic thing because it did separate the two people, so perhaps the person – if it is a child – who stood in between could have felt that it is tragic and for the adults it would have seemed funny. I pointed out that the child which forms the wall between father and mother, puts himself between, separates them and makes trouble between them, would feel full of guilt (being himself in childhood). The hope is that the adults won't take it as seriously.

'Next day'

Mr B remarks that Klein looks scared of him. He

again complains about the state of his wife, but with a feeling that he might increasingly come to detach himself more from that misfortune. Complaints about his wife not doing what he wants, and about her health, are much less bitter than on other occasions. He had a dream which he did not write down as he often does because he really did not wish to, but at the same time he knew that he would not forget it. He still does not want to tell it and wonders about the inhibition in that. It was a very unpleasant dream and yet he feels he should tell it and so he does.

The dream:

He was in a place which had walls around it and an iron roof. It made an impression of having been blitzed, destroyed, drab, grey, without life – no flowers, no colours, no birds, no moths. An excavation went on and he was on the ground level as far as the excavation goes but not as far as the outside goes. He saw pipes which again remind him of iron mechanical things. The pipes were black and he was slewed round, feeling in a very precarious position. There were other people there, but they were vague, dim – also drab grey – and he suddenly says 'You were among them (speaking to me). They were not directly hostile – perhaps did they take a little interest in the excavation and him? But suddenly he adds, 'I wished to kill them'. Also suddenly, after a silence, he adds, 'The whole thing is like analysis tearing one's guts out'.

Klein interprets that the pipes are,

the guts and says the blackness pointed at guts and faeces. Excavation is meant often in a very good sense – a special interest of Mr B's in archaeology. It has often in dreams and associations represented the analytic procedure. Since this represents analysis digging, as it were, into his insides and his mind, the situation refers to his own inside. The figures are so dim and vague because they are the same as the people in the car – his internal figures. That I am one of them shows that they are his important figures – his parents, brother, sister – but they have become so vague, dim, grey, etc because they have become part of himself – a lifeless, blitzed, endangered and horrible place – his inside being represented in that way. His being slewed expresses also part of his internal situation, for he often does not know which way he is moved, who moves him, what is his 'me'.

Klein suggests that the dream is a direct continuation of the game dream of the preceding day. She reminds Mr B that,

one association when he spoke of his wife, preceding report of dream, was that if she could recognise the psychological reasons for her illness, if she could alter her point of view, it would make all the difference in the world. He adds the same thing must apply to himself and to his cure. Now I point out that the recognition of the material of the preceding day might already have been felt by him as his changing his point of view and expresses the feeling that if he could accept and work through these painful feelings that might mean his cure. Mr B then adds that towards the end of the dream there was a hopeful feeling. He felt that he was not really quite in the depths but that he would come up.

Klein counters this thought, however, saying:

that he had spoken of his being on the ground level of the excavation, but that from what he said now it appears he must have been very much in the depths. Feeling he was on the ground level was a defence against being very deep down and quite imprisoned there. This, I link with the early masturbation phantasy which he had reported. In his phantasy, he pictured himself travelling inside his aunt's body. It was a most interesting exploration and expedition – only pleasurable. Further, analysis had shown that there was complete denial of the fact that there was an entry or exit to the body, again that did not appear in his phantasy, and the frightening part of the phantasy was that he had forced an entry into the body and was cut off and exposed to dangers. We had since had much material to confirm the fact of attacking mother's body and endangering himself and her by this.

Klein relates this to Mr B's ongoing concern about his wife's illness and his feeling of guilt when she is ill. She also remarks that,

on the preceding day there was one element in the dream which pointed to this attack. That was his taking the rabbit out of the hole, being helped by his good dog in finding it, and that this had on earlier occasions represented the babies he took out of mother's body. In that sense the hole was his mother's body. The stone wall with the game, etc must also have been standing for mother's body, and the situation in today's dream is not only a representation of his own inside in which he carries these hostile figures, but also mother's body which he has injured and cannot get out from again. But in the end, he knew he could get out, which confirms his feeling that analysis would help him out of his difficulties.

Klein continues to ask for associations to parts of the dream:

I ask about the iron which has reappeared in present dream with reference to the pipes, etc. Also, that everything was at right angles, which always meant to him the mechanical, the unpleasant, the dead things, as well as on one occasion representing the two legs and what is in between them. Mr B associates with difficulty to the 'apparatus', as he had called the corrugated iron which came down on the wall. He suddenly says it reminds him of circumcision, about which he accuses the parents and particularly the doctor who did it when he was a baby. Apparatus is then an instrument. He says it has something sexual in his mind too. I suggest that the apparatus which came down, injuring the nice wall, seems to have stood also for his father's genital which the patient remembers having seen on various occasions as a child. I suggest again the hypothesis of primal scene, particularly linked with the nightmare when he slept in father's dressing room next to bedroom and had a dream that a dog was biting off his genital. He called for help but mother was not enough sympathetic. Mr B replies that my interpretation that the corrugated iron is father's genital is very surprising. He then explains that he does not really mean it is not true, rather, it could be true but it seems so far-fetched; far-fetched does not mean untrue. I note that the far-fetchedness is the dimness of the memory and of the surprise he had when he saw the sexual intercourse, but it would include that this genital was bad and destructive, soiled and spoilt mother's inside and prevented him from seeing and entering mother.

The following day, Mr B returns to Klein's interpretation of the iron roof coming down, which,

he had not been quite satisfied with. He feels that it has another meaning as well. He reminds me that he had an association to it which was not taken up, to a roof over some place where there are no walls – like a bicycle stand where bicycles are stored. Also that the wall was not really attractive. He had felt about it that there was nothing artificial but good Scotch stone. It was not part of a house or something like that with warmth etc between it, but rather like something between two other things separating two other things. Also, thinking of the game, it strikes him that he was thinking particularly of grouse. He feels that all his life he has been grousing. Is grouse then hidden inside him as was the game which disappeared into the wall? He expands on this feeling that from whenever he remembers he has had a grouse [meaning a complaint], and there are some further associations which point to his earliest grouse of not having had sufficient of milk and mother. At the same time his rejecting it because of grouse. He goes back to the bicycle and says he has a strong feeling that it is something sexual.

This memory of the bicycle reminds Klein of an earlier dream:

in which a boy was injured by him and his brother driving in a car. He thought the boy was killed, then noticed him driving off with the bicycle shattered or broken or wobbly or something wrong with the bicycle. That definitely showed that both he and brother had injured their genitals in sexual activities.

The following material is clearly dated 1948, which seems to confirm there is a period of about 4 years for which no notes about Mr B have so far been found. Further searching in the archive may of course reveal other sessional notes belonging to the years in between 1943 and 1948. Indeed, Spillius (2007) already published an excerpt from Klein's notes about a patient, whom I believe is Mr B but who remains unnamed there, from 1947, which suggests that more material may be found. This material is headed, 'An illustration of the schizoid mechanisms', and comes shortly after the publication of Klein's important 1946 paper, 'Notes on Some Schizoid Mechanisms', which was presented to the British Psychoanalytical Society on 4 December 1946. It is interesting material which suggests Mr B may have seen active service during the War, describing as it does an experience in a trench.

Thursday 10th June 1948

Mr B reports a dream:

> *He was in Cornhill, not the real Cornhill associated with his father's work as well as his own, but another Cornhill – not one associated with an early love – a place where one catches salmon (decided it was not this Cornhill either). 'It was a hedgerow, grass and bushes and a blackbird's nest. She was sitting on her eggs or young and I was slashing down all the grass and bushes and unintentionally exposed her to view and to danger. I was full of remorse and wondered whether by cutting some nearby foxgloves and erecting them around her I could replace the protection I had removed. Then I turned down Cornhill and met a gay young thing and thought she might help me. I am feeling very distraught and unanchored'.*

Klein records, 'These notes are verbatim because the patient had written down, as he often does, the dream, and handed it over to me'. In association to the dream, Mr B remarks that they,

> *have had a flycatcher nesting on the house. He was anxious that she should not be disturbed and 'desert'. When the eggs are hatched she won't desert the young but until they are hatched she might be rather touchy. Mr B adds that he has once frightened her unintentionally.*

In association to foxgloves, Mr B says that it,

> *sounds a sexual thing. The glove reminds him of the female genital and the hand of the male. It was quite useless to try to provide this protective hedge. He felt it hopeless. Mr B expresses, as often, that he is worried about the health of his wife. In this hour there are no more associations to be got. He is deeply depressed and grieved, the mood of the dream persisting. He seems very much afraid of any interpretation I could give.*

Klein reminds Mr B of former dream material in which he had watched 'a jay attacking the nests of other birds', and thought of this as representing himself.

> *Mr B's first association – even the one preceding that of the foxgloves – was that in Regents Park some hemlock had been slashed down by hooligans. I point to his feelings when his mother was pregnant with his sister, his desire to attack her and to injure the baby inside her, and to much former material which substantiated this suggestion; his whole relation to his sister was influenced by early jealousy and guilt. The blackbird then stood for his mother and his feeling that he exposed her to danger, in fact he was attacking her – the hooligans in Regents Park slashing down the herbage 'unintentionally' was one way of defending himself*

against his guilt. Mr B remarks that not even in the dream did he quite believe that it was unintentional.

Klein notes that further,

the illness of his wife stirs such feelings of guilt in relation to mother. I refer to his great grief about not being able to give more children to his wife. There is also, I suggest, a reference to me – he had recently expressed concern about my health. Was it then possible that Cornhill also contains a reference to Clifton Hill? Mr B says 'I shall think about this interpretation', but he did not disagree. Finally, I remind him of how often I had been represented in dreams by birds in danger.

Friday 11 June 1948

Mr B's mood has changed. He says he knows a good deal about the dream and is going to tell me. He had just re-read Cymbeline by Shakespeare, an extraordinary story. He had read it before repeatedly and only now seemed to be able to understand its complications. There is a queen and a king who becomes separated from the queen. An evil brother is after the queen. Two sons are taken away early in childhood and don't know the queen and the king and in the end, there are two supposed corpses on the stage – the queen and the evil brother dressed up like the king. The evil brother is in fact dead, the queen revives and is reunited in the end with the king and reconciled with her sons. Mr B is particularly taken by these two corpses who are unreal in so far as one is not a corpse and the other is the corpse of somebody else.

In association, Mr B thinks of,

a museum abroad in which a medieval nunnery was reconstructed and there was a nun sitting there. Of course, she was only stuffed, but for a moment one could wonder – was she stuffed or was she real? The blackbird in the dream appeared to be stuffed and he was male. I point out that this seems as unreal and un-understandable as the story of Shakespeare's Cymbeline. There seemed to be a particular confusion regarding the sexes – the blackbird was hatching eggs, but now it appears to be male – the blackbird was alive but now it appears to be stuffed.

Klein interprets that,

the male blackbird and the nun represent here the two parents and his uncertainty about their sexual relation, whether they are alive or dead, mixed up with one another, and which is male, which is female. His early fears on seeing his mother in the morning in bed and his worry about her looks. What has happened during the night? In this connection his slashing the protective herbage means slashing at the two parents in sexual intercourse at night. Also the herbage representing the pubic hair which would expose the father's and mother's genitals to danger by him or the mother to danger by the father. In the 'foxglove' association there is an attempt to reunite the two. He brings the two genitals together in a protective way, making good the preceding action of slashing and killing the parents and their babies.

Klein notes that,

the mood in this hour was completely different from the preceding hour. Obviously, the interpretations given had released feelings and Mr B could actively cooperate in the interpretation of the dream.

Friday 14 June 1948

This is a particularly poignant session, with highly symbolic contents, which must surely be regarded as a culmination of many years of analysis. Mr B reports 'a very pleasant dream':

Throughout it, he had a very pleasant feeling and, unusually for him, no feeling to the contrary entered. He was in Cornwall and he found in a river a little crystal bottle, very nicely made, which had the initials of both his father and mother in gold on it. He knew that it must have been there for many years and was surprised how well it had kept.

To this place in Cornwall, Mr B associates,

pleasant childhood memories, particularly the fact that they could eat seaweed, 'picking it up as they went along'. The fact that they were allowed this unconventional food ad libitum, stands out against the other aspects of his upbringing. Great care was taken over food precautions, the Victorian way of looking after children, the mother's and nurse's care regarding the food and other arrangements, great concern with hygiene. Mr B speaks very warmly about the parents' kindness in this respect.

This warm feeling seems to extend to Klein, for she notes that,

the first remark of Mr B before he told me the dream, had been an appreciation of analysis (which is very rare with him). I suggest that the unconventional food is the analysis. He had been very careful not to let people know he is in analysis and the analysis had shown that he was concerned about his parents, who might not have agreed to his being analysed. Now this unconventional food is appreciated and brings up the unconventional food allowed by mother – in the first place the breast feeding in which no such rules as later on would enter – at least that was his wish; unlimited and un-interfered with gratification by mother and her breast which was later on revived when the seaweed was allowed.

Mr B then says that 'he felt that the bottle with the mixed initials of both parents was as if they had, after all, been happily united'. Klein writes that this is a thought that had been very repressed in Mr B, who had 'always felt the unhappiness of the parents, particularly also their sexual unhappiness'. Klein interprets that,

> the *depths of rivers and sea had so often in his analysis stood for the inside of the body, his own as well as mother's, also for the analysis which finds things in the depths. He had now discovered that through analysis, the unconventional food, that there is an aspect of the parents, sexually, which is good and also that they are united and preserved in his own mind, in his own inside, which is a way of keeping them alive. The river here is standing for his unconscious as well as for his inside. This implies a return to a happy earliest relation to mother – a good feeding situation revived in relation to me and to the analysis. Mr B responds by saying that he had brought a jar of goat's milk to town and when coming into my house thought that he would like to offer it to me and he adds, 'there seems to be milk all around'. I say that this milk is the return for the food received in analysis and for the early food which he would like to return to mother.*

Mr B remarks,

> *that he is rather surprised that there should have been nothing evil in this dream, and that he can hardly believe that it could all have felt so good. In the same hour, he has all sorts of associations regarding family life, his relation to his children, to his wife – all of a confident nature. His worry about his wife's health is much lessened. He also expresses his belief in the analysis quite strongly. I suggest that this change in mood and the complete contrast between the dream with the bottle and the blackbird dream are inter-connected. There is some relief from his guilt relating to the sexual life of his parents and their relationship, which has led to a greater conviction that there is an aspect of the parents' early married life which is good and which he can preserve inside himself. The little bottle of course, represents the breast as well as the two genitals of the parents united in a happy way. Mr B agrees but says the bottle was a very fragile object after all and could be broken, which indicates anxiety about his being able to preserve these precious objects against his own attacks.*

The following material, the latest I have so far found in the archive, comes almost fourteen months after the preceding notes. It too seems to have been used for teaching, as the notes are headed,

> *'Making use of apparently not very significant material'*

Klein notes that the session comes just days before the summer break.

Friday 5 August 1949

Mr B reports a dream:

> *He dreamt that he had sent off a cheque and somebody raised the question whether it would be met. He seemed to think that there was no risk that it would not be met.*

In association to the dream, he recalls,

> *A tenant in the past who repeatedly gave cheques which would not be met. But he was not much upset by that. He already knew that he was unreliable, but it never happened that one of his own cheques was not met.*

Further,

> *He was thinking of the work in the fields done during the weekend. His sickle was broken. He must have misused it, pushing it too hard into the ground, weeding onions in the fields and weeding thistles, the most urgent ones first, the others to be left until later. The most urgent are those which seed. The others are only spread by plants. In between, relations with his wife. They had sexual intercourse after some time of abstinence – she had been unwell and therefore not willing. He feels that her physical trouble is only imaginary – that there is nothing physically wrong with her. Then goes back to the cheque dream. Who was the person who raised the question whether it would be met? He thinks it was me. He had sent me a cheque a day before the dream. He feels that such pertinent questions would always be raised by me. Mr B loves puns and excels in them unconsciously. The Czechs, he said, might say they have not been very well treated by the English and that the English let them down in 1939. But the Czechs should remember that they owed 20 years of freedom to the British after the preceding war, and that is something.*

Klein interprets,

> *The English in this case are obviously the parents and the authority, and in this case also stand for me, he being the Czech. He feels he should not be too dissatisfied with what he has received from his parents and me, even if I am going to leave him. The period of freedom would then refer to things in childhood and to gains made in analysis. But the fact that the Czechs in the bad aspect of the situation had been delivered to Hitler, the bad father, show his great fear before the holidays that I leave him with what are still his persecutors. Relevant are constant accusations about his mother, wife, analysis. Persecution is much reduced, but guilt and depression have come to the fore.*

> *Since there was no danger of the money not being paid, it must refer to other obligations which he could not meet, and the question apparently raised by me in the dream (but actually by himself), was a very important one. Only recently he had again and again expressed his doubt in himself including in relation to his not being a productive, cooperative patient, taking too little advantage from the analysis, misusing me. He agrees to this very familiar feeling which is in keeping with his conscious feelings.*

Klein remarks,

> *The broken sickle which came up before and after the dream reported, was broken, but in a sense the ground was hurt. I remind him of material of injuring the mother's breast ... The*

whole way in which he dealt with the field, [his description of which] intermingled with the dream report, and in between the reference to the sexual intercourse with his wife. His need to say there is nothing physically wrong with her. But the thistles which should urgently be weeded because they are spread by seeds implied that his seeds are harmful and should be eliminated. In contrast to that, other references about things he plants and cultivates, and the great wish for more children increased by this fear. If his wife is ill, that is proof of his own dangerous and destructive planting, or not weeding in the right way. Transferring this to me (the mother whom he did not keep alive), not giving her the right thing, injuring her and therefore not meeting obligations. All this is of course accentuated by the fear of parting before the holidays.

Here ends Klein's record of her analysis with Mr B.

Notes

1 There is, very unfortunately, a gap in Klein's notes here, so we don't learn why he felt reassured about his wife's analysis.
2 This seems to support the idea that earlier clinical material was used in later teaching.

Conclusion

In her 1937 paper, 'Love, Guilt and Reparation,' Klein writes,

> We all know that if we detect in ourselves impulses of hate towards a person we love, we feel concerned or guilty. As Coleridge puts it: … to be wroth with one we love, Doth work like madness in the brain. (p. 309)

During his analysis, Mr B misquotes this line from Coleridge to Klein, telling her, 'If we fall out with those we love, it works like poison on the brain.' He must so clearly have had his mother in mind when he said this, and it takes a long analysis, as Klein puts it, for him to develop more loving concern for his objects, including his mother.

Right at the end of her 1937 paper, Klein writes,

> If we have become able, deep in our unconscious minds, to clear our feelings to some extent towards our parents of grievances, and have forgiven them for the frustrations we had to bear, then we can be at peace with ourselves and are able to love others in the true sense of the word. (p. 343)

This does seem to be true of Mr B in the later stages of his analysis. The 'long rope' that Klein gives to his many grievances does seem, in the end, to result in a 'straightening out' of the objects in Mr B's mind, and in turn to a more constructive and creative intercourse between them. The implications of this for Mr B's life, though we know nothing of it beyond 1949, one can only imagine were profound.

Mr B had come to Klein full of hate and accusations against his mother in particular, and these powerful feelings initially obstructed his mourning of her. A very difficult early feeding situation, followed by the unexpected and traumatic arrival of a baby sister and some worrying sexual activity between siblings (or phantasies about this), had all contributed to very great internal conflict and profound unhappiness. Regarding the birth of Mr B's sister, Klein felt this was so harrowing an experience, and indeed one for which Mr B was in no way prepared,

DOI: 10.4324/9781003373414-9

that 'many later complaints and experiences were added to this old experience.' Concerning the possible violation of Mr B by his older brother, and of their younger sister by Mr B himself, the internal consequences are shown by this analysis to have been ruinous. Mr B demonstrates significant insight when he tells Klein that he knows many of his external troubles are 'only something for his inner misery to rest on,' and Klein is to concur many times with him that it is an internal situation she is analysing, and which is at the root of his deeply entrenched depression. This, he works through to a great extent in the course of his analysis.

In the early years of treatment, following the death of his mother, Mr B claims that analysis is 'disintegrating him.' Klein shows him that rather it is the disintegrating state of his objects inside which is so utterly debilitating. Indeed, the very hostile, 'scorched turf' of his internal landscape is often felt by Mr B not to be able to sustain life at all, and as such there is little chance of mourning getting going, or of him beginning to install a peaceful maternal object inside. Before this can happen there is much necessary working through of hatred and despair, and as one would expect, the transference becomes a battleground as Mr B's at times cruel and sadistic treatment of objects extends to his relationship with Klein. At such times, he is in almost complete denial that his mother's death is impacting him at all; everything is Klein's fault as she becomes the depriving and with-holding mother of his earliest feeding experience – the flat fish or stormy petrel[1] mother who struggles so much to attend to her young. Guilt too plays its part: so responsible does Mr B feel for not having saved his mother from a deadly parental intercourse, and for harming her himself with his own hatred and grievances, that he cannot bear to think of her in a more loving way. Guilt thus drives him to hatred. In the transference too, Mr B is in turn full of hate and then despair concerning his treatment of Klein. The unrelenting back and forth between love and hate becomes more understandable as Klein grasps that love, and indeed any affectionate or co-operative feelings that approach it, including hope, feel just too close to destructive sexuality for Mr B to bear.

Much analysis of Mr B's conception of parental intercourse has to take place before he can begin to recover some sense of the more constructive aspects of sexuality, yet as the 'Cornhill dream' he reports in 1948 shows, analysis does appear to have unearthed a (precarious albeit) sense of a happily united couple. This I think could only have followed from the significant restitution of Mr B's objects, and particularly of his internal mother, which the analysis enabled. Hatred, once thoroughly analysed, really is seen to give way to love. The long rope given to Mr B's 'grousing' about his mother, as well as much later on in the analysis to his railing against his father (and of course against Klein throughout the whole analysis), sees a freeing up of love and gratitude. In this way, analysis helps substantially to strengthen Mr B's belief in his own constructive and reparative capacities, which are evident from the beginning, Klein recognises.

One of the very important outcomes of his analysis is that the ground is prepared for a far happier coexistence of objects inside. Mr B's re-emerging love of observing others (he tells Klein how much he had loved to observe all the staff of his house as a small child) is taken by Klein as evidence of his belief that he can, after so much analysis of anxiety concerning internalisation, safely take in objects and experiences, and can even enjoy doing so. His profound gratitude for this is conveyed through his exaltation of the 'Indore process,' a process by which earth or soil, standing for the internal landscape, Klein argues, is enriched and preserved. While Mr B was for so long in a state of almost total despair about his 'insides' and his own destructiveness, which indeed he felt Klein regularly highlighted, Klein consistently holds on to the hope that analysis can help him recover good experiences of objects and of himself, and preserve these, just as he recovers and hopes he can preserve the bottle of his dream, with the parents' initials inscribed on it.

I think readers will agree that this account of Klein's analysis of Mr B shows her to have been an incredibly sensitive, as well as robust analyst, capable of withstanding much hatred and despair. She demonstrates enormous compassion when she asserts for example that there must be good reasons why Mr B cannot emerge from his depressed state; and when he suffers so much when he bumps into other patients, so much that he can barely stand to attend at all, she tells him they'll just have to do as much work as they can until the storm is analysed, and passes. And it does. Klein's capacity to stay with her patient, and to go on trying to understand him even in the face of frightening threats, is remarkable. Importantly, what I think this work shows is that while she is frequently analysing her patient's hate and destructiveness, such activity is shown to be in the service of liberating the more constructive and loving aspects of Mr B's character which might otherwise remain hidden. Indeed, this work is instructive in respect of how Klein approached aggression directly, and may deepen critical exploration of her belief in the need to analyse destructiveness.

Elliott Jaques, in his foreword to Klein's (1961) *Narrative of a Child Analysis*, commented that it had long been Klein's ambition to publish a full account of a child's analysis, but that 'the problem of scale in giving a satisfactory account of a total analysis seemed insurmountable' (foreword). In the case of Richard, it was the war which 'threw up a circumstance which suddenly offered a possible solution' (Ibid.). This necessarily short analysis was one about which Klein kept extensive notes in the full knowledge that she would later publish an account of it. Her record of Mr B's analysis is more sporadic: for some periods notes are very full indeed, but for others much less so, and for long stretches no notes survive at all, assuming Klein made them. However, partly on account of its length, Mr B's analysis did offer the opportunity to really work through a range of anxieties and conflicts that Richard's analysis did not. Indeed, as the reader will note, even in the last set of notes from 1949, Mr B is grappling with, and Klein is analysing, anxieties which have been present to differing degrees from the beginning of, and throughout his analysis. One can only speculate that had Klein lived longer, she might herself have published a *Narrative* of Mr B's analysis.

The record of treatment revealed in this book is certainly a window into Klein's highly original and influential way of conducting psychoanalysis, and it lends much support to her many and varied theoretical contributions. For example, that relationships with objects endure in the mind, and can be modified long after the death of the external others on whose image those objects were based, is abundantly clear in the analysis of Mr B. That depression may offer some protection from a sense 'badness' or poisonousness inside, is also evidenced. The terrible implications of a belief in the ruinous nature of parental sexuality, are also movingly shown. Material throws light on the experience of the arrival of a sibling, as well as on the phantasies bound up with this. While Mr B's sister's birth is obviously traumatic for him, what is also evoked as he observes her infantile suffering, are Mr B's own early feelings of distress and helplessness which he felt were not attended to. Thus, further light is thrown by Klein in this particular case on the way in which a child may be retraumatised by the arrival of a sibling in a different sense than is usually understood; that is to say, it is not simply the displacement that is traumatic.

I have included in this book all of Klein's previously unpublished clinical notes on Mr B that I have so far found in the Melanie Klein Archive. I strongly suspect that more shall be unearthed, and assuming this is the case I very much look forward to continuing to fill out the picture of his analysis. As I write, as part of my role as archivist for the Melanie Klein Trust, I am involved in the process of more fully cataloguing the contents of the archive, a process which was begun by Elizabeth Spillius. This will make the archive much easier to navigate, and will enable scholars, psychoanalytic candidates, and Melanie Klein enthusiasts alike to more easily conduct their own research into Klein's fascinating psychoanalytic work. Such work is perhaps 'unconventional food,' a term Klein used to describe her offering to Mr B, but it is work which many will likely find both satisfying and important for decades to come.

Note

1 'In Klein's notes, she writes 'stormy petrel', though the correct name of the bird is Storm Petrel. Mr B, who was so knowledgeable about the natural world, presumably knew this. We cannot know for certain which term he used. The term 'stormy petrel', however, was once used to denote 'a person who brings or portends trouble' (Collins English Dictionary) deriving, apparently, from a belief held by sailors that storm petrels foretold or caused bad weather at sea. One can imagine Mr B may also have used this term, which seems not unconnected with his experience of his mother.

References

Klein, M. (1937) 'Love, Guilt and Reparation'. In *Love, Guilt and Reparation and Other Works 1921–1945* (1975). Virago.

Klein, M. (1961/1998) *Narrative of a Child Analysis*. Vintage.

Index

Page numbers followed by "n" indicate notes.

Dream Index

Ingram Content Group UK Ltd.
Milton Keynes UK
UKHW022003240723
425724UK00009B/35